HOWE LIBRARY
SHENANDOAH COLLEGE &
CONSERVATORY OF MUSIC.
WINCHESTER, VA.

WITHDRAWN

D1565964

A SACRED CIRCLE

HOWE LIBRARY
SHENANDOAH COLLEGE &
CONSERVATORY OF MUSIC
WINCHESTER, VA.

A SACRED CIRCLE

The Dilemma of the Intellectual
in the Old South,
1840–1860

DREW GILPIN FAUST

The Johns Hopkins University Press
Baltimore and London

This book has been brought to publication with the generous assistance
of the Andrew W. Mellon Foundation.

Copyright © 1977 by The Johns Hopkins University Press

All rights reserved. No part of this book may be reproduced or transmitted in any
form or by any means, electronic or mechanical, including photocopying, recording,
xerography, or any information storage and retrieval system, without permission in
writing from the publisher. Manufactured in the United States of America

The Johns Hopkins University Press, Baltimore, Maryland 21218
The Johns Hopkins Press Ltd., London

Library of Congress Catalog Card Number 77–4547
ISBN 0–8018–1967–9
Library of Congress Cataloging in Publication data will be found
on the last printed page of this book.

E   Faust, Drew Gilpin.
449
.F2   A sacred circle

975.03 F275s

For Lawrence, Donald, and Tys

9.90 Goldberg 11-7-78

Contents

Preface

While Americans generally have regarded the South as singular and enigmatic, Southerners have felt compelled to explain and justify the peculiarity of their section. Yet from Thomas Jefferson to William Faulkner, W. J. Cash, and C. Vann Woodward, they have been unable to resolve a profound ambivalence toward their region and its institutions. Because the South has been so long and so intensely occupied with explaining itself, studying the "mind of the South" is like looking at a reflection of a reflection. Attempts at self-interpretation have become one of the region's most characteristic cultural products.[1]

As Cash and others have applied it to the South, "mind" has several meanings: it is the active faculty of cognition and feeling in man as well as the abstract body of thought, belief, and values he has produced. In the relationship between these elements—between how he thinks and what he thinks, between the influences upon his intellectual process and its actual substantive products—lies the key to understanding the Southern world view. Studying the "mind of the South," therefore, goes well beyond an exercise in intellectual history. A convergence of cognition, belief, feeling, and temperament, the Southern mind is at once a cultural, a social, and a psychological phenomenon that best can be explicated by analyzing the interaction and interdependence of these factors.

But the development of Southern thought over the past four centuries is incomprehensible apart from the specific and changing contexts in which the mind of the South has been located. As the section entered an era of crisis in the years leading up to the Civil War, the relationship between Southern thought and society came under increasing scrutiny. Many outsiders both at the time and afterward believed that the Old South responded to any challenge to its way of life in a monolithic and defensive fashion. Because such a society was at best infertile ground for the growth and nurture of an intellectual class, the dilemmas of the Southern man of knowledge appeared with particular acuteness in this era. During these years, the South became intensely conscious of its cultural uniqueness—what it liked to call the "peculiarity" of its institutions. In response to the social and cultural turmoil that accompanied this awareness, the South called upon the intellectual to imbue his work with direct social relevance—to serve the Southern cause. Inevitably, the man of knowledge had to confront his own ambivalence toward his region, to define and redefine his social role and its relationship to Southern institutions and values.

Because a society is least tolerant of nonconformity in times of crisis, it is often—paradoxically—in such periods that intellectual criticisms become most fully articulated. The pervasive sense of social urgency and the consequent insistence upon solidarity may prompt or even require a thinker to produce elaborate justification for criticism or dissent. Between 1840 and 1860, intellectuals in the South confronted just such a situation. As violent conflict with the North approached, Southerners exhibited decreasing patience with individuals whose primary allegiance was to abstract and disinterested speculation. Because they lived in a society that on the whole regarded their intellectual commitments as frivolous, men of mind in the Old South were forced to explore the nature of their relationship to their region to explain and justify their role. Their search for an intellectual identity thus reveals a great deal not just about the thinkers themselves, but about the social context to which they were responding, the ante-bellum South.

During the 1840s a number of Southern thinkers united in an effort to establish a role for men of mind in their region. Novelist William Gilmore Simms, politician James Henry Hammond, agricultural reformer Edmund Ruffin, and professors Nathaniel Beverley Tucker and George Frederick Holmes all believed that their innate genius had exiled them from their society. This common sense of alienation provided the basis for intense personal friendship that evolved into what Simms christened a "sacred circle"[2]—a network of mutual emotional and intellectual support. In letters and visits, they explored their common plight and defined a common purpose: to reform the South to make a place for their particular talents. In jeremiads against their region, they explained all the South's shortcomings—from soil depletion to political corruption—as the result of her neglect of the intellectual's transcendent moral concerns.

Within this legitimating framework, the Southerners defined themselves both as neglected prophets, speaking truth to an unheeding world, and as stewards, destined to provide practical guidance for the human race. To realize this self-conception, the group undertook first to "reform the works of mind," to render speculations on society and history as relevant and reliable as the widely celebrated discoveries of empirical natural science. The products of intellect must guide a truly moral society; mind would direct the social improvement that seemed as imperative to these Southerners as it did to the moral philosophers who were their Northern counterparts. Because all social questions

appeared as essentially moral issues, reform was the particular responsibility of the intellectual, who alone was committed to the primacy
of the transcendent.

But for these Southerners, the most important reform effort was the
defense of slavery. They identified their values with the South's distinctive way of life by defining moral stewardship as the ultimate basis
for the system of human bondage. Ironically, they turned to the evangelical conceptions that underlay reform sentiment throughout the
nation to justify the South's peculiar institution. Yet even their defense
of slavery failed to earn them the social recognition they coveted. As
war approached, pressures for conformity within the South placed
insurmountable obstacles between the group and the achievement of
its purpose. The beleagured South had neither time nor resources for
disinterested speculation.

Despite their ultimate failure, these Southerners' parallel careers
demonstrate that critical thinking existed within a society too often
regarded by historians as monolithic.[3] Moreover, their lives serve as an
example of how belief systems simultaneously influence and reflect
social reality and individual psychological needs. These intellectuals'
conception of their genius did not simply legitimate their more self-
interested aspirations, but organized and even prescribed their relationship to the world. In addition, the interaction among the five dem-
onstrates how informal groups may function as contexts for the development of ideas, as well as vehicles for their social expression. The
Sacred Circle transformed friendship into an important social and
cultural force.

This study attempts as well to address more general questions. The
problems facing these five Southerners illustrate issues that have confronted the thinker throughout history. The primacy of the intellectual's dedication to cultural concerns always has tended to produce a
kind of social marginality. In the words of sociologist Edward Shils,
the intellectual's "need to penetrate beyond the screen of immediate
concrete experience" to find a more general realm of meaning and
values has imparted to the man of ideas a certain semblance of irrelevance.[4] The relationship between the intellectual and the rest of society
always has been problematical, for while his talents have craved
expression and recognition, his commitment to disinterested truth
usually has prescribed that he remain distant from the centers of social
prestige and peripheral to the exercise of power. The situation of the
intellectual in the Old South represents a particular instance of these
recurrent themes and of the perennial tension between thought and
action in human life. Understanding the mind of the South, therefore,
does not involve just describing a part of the internal dynamics of the
section's ante-bellum culture, but promises as well to link the regional

experience with larger historical issues: the relationship between knowledge and society, between the thinker and his world. In their simultaneous love and hate for the South, in their need both to justify and to reform, Hammond, Holmes, Ruffin, Tucker, and Simms embody not just the dilemma of the thinking Southerner, but the universal plight of the intellectual.

In my efforts to reconstruct the texture of these Southerners' lives, I have profited from the assistance, advice, and support of a myriad of scholars and friends. Unlike my five Southern men of mind, I never have had cause to complain of intellectual isolation, and I am deeply grateful for the ministrations of this twentieth-century "sacred circle." I shall not attempt to list all those whose personal friendship and support have made my work easier. I hope and trust they know who they are and feel my gratitude in other ways.

Material assistance from the University of Pennsylvania, the Social Science Research Council, and the Spencer Foundation has supported this undertaking generously. Archivists at Duke University, the Library of Congress, South Caroliniana Library of the University of South Carolina, South Carolina State Archives, University of Pennsylvania, Southern Historical Collection, University of Virginia, Virginia Historical Society, South Carolina Historical Society, and William and Mary were unfailingly helpful. I am especially indebted to Allen Stokes at the South Caroliniana Library whose detailed knowledge of the Hammond material greatly facilitated my research. I owe special thanks to Mary C. Simms Oliphant for providing me with Simms material that was otherwise unavailable. Robert Brugger, John Caughey, Robert Engs, Clifford Geertz, Deborah Hood, Neil Leonard, Donald Mathews, Murray Murphey, Anthony Wallace, Ronald Walters, and C. Vann Woodward all have criticized my ideas forcefully and helpfully. I am particularly grateful to Bertram Wyatt-Brown for the detailed comments he offered on an earlier version of the manuscript and to Richard Beeman for his constant and loyal support.

My greatest debt, however, is to Charles Rosenberg, who has both encouraged and challenged me from the beginning of my graduate work. As my dissertation director, he was generous with his time and insights. But I most appreciate the way he always has made me feel I could do better and so often has shown me how.

A SACRED CIRCLE

Introduction:

A SACRED CIRCLE

n the winter darkness of 26 January 1843, a striking figure stood on the railroad platform at Petersburg, Virginia. The traveler's shoulder-length hair had turned nearly white, yet his complexion was rosy, almost childlike, his grey eyes clear and quick, his posture erect and self-assured. Edmund Ruffin's appearance of confidence arose in part from the sense of satisfaction he felt as he contemplated the purpose of his journey. He was embarking not simply on a trip, but a mission on behalf of science, truth, and Southern salvation.[1]

In the last days of December, Ruffin had been chosen by the governor and legislature of South Carolina to direct an agricultural and geological survey designed to identify the sources of the state's disastrous economic decline. "This appointment," Ruffin confessed, was "highly honorable to me and therefore highly gratifying," perhaps the more so because of his neglect by his own state, whose economic situation was scarcely better than that of her sister to the south.[2]

Only months before, Ruffin had been forced to abandon an enterprise to which he had devoted the preceding decade of his life. As early as the 1820s Ruffin had become alarmed at the diminishing profitability of Virginia's agriculture, which long had constituted the source of her wealth and the foundation of her civilization. Ruffin was determined to enlist the forces of science in her behalf, and in 1833 had founded the *Farmers' Register*, an agricultural periodical that served as the focus of his program to reform and save Virginia. But for the publisher, as for the planter, Virginia constituted a "barren field." Her citizens, Ruffin found, lacked "all public spirit and even . . . enlightened self interest." In January of 1842, Ruffin announced his intention to retire from his editorial work at the end of the year, and, in tones of angry self-pity, promised no longer "to obtrude on the . . . public, services which seem to be so little appreciated and . . . so little aided."[3]

1

In light of such discouragement, Ruffin felt particularly gratified by the recognition of his work in South Carolina and looked forward to a warm reception in Charleston. But as he awaited his train in the winter evening, Ruffin little anticipated the special significance of the 180 miles by rail and 200 miles by sea he would travel in the next few days. This trip was to provide the occasion for his introduction to South Carolina's young Governor Hammond, self-designated "apostle" to Ruffin in the cause of scientific agricultural reform. In the course of the next few years, James Henry Hammond would become Ruffin's devoted correspondent and perhaps most intimate friend.[4]

From the time of their first meeting in Charleston, Hammond displayed a hospitality which the visitor found "altogether agreeable," inviting the Virginian to share his "mess" and sitting room in the hotel suite he occupied on his visits from the capital at Columbia. From the first, Ruffin was taken with the tall and handsome governor. Soon he recognized that Hammond's impressive physical appearance was matched by a remarkably astute and inquiring mind, "unquestionably," in Ruffin's estimation, "the most powerful . . . in the Southern states." Despite more than a decade's difference in age, the two had by summer become friends, passing long June evenings at Hammond's plantation high on a bluff above the Savannah River where together they analyzed specimens of South Carolina soil, as well as samples of Hammond's stock of tobacco, port, and madeira.[5]

As the summer wore on, Ruffin discovered that he and Hammond shared a good deal more than their commitment to agricultural reform of the seaboard South. The Carolinian seemed like Ruffin himself to view the wasting of the Southern soil as manifestation of growing barrenness of the Southern mind and erosion of the Southern character. Hammond not only provided the appreciation for Ruffin's ideas he had sought long and futilely in Virginia; Hammond shared Ruffin's bitter sense of alienation. Despite his position as governor, Hammond felt his true worth unrecognized and knew the desperate loneliness that seemed the lot of the scientist, the thinker, or the reformer in the Old South. "I am as you only laughed at," Hammond confided to the Virginian. "I have no assistant, no sympathizer, no consoler," he lamented. "If it be of any consolation to you to know of others suffering like yourself," Ruffin reassured him, "I can afford you some of it."[6]

These feelings of personal loneliness, social alienation, and intellectual futility were not peculiar to Edmund Ruffin and J. H. Hammond, nor was the close and comforting friendship the two forged in response to serve as solace in their trials. Indeed, Hammond and Ruffin shared analogous relationships with other Southerners who regarded themselves as similarly lonely and unappreciated: the intellect they all saw as their defining attribute seemed to have no place within the South and no role in arresting regional decline.[7] Drawn to one another by a shared feeling of "exile" and a common perception of Southern crisis, a number of intellectuals in the late 1830s and 1840s evolved a network of mutual support that functioned through the frequent exchange of letters and visits, a pattern of interaction in which Ruffin's trip to South Carolina proved only an inaugural venture.

Upon his return to Virginia, Ruffin corresponded regularly with Hammond, and the two exchanged not only letters, but samples of their work in forms that varied from political and agricultural pamphlets to new hybrids of peas. Ruffin returned to Hammond's plantation for occasional visits, and after the death of the Virginian's wife in 1846, Hammond repeatedly urged him to settled permanently in South Carolina.

Hammond meanwhile was developing similarly intense friendships a bit closer to home. After their joint participation in the foundation of the State Agricultural Society in 1839, Hammond began to receive letters requesting "agricultural enlightenment" from William Gilmore Simms, a South Carolina poet and novelist who resided about fifty miles away.[8] Before long, the two planters began to discuss other topics as well—the politics of their native Barnwell District and of the state, the condition of Southern literature, and the decline of the South more generally. Fifty miles was sufficient distance to make letters their chief mode of interaction, but after a few meetings at Barnwell Courthouse, where both occasionally were required to transact business, Simms and Hammond discovered themselves eager to share each other's company whenever possible. Hammond found Simms a "most incessant talker" and a highly entertaining visitor. "Large of stature, erect in port, with a proud pose of the head," Simms seemed "perfectly at home in whatever company he happened to find himself." His sense of humor, "bold, bluff and masculine—with a touch of satirical innuendo and sly sarcasm" was legendary among his contemporaries, who often heard "his voice rolling in jovial thunder above a murmurous sea of conversation." It is easy to imagine him entertaining his friend as the two sat at Hammond's fireside talking, playing billiards, and drinking wine, or sipping their favorite Carolina punch in front of the walls of books in the brick library at Simms's "Woodlands." The novelist undoubtedly also was an asset to Hammond as a guest in his ostentatious new town house in Columbia. Not only would Simms's skills as conversationalist and raconteur make him shine in any group; his taste and intellectual sophistication enabled him to appreciate the expensive Brussels carpets, the De La Tour and Gilbert Stuart paintings Hammond had brought from Europe, treasures other

South Carolinians regarded "with the apathy of Indians."[9]

But Simms was more than joviality, taste, and intellect. Like Hammond, he had an introspective, morbid streak, a similar sense of frustration and resentment at what he perceived as neglect by his region. Perhaps on their rides together about Hammond's estate this darker side of their rapport emerged, for, as Simms recalled two decades later, Hammond had been his

most confidential friend for near Twenty-five years. Never were thoughts more intimate than his and mine. We had few or no secrets from each other. . . . I felt that there was something kindred in our intellectual nature. Certainly there was much, very much in common between us. Never did man more thoroughly appreciate his genius—its grasp—its subtlety—its superiority of aim. And most deeply did I sympathize with him under the denial of his aim and the exercise of his powers.[10]

From the first, however, Simms endeavored to draw Hammond out of his "morbid moping." As novelist, editor, critic, and, in Hammond's words, the "most distinguished literary character of the South," Simms maintained "a constant intercourse" with a multitude of Southerners of intellectual inclination, and he began to introduce Hammond to this regional intelligentsia.[11]

Despite the discouraging state of letters in his section, Simms found consolation in the reverence of at least some Southerners for the life of the mind. "The existence of these men," he proclaimed in 1841, "is testified by their frequent struggles in the cause they espoused, for the divinities whom they loved. Their labors have made themselves known, if not felt, in unremitted and still continued though feeble exertions to extend their sacred circle—to diffuse its hallowing influences and pursuade [sic] the friends whom they would serve and elevate, to the altars where they themselves are only too glad to bow."[12]

Simms was acquainted with a number of such Southerners in Virginia and South Carolina and even some from Louisiana and other states to the west. But this group was too large, too undifferentiated, and too scattered to serve as the "sacred circle," a nucleus for the Southern reform movement he hoped to create. His was to be—as his choice of metaphor made clear—a religious effort at proselytism that would begin among those who understood his goals and shared with him a sense of common plight and common purpose.

Not long after the beginning of their own friendship, Simms and Hammond found another potential convert in George Frederick Holmes, a considerably younger but highly learned resident of Orangeburg District who had emigrated from England in 1837. Simms was eager to secure Holmes's contributions for his editorial endeavors and, as the transplanted Englishman described it, set about "to transmute me into one of the Brotherhood of the Quill." When circumstances prevented their more usual leisurely meeting to "crack a bottle together" at Simms's plantation, Holmes joined his friend at the Orangeburg train depot as Simms passed through town en route to business in Columbia. While the cars paused in the station, the two authors exchanged their latest manuscripts and Simms presented Holmes with new books to review. Such circumstances were far from ideal for an editor's supervision of his protégé, but in the rural South, writers had to make the best of any opportunities for personal interaction. Soon Holmes started to write about these difficulties, publishing open letters to Simms on the burdens they shared as intellectuals in the South. "I do not think," Holmes began, "I can address my remarks with greater propriety to anyone than yourself, who were the original cause of their formation."[13]

In 1846, Holmes's assumption of a faculty position at William and Mary provided the occasion for induction of another thinker into full membership within the Sacred Circle. A professor of law at William and Mary, Nathaniel Beverley Tucker was a distant cousin of Edmund Ruffin and had been involved with him the effort to establish the *Southern Magazine* in 1841.[14] Hammond, too, was acquainted with the older Virginian, for they had corresponded intermittently about Southern politics since Hammond's congressional term in 1835, and so he gave Tucker advance notice of Holmes's arrival. "I think you will find him an acquisition. Do give my best regards to him." Tucker responded enthusiastically: "I am delighted with Holmes. I invited him to make my house his home . . . and he has been with me six weeks. We harmonize perfectly in everything." Soon Hammond introduced Simms to Tucker through the mail, entering the novelist "as a colleague with myself under your tuition." Before long, Simms, too, was corresponding with the old professor. Their exchanges, they agreed, were of a character far too rare among ante-bellum Southerners. "We do," Tucker summarized, "but express the pleasure with which . . . men of candid minds who think their own thoughts and say what they think naturally find in the intercommunication of their ideas."[15]

Frustrated by the geographic distances between them, the members of the group yearned for the day when they no longer would be separated, for a different South in which the intellectual no longer would feel isolated. "Holmes was saying last night," Tucker reported, " 'O! if we could get a visit from Hammond.' " And Simms similarly assured the Virginian, "We drank your health in joyous bumpers at Hammond's. . . . We greatly wished for your presence, and concluded with the congratulatory thought that the formation of a new republic would bring us wonderfully nearer to one another."[16]

Because they needed to find appreciation for their talents, Southern men of mind united with others similarly inclined—and equally frustrated—both to console one another and to assert their right to social recognition and status. Patterns of personal friendship thus assumed both social and cultural significance, for the psychological, intellectual and professional concerns of these articulate Southerners all became intertwined within the framework of their Sacred Circle. While the members of the network provided one another with emotional sustenance, the group itself served as surrogate for the formalized cultural institutions the Old South seemed conspicuously to lack. Because the Sacred Circle endeavored explicitly to define the larger cultural meaning of the personal relationships that comprised its essence, it provides a particularly striking illustration of the social significance of friendship, a subject too often overlooked by historians.[17]

Because of its informality, however, this group cannot be defined with precision. It had no explicit organizational structure, no specific date of foundation or dissolution; its boundaries are similarly unclear. Hammond, Ruffin, Simms, Holmes, and Tucker seem unquestionably to have participated in the network. But others had intermittent contact with this group, shared many of its views, yet their exact relationship cannot be determined from existing evidence.[18] The particular friendship among the five members of the Sacred Circle is richly documented by surviving personal and public papers that delineate the relationship between their lives and their perception of their role as intellectuals. There is reason to think, however, that except for the quantity of material they left to posterity, the group was not atypical. Informal networks such as this one seem to have been a central institution in Southern intellectual life. Holmes, for example, was involved briefly with a group called the Alligator Club near Orangeburg; Simms participated in a literary coterie based in Russell's Bookstore in Charleston; Charles Gayarre belonged to similar networks in New Orleans. Moreover, the critical attitude Hammond, Holmes, Ruffin, Tucker, and Simms assumed toward their region was not unique, for one finds many of their concerns echoed repeatedly in the Southern periodical and popular press.

Whatever their feelings of isolation and marginality, these five thinkers were acknowledged to be among the foremost minds of their region, and their views consistently reflect those of the Southern intelligentsia generally. But this intellectual class—as its members knew all too well—was not the South and often felt it had no place within it. The members of the Sacred Circle found themselves alienated from their society and denied the recognition they were certain their talents deserved.

ONE

Bald and Sterile Fields:

THE CONTEXT OF INTELLECTUAL DISCONTENT

Although the planter frequently invoked the "learned leisure"[1] permitted by slavery as one defense of his way of life, many Southerners of the late ante-bellum period were well aware of the intellectual deficiencies of their region. Achievement in the realm of mind brought neither fame nor fortune, and explanations for the "hindrances to the Progress of Literature at the South"[2] abounded in popular oratory and the press. The absence of cities to stimulate intellectual interchange and the general sparseness of Southern population were the most commonly cited impediments to diffusion of knowledge. But many sharper critics agreed that the region's natural resources had seduced the Southerner into "mental indolence," a far-from-learned leisure that "deadens his energies and impairs his vigor."[3] Whatever the explanations advanced for the section's intellectual shortcomings, there could be little disagreement that on an objective, institutional level the South did little to encourage or support the life of the mind.

The most telling indication of the South's neglect of letters was undoubtedly her failure to provide for public education. Although the last years of the ante-bellum period were to foster widespread efforts to remedy this situation, no Southern state had an effective common school system before the Civil War. While most made some provision for instructing paupers, these arrangements were almost universally unsatisfactory—described in South Carolina as "radically defective," in Louisiana as "a reproach," in Virginia as "disgraceful."[4] This lack of basic educational opportunity resulted in a shortage of qualified teachers, which in turn guaranteed the inadequacies of the system at all levels. In 1853 the Grand Jury of Barnwell District complained to the South Carolina legislature, "There is not a decent Free School teacher in the District. The Majority . . . are men who are ignorant of the very first principals [sic] of education, illiterate themselves, and

7

sometimes of such bad habits that they have been known to be drunk
for days after drawing their pay."[5]

Criticisms of primary schooling in the region appeared repeatedly
in Southern journals and newspapers. "It may convey a just notion of
the benighted condition of our state," wrote one Virginia editor, "to
say that on the 1st of October last, there were thirty thousand poor
children over the age of five . . . without any means of instruction
whatever."[6] As the ante-bellum period wore on, Southern deficiencies
increasingly were seen in terms of objective comparisons with the
North. "The number of those who cannot read and write in Virginia
is 58,787," the Richmond Education Convention of 1847 reported omi-
nously. "In Massachusetts it is only 4448." The census of 1850 impressed
this striking discrepancy upon the nation as a whole, disclosing the
illiteracy rate among white Southern adults at 20.3 percent as contrasted with 3 percent in the Middle States and .42 percent in New
England.[7]

In the Old South, elementary education, even to the level of basic
literacy, was a privilege rather than a right. South Carolina's Governor
John Manning exaggerated only slightly when he observed in 1853,
"Education has been provided . . . but for one class of the citizens of
the state, which is the wealthy class. For the middle and poorer
classes of society it has done nothing."[8] These deficiencies did not
affect only the individuals left ignorant and untaught. Perhaps more
important, they represented a general lack of intellectual leadership
and commitment on the part of the literate majority.[9]

Given the aristocratic social views of many Southerners, one might
expect the region to have developed a hierarchical system of education that, despite inadequate elementary public instruction, would
provide rigorous intellectual training for an elite. While the number
of colleges, universities, and private academies within the region might
seem to support such an interpretation, for a number of reasons these
institutions were less than ideal centers for a thriving intellectual life.
Colleges in nearly every Southern state confronted inadequately prepared matriculants, some, as one South Carolina College professor
observed, "entirely untutored in even an ordinary correct pronuncia-
tion."[10] Because of the inadequacies of elementary education, universities necessarily had to lower their standards to compensate for deficiencies in student preparation. Most such institutions in the South,
DeBow's noted in 1861, were universities "in name only—being really
inferior . . . to the best high schools of which England can boast." A
staunch defender of Southern rights, *DeBow's* nevertheless was unre-
strained in its criticisms of the region's system of higher education,
which it described as "one for SHOW and not for use. The great object
of education, viz: the training and developing all the powers of the

mind into active and vigorous exercise is quite ignored. The knowledge imparted is a mere smattering; the accomplishments mere tinsel glass."[11]

But Southern colleges and universities encountered obstacles perhaps more distressing than the ill-preparedness of their students. Many of the youths who attended these institutions were not merely ignorant, but entirely uncontrollable. Discipline—not instruction—was the overriding concern of nearly every faculty. The extremes of student unruliness occasionally threatened the lives of instructors and the residents of college towns. In 1856 one of a number of ante-bellum "riots" at South Carolina College was quelled only after five militia companies were mobilized. College buildings and professors were subject to "wanton destruction" from "brickbats and other missiles." One of Tucker's colleagues at William and Mary recorded a particularly memorable evening in the faculty minutes. A professor discovered three disguised students hurling objects at the president's house. He pursued them, but one turned and "snapped a pistol at him," then ran inside the main college building where he was heard "breaking the windows and furniture of one of the lecture rooms on the second floor." The instructor retreated in fear but the next day found the room "more or less polluted" and the faculty record books defiled with "human ordure and other filth."[12]

Any dissatisfaction with college life or supposed mistreatment by the faculty provided an occasion for student uprising, for notions of honor seemed to these young Southern gentlemen adequate justification for any act of violence. One South Carolina father lamenting a recent disturbance at the college explained that "a majority of those who go to college are desirous of doing nothing more than what is absolutely required" and thus looked upon their professors as "hard task masters. . . . And boys . . . are apt as soon as they get to College to imagine that they are quite gentlemen, and consider any thing they fancy to be harsh as an insult to their assumed dignity not to be submitted to without an apology or forsooth they will rebel & break up the college."[13]

This atmosphere was far from conducive to dispassionate contemplation, and a professorship in such an institution hardly encouraged sophisticated intellectual speculation. The faculty in Southern colleges were in a sense prisoners of the often arrogant and fractious sons of the gentry who paid the instruction fees.[14] Assaults on professors were almost commonplace; George Frederick Holmes was scarcely moved to comment when he heard that one of his colleagues at the University of Virginia had been struck with a slingshot by a student who then tried to bite off his teacher's thumb. Perhaps by the time of this incident in 1857, Holmes was accustomed to the unruliness of

Southern students, for a decade earlier he had lost his job as the first president of the University of Mississippi when his introduction of an honor system there produced a complete breakdown of order. Perhaps, too, Holmes considered his colleague at Virginia fortunate only to have his thumb threatened, for in an earlier incident a professor at the university had been shot and killed.[15]

The indignities to which professors submitted in return for inadequate and often uncertain financial compensation are probably the best testimony to the scarcity of roles for men of knowledge in the Old South. The educational system, deficient as it was from the lowest to the highest levels, nevertheless constituted almost the only institutional framework for the life of the mind in the region. The South lacked the demand for intellectual products that increasingly characterized the North, where a large reading public, concentrated to a considerable degree in urban centers, provided a market for a great variety of books, newspapers, and periodicals. In the South, however, neither a healthy publishing industry nor a vigorous periodical press developed. Northern houses such as Harper and Lippincott distributed books in Southern cities, but native writers were distant from editorial encouragement, and subjects of particular interest to Southerners tended to be neglected by the press. The paucity of urban centers not only limited the availability of books, but rendered intellectual interchange difficult and accounted at least in part for the scarcity of Southern libraries, philosophical societies, and lycea until the very last years of the ante-bellum period.[16]

In such an environment, the individual attracted to the life of the mind confronted serious difficulties. One Charleston poet felt that "at no time and in no country" had the writer been so beset. "It would scarcely be too extravagant," he declared, "to entitle the Southern author the Pariah of modern literature."[17] A contributor to the *Southern Literary Messenger* in 1854 described the situation more matter-of-factly, noting "we have not a self-supporting class of literati. The genius of our institutions does not provide for it—much less our tastes and the structure of society." Perhaps, he mused, by that far distant day when the Pacific coast had become as densely populated as the Atlantic, "we may have princely endowments of literary institutions . . . with a literati recognized as a class. But," he wondered, " 'Cui bono'?"[18] Most aspiring writers and intellectuals responded far less dispassionately. Indeed, such men saw the region's shortcomings not simply as matters of taste or institutional arrangement, but as a crucial factor in their own lives and, they were convinced, the central factor in the condition and future prospect of Southern society.

A common perception of this Southern "barrenness"—both intellectual and agricultural—had generated the initial rapport between Hammond and Ruffin, and a similarly shared sense of Southern desolation provided the impetus for formation of the larger intellectual network that came to include Simms, Holmes, and Tucker in the course of the decade. For these five, an overriding reality of their own lives was their sense of neglect by their society, a rejection they viewed as both cause and effect within a pattern of more general regional decline.

There was indeed considerable objective basis for such a view of Southern civilization during the early 1840s, especially in the seaboard states where these five men lived. Although cotton prices had increased steadily up to 1837, the Panic of that year reversed this trend, and in 1839 the agricultural market collapsed. For South Carolina and Virginia, this depression was but the culmination of a long period of economic difficulty. From the turn of the century in Virginia and after the mid-twenties in South Carolina, the decreasing productivity of land and the ready availability of virgin acreage in the Southwest had produced a steady outflow of both men and capital. In the forty years before the Civil War, South Carolina lost through emigration more than two hundred thousand whites, nearly half the number born in the state after 1800.[19] The high agricultural prices of the 1830s served as a special impetus for migration to western areas where highly productive land awaited cultivation. By the 1840s, whole sections of South Carolina were virtually deserted, prompting Ruffin to lament on his visit to that state in 1843, "How many well located plantations . . . once highly improved and still with fine buildings and noble avenues of oaks remain dilapidated and abandoned!"[20] Virginia, too, was experiencing severe economic and demographic crisis. Between 1830 and 1840, the total increase in white population in the state was only 3 percent, and eastern Virginia lost twenty-six thousand inhabitants in the course of the decade. Land values in the state declined by more than half between 1817 and 1829, and Virginia's exports slumped by two-thirds.[21]

Nationwide economic difficulties thus were intensified in Virginia and South Carolina by deteriorating productivity, which encouraged a steady westward exodus. Because these two states long had considered themselves the leaders of the South, the discontinuity between economic reality and traditional pretension was particularly troubling, and many thinking inhabitants of the two states gave themselves up to a sense of doom. To the Sacred Circle and to many other Southerners as well, their section appeared a "region of tombs."[22]

Simms, Hammond, Ruffin, Tucker, and Holmes had grown aware of the economic plight of their states independently, for all had been personally affected by these unfavorable economic realities. As young men, four of the five had seriously considered joining the movement of emigration from the seaboard South. At frequent intervals throughout his life, Holmes talked of moving West, to Missouri, or Wisconsin, or Minnesota, where economic opportunity would satisfy his "determination of making a fortune."[23] Hammond, too, thought of leaving South Carolina on a number of occasions and in 1836 purchased fifty thousand acres of cotton land in Texas. Simms often spoke of moving North where he believed authors were accorded financial recognition they were denied in the South. Tucker, who was considerably older than his three friends, first confronted the economic troubles of his native state in the years just prior to the War of 1812, when the embargo and consequent dislocation of shipping disrupted Virginia's commercial life. A dearth of business coupled with a severe shortage of money often kept even those few clients the young lawyer secured from paying their bills. Tucker believed this early poverty was the direct result of weaknesses in the Virginia economy. "Never again," he vowed, would he "live in a country which does not abound in necessaries," and soon after the war, he moved to Missouri where he remained for twenty years.[24]

The effect of the decreasing productivity and wealth of the seaboard South upon their individual livelihoods made all five thinkers deeply troubled about the exploitive—and as they saw it, disastrous—methods of Southern agriculture. "Nothing," Simms declared indignantly, "could be more wretched and slovenly." But soil erosion also symbolized a more pervasive Southern crisis; wasted lands were a result, not a cause, of the South's lamentable state. "It is not," Simms emphasized, "the poverty of the soil which has made us poor." The sources of Southern decline were deeper; the "true deficiency" of Southern agriculture arose from a failure of mind, in both its intellectual and moral capacities. "The great evils which serve to prevent agriculture being prosperous in Virginia," Ruffin wrote, "may be summed up in the single word, *ignorance*." And because these deficiencies were failures of mind, they were simultaneously—in the mid-nineteenth-century understanding of mental structures and processes—ethical shortcomings as well. Simms found the Southerner victim of "vast temptations to cupidity and mercenary enterprise held out by the immense, and but partially opened tracts of plain and prairie in the west." The planter yielded to his greed, exhausted his land, and moved on, little caring that "the constant disruption of the bonds of society which is produced by the wandering habits of its members results invariably in moral loss to the whole." Possessed by an "insatiate rage for gain," the Southerner had all but forgotten his "sacred obligations" to his homeland. The decline of Southern agriculture evoked in Hammond similar "feelings of profound emotion. Not only on account of its immediate pecuniary consequences, but its great moral effects."[25]

The only salvation for agriculture, indeed the only hope for the South, Simms concluded, lay in "the loyalty of . . . the people to their leading intellects," for the region had been stricken by a "wasting process which in the moral as in the physical culture has left us to the possession of . . . bald and sterile fields."[26]

For the men of mind, imagery of degeneration came to represent what they viewed as the decline of Southern civilization on every level, from the erosion of its physical resources to the decay of its moral and intellectual endowment. "The productions of the brain," Hammond observed, "seem to be in so bad stock as those of the soil." In its identification of the agricultural with the intellectual and moral, this recurring metaphor did not simply describe the plight of the man of mind, but rather implied that such individuals ought to possess a primary significance. Just as society had to nurture the land and produce food to survive physically, so, too, the image suggested, it must cultivate the thinker; his contributions were as indispensable as the fruits of the earth. "Books," Simms declared, must "become an aliment as absolutely necessary to us as any other."[27]

By the time they met in the early 1840s, each of these intellectuals had come to recognize the simultaneous existence of several dimensions of crisis. First, all five had experienced personal economic and social setbacks, difficulties they chose to define as the result of a general regional neglect of intellect. Because the thinker occupied no specific niche within Southern society, Hammond regarded himself in 1839 as "in danger of having no *caste* whatever, which will not do." Simms's insecure personal finances rendered him particularly sensitive to the economic disadvantages of being a Southern intellectual and prompted him in 1841 to proclaim in disgust, "We have not one native professional author from the Potomac to the Sabine who, if he relied on the South purely for his resources, would not in half the number of months of the year, go without his porridge." The region's failure, as Holmes put it, to "maintain suitably its intellectual and spiritual teachers" thus had a direct impact upon the lives of these five, and their perception of a Southern indifference to letters served as an explanation—and even justification—for their failure to achieve the economic and social position to which they aspired.[28]

Their personal difficulties and frustrations were paralleled by a more general regional crisis—the rapid decline in the population, wealth, and political power of the Old South of Virginia and South Carolina relative to the rest of the nation. And this situation, like their own hardships, they attributed to their section's intellectual and moral deficiencies. The same indifference to the role of mind, they found, had impoverished both the South and the Southern intellectual.

Thus at the time of their first meeting, each of the five thinkers had

come independently to regard his feelings of marginality as the inescapable product of social forces and to identify his own plight with
that of his region. In such an explanation of their situation, Hammond,
Holmes, Ruffin, Tucker, and Simms discovered the foundation for a
common social vision and a shared discontent with the Southern status
quo.

TWO

As Men and Authors:

ROMANTIC GENIUS AND ROMANTIC FRIENDSHIP

estined to till the bald and sterile intellectual fields of the South, the members of the Sacred Circle had little doubt that they necessarily shared a "mutual career" of professional frustrations and difficulties. But what began as a sense of common grievance soon evolved into a relationship encompassing their personal as well as intellectual concerns. Their shared problems, the five gradually recognized, arose not just from the social isolation of the man of knowledge, but from their common temperamental and emotional idiosyncrasies, peculiarities they identified as an inevitable concomitant of their innate genius. Because this "born allotment" served as the foundation of their growing intimacy, the course of friendship encouraged them to explore the nature and meaning of their psychological similarities. The Sacred Circle thus developed into an institution that nurtured both mind and heart; it came to sustain its members, as Simms described, "at once as men and authors."[1]

OUR MUTUAL CAREER

At first Hammond, Holmes, Ruffin, Tucker, and Simms endeavored to provide one another with essentially intellectual support. Because they felt themselves deprived of mental companionship, they delighted in the purely cerebral aspect of their association, and their interaction "as authors" in large measure shaped the texture of their entire relationship.

As a framework for intellectual exchange, the network they established served a number of clearly identifiable professional functions. Most important, perhaps, the five Southerners served as catalysts for one another's thoughts. All recognized the intellectual's need for "someone to test ideas with," and Hammond and Holmes independently arrived at the same metaphor of flint and steel to represent the dynamic quality of the relationship between thinkers. The five also sought from one another the rigorous and constructive criticism they received nowhere else in Southern society. "I am not fishing for compliments," Hammond insisted as he requested Simms's advice. "I want the discriminating opinion of one capable of giving one that may be of real service to me." In regard to a projected article on Ruffin's specialty, agricultural chemistry, Hammond turned to the Virginian for similar aid. "I want your *candid* & *entire* opinion. . . . I want you to point out its *errors* and *defects*. . . . If you let me make a fool of myself. I shall throw the responsibility on you."[2]

The members of the group did take considerable intellectual responsibility for one another. With Simms, for example, Hammond saw his role as that of an intellectual conscience and continually urged the novelist to write more slowly, more carefully, with an eye to posterity rather than popularity. "Why will you not," he demanded, "for godsake spare one month in the year to devote annually to something *great*." Simms, by contrast, expended much effort helping Holmes attune his abstract and scholarly mind to an uncultivated Southern audience. Holmes's work, Simms warned, must not be "cumbered with learning, only freshened by it." Above all, he advised soberly, "Do not be too profound in your jokes."[3]

The members of the group sought to capitalize upon their differences in intellectual style and perspective, and at the same time to provide one another with tangible assistance in achieving the intellectual goals each had defined as particularly his own. Holmes requested recommendations for professorships from Simms and Hammond and in turn served as Simms's lieutenant in the battle for a comprehensive copyright law protecting American authors. Each wrote for the publications sponsored by the others: Tucker and Hammond contributed to Ruffin's *Southern Magazine* and *Farmers' Register*, while work by Hammond, Holmes, and Tucker appeared in Simms's editorial ventures: the *Magnolia*, the *Southern and Western Monthly Magazine*, and the *Southern Quarterly Review*. Their flattering reviews of one another's speeches and publications helped gain acceptance for the opinions they held in common, and all five assisted in disseminating the work and ideas of other members of the circle.[4]

Because areas of intellectual inquiry were relatively unspecialized in the nineteenth century, almost all men of mind maintained a wide variety of interests and institutional commitments. The members of the Sacred Circle found their diverse contacts and involvements distinctly advantageous to the group as a whole. Upon his election to the state legislature in 1844, for example, Simms promised Holmes he would take advantage of his political position to "promulgate your literary and professional views." Similarly, Hammond's entry into the United States Senate in 1857 would enable him to distribute Ruffin's pamphlets on slavery and scientific agriculture postage-free and, in addition, to insert his friend's essays in the *Congressional Globe*. Tucker supplied Hammond's writings on slavery and Ruffin's pieces on politics to his friends in Virginia's academic and political circles; Hammond offered to subsidize a collection of Tucker's works and, on another occasion, to pay off some of Simms's debts. Simms, in turn, used his contacts with Northern publishers to arrange for a reprint of Tucker's novel *The Partisan Leader* and for an edition of Hammond's essays and speeches.[5]

The members of the network recognized that their differing intellectual specialties and varying institutional and personal contacts could be used to advance the more general aims of the group. Hammond and Ruffin were conceded to be expert both in politics and agriculture, while Simms was pre-eminent in belles-lettres. Tucker contributed most on legal and constitutional questions, especially those relating to states' rights. Holmes was the most abstract thinker in the network, as well as the most scholarly.

Despite these differences, all participated in each others' interests to a considerable degree, with Ruffin and Tucker producing novels, Holmes and Simms writing occasionally on agriculture, and Hammond composing poetry and treatises on metaphysics. Whatever their specific area of endeavor, the five thinkers recognized that each separate effort was dedicated to a common purpose; every undertaking was designed ultimately to advance their shared goals of establishing a social role for knowledge and for the intellectual. In large measure they were, as they proudly acknowledged, "echoes" of one another, and thus they could speak almost interchangeably. As Hammond explained in regard to his offer to finance an edition of Tucker's writing, "I wish all could think as you and I do & I know of no way of accomplishing so much as by the publication of your works."[6]

THE FATE OF GENIUS

The relationship among the five soon became much more than a professional convenience. Almost from the beginning, the emotional and psychological functions of the network rivaled its purely intellectual purposes. "I once wrote a letter to old B. Tucker," Simms reminisced in 1859, "and closed it with 'Yours lovingly.' I forget what were the exact terms of the old man's response, but it showed that his heart was touched by the use of a word which men employ femininely only,—and in their dealings with women. Surely, . . . in a guild like ours, which the world never welcomes to *its* love . . . there should be much love among ourselves! *We,* at least, will try to love one another at once as men and authors."[7]

Because the members of the group saw themselves "at once as men and authors"—with each element of that juxtaposition inseparable from the other—personal and professional interests fused; the network provided its members with emotional support at the same time it assisted them in relating to the rest of their society and the seeming crisis of their culture. Their shared vision thus extended well beyond the professional realm and encompassed far more than a simple concern about the sources of their livelihood—what Simms called their "porridge." The neglect of intellect in the South resonated within each of these thinkers as a sense of deep personal loneliness, expressed in what Simms described as "fits of despondency" and Hammond called his "morbid moping." Recurrent bouts of depression and gloomy introspection characterized all the members of the circle. "I have never known what was cordial sympathy in any of my pursuits among men," Simms lamented. "I have been an exile from my birth." Hammond felt much the same, finding himself "as solitary . . . as if I were in the Great Sahara." Ruffin complained of a "popular aversion" to him; Holmes regarded himself as "an alien on a desert shore"; Tucker remarked that Robinson Crusoe had been "hardly more completely isolated than I." Indeed, he concluded a bit peevishly, his own lot was worse, for Crusoe had been "at least permitted to persuade himself that if they knew where he was they would have taken some notice of him."[8]

The five thinkers found themselves to be remarkably alike—not just in their views or their relationship to Southern society, but, most important, in what they saw as their shared temperaments and emotional needs. For until they had discovered one another, it had seemed, in Simms's words, that as a "peculiarly intellectual individual," each was doomed both to "eminent solitude in the world of fame" and to "corresponding solitude in the world of the affections." The intensity of their friendship therefore arose from recognition of the similarities of their careers, not just as thinkers, but "as men"—their shared depression and despair, their parallel family experience, their common psychological structure, which Simms described as the "peculiar moral constitution" of the man of knowledge.[9]

However alienated these Southerners may have felt, Hammond, Holmes, Ruffin, Tucker, and Simms nevertheless shared in a European and American intellectual world view that structured their perceptions and provided them with a very specific range of categories with which to formulate their view of their environment and themselves. Indeed, their very feelings of isolation were in large part an artifact of mid-

nineteenth-century culture. In the process of their intellectual socialization, all five thinkers had been significantly influenced by what since
has been described as the prevailing Romantic outlook. For all the
members of the group, this outlook defined not just an approach to
literature, but an ideology that provided a system of values, a set of
behavioral attitudes, and a common vocabulary in terms of which
each thinker construed his past experiences and his present misfor-
tunes.

In recent years, it has become fashionable for literary critics and
historians to discriminate among different phases and styles of Romanticism, to emphasize differences between Blake and Tennyson, for
example, or sharply to distinguish the English, French, and the Ger-
mans.[10] But to the members of the Sacred Circle, such efforts would
have appeared in large measure meaningless. These Southerners were
cultural provincials who lacked the sophistication of modern or even
of the most prominent nineteenth-century critics. Yet, anxious to identify themselves with the mainstreams of the intellectual life of their
era, they eagerly, syncretically, and somewhat indiscriminately adopted
any available ideas that seemed appropriate to their situation. Thus,
for example, they minimized the growing estrangement between
science and religion in order to continue to derive legitimation for their
own ideas from both sources of cultural authority. In a sense, their
minds may likened to the commonplace books in which several members of the group, like many educated individuals of their time, recorded
any literary excerpts that seemed relevant to their particular concerns.
In their commonplace books, as in their lives, ideas from sources as
disparate as Coleridge, Montaigne, Vico, and the Bible were removed
from their contexts and appropriated for these Southern thinkers' own
purposes. The members of the Sacred Circle sought to use ideas to
place themselves and their plight within a broader context than simply
that of the ante-bellum South. By identifying their regional dilemma
with larger cultural issues, they hoped to enhance the significance of
their own situation, imparting to it a degree of transcendence. Any
idea or posture available in the cultural repertoire might help to
advance their ends. Thus they emphasized, cultivated, and undoubtedly exaggerated the similarities they found between the experiences
of a Byron or a Shelley and their own life and thought. By assuming
Romantic poses and attitudes, by styling themselves after the literary
giants of their age, they hoped to prove themselves legitimate intellectuals, to gain a confirmation of their identity they seemed unable to
secure from the philistine inhabitants of the South. Their writings are
thus replete with images and perceptions which later literary historians
have identified as characteristic of Romanticism in its most general
sense with its emphasis on the exceptional, on exaggerated feeling, on

the importance of the self, on feelings of exile and alienation. These attitudes and categories of understanding provided a framework in terms of which the members of the Sacred Circle could explain their personal disaffection. But their use of this vocabulary signified as well the adoption of a number of more widely accepted Romantic assumptions about the state of the world and, most especially, the place of the artist or thinker within it. Indeed, the stereotype of the alienated Romantic artist seemed so accurately to represent their own existence that it became both an explanation of their experience and an influence upon it, a model both of and for their lives. Life and feeling began to imitate Romantic art.[11]

As young men, each of the five thinkers had read widely in Romantic literature and had endeavored to compose poetry. During his student days at South Carolina College, Hammond wandered around Columbia communing with the "woods and wilds and melancholy groves," gleaning poetry from the "demoniac spirit which preys upon me." Quite self-consciously, Hammond planned a work with "some resemblance" to Byron's *Childe Harold* and recorded—or perhaps encouraged—his own morbid moods with a typically elegiac variety of Romantic verse:

> Thou loveliest flower that ever bloomed
> In Woodland wild or meadow gay
> Oh why wert thou so early doom'd
> To drop & fall & fade away.[12]

In a similar manner, Beverley Tucker depicted his frustration in a melancholy work that clearly reflects the Romantic image of the *poete maudit*. Dramatically entitled "Midnight. March 23, 1830," Tucker's lament began:

> And this is life; and this it is to live
>   To toil, for what? For that I prize no more,
> Tho' others prize it still: to tug and strive.
>   To heap up wealth's unprofitable store,
>   Which no delight can purchase: to endure
> The applause or censure of the worthless crowd,
>   Whose breath is poison; whether we secure
> Their mercenary praise, or sternly proud,
>   Provoke their brutal rage to execration loud.[13]

Although these excursions into sentiment and self-indulgence have no discernible literary merit, they were nevertheless important to their authors as exercises in self-realization. Bewailing loneliness or lamenting the ephemerality of life or love, such poetic endeavors encouraged the Southerners to view their own trials as equivalent to the dramatic sufferings of the most tortured Romantic. Through the process of literary creation, the thinkers identified themselves with the spirit of their age. Their own sense of alienation within the South was unquestionably what made Romanticism so meaningful to these five thinkers. Like Shelley, they felt that their "weak and sensitive" natures rendered them unfit to "run further the gauntlet through this hellish society of men"; like Keats they seemed to be "literally hooted from the stage of life"; like Carlyle plagued by isolation; like Goethe and his Faust desperately lonely within the solitude of knowledge.[14]

In some ways the Southerners did share the dilemma of these literary luminaries. For although Byron and Shelley were far more gifted, they experienced many of the same social and cultural stresses as did the five Southern men of mind. The kinds of dilemmas of which the Southern intellectual complained seem in many ways identical to the more general dislocations Raymond Williams has described as characteristic of the role of the artist or thinker in the nineteenth century.[15]

The process of modernization—with its implication of concomitant changes in both values and social structure—was transforming the relationship of the intellectual to Western society. Social democratization, new methods of industrial production, and the emerging primacy of the marketplace had introduced widespread changes in the social environment of art as the "cash-nexus" intruded forcefully into this formerly transcendent realm. Advances in printing processes and the rise of a middle-class reading public in both Europe and America during the last years of the eighteenth century had revolutionized the relationship of the artist to his audience. Instead of interacting directly with a patron or an immediate circle of cognoscenti who shared his tastes, the writer felt himself thrust into the marketplace as but another producer within an industrialized mass society. As George Frederick Holmes observed, "The age of steam in things mechanical has produced an age of steam in things intellectual." In a statement Holmes found sufficiently striking to copy into a manuscript volume of notes, Coleridge explained the meaning of this mechanization of literature. "In times of old," he observed, "books were as religious oracles; as literature advanced, they next became venerable preceptors: they then descended to the rank of instructive friends: and as their numbers increased they sunk still lower, to that of entertaining companions." Art seemed to have become merely a specialized form of manufacture, but another commodity.[16]

In this environment, the artist experienced a structural alienation from his public that seemed qualitatively different from the traditional sense of isolation that had troubled intellectuals from at least the time of Socrates. The nineteenth-century thinker bewailed the seeming historical uniqueness of his own plight and began self-consciously to distinguish himself and his realm of "culture" from the philistine concerns of the uncultivated masses. When Hammond declared to Simms that he "felt a very wholesome contempt for my audience,"[17] he simply mirrored a sentiment—or perhaps a pose—which Williams has suggested typified this era.[18]

Such perceptions of change in social and cultural realities, Williams believes, produced a new aesthetic ideology designed to combat art's apparent irrelevance within an increasingly utilitarian world. Culture emerged as an "abstraction and absolute," distinguished from "society" as a superior dimension by which the world of the cash-nexus might be condemned. Belief in the higher reality of intellect and art implied as well the superiority of the artist, who emerged in Romantic theory as the custodian of truth, morality, and order in the midst of cultural and social upheaval.[19]

Such notions culminated logically in the Romantic notion of the creative but alienated genius, an image that was central not just to the ideology of Romanticism but to the dynamics of the Sacred Circle. Within a single framework of explanation, this construct seemed to encompass the varied aspects of their plight—to serve as both interpretation and legitimation of their individual dilemmas. The idea of genius enjoyed widespread currency in nineteenth-century thought, and from the mid 1700s essays on the topic had issued from English and American presses at a rapid rate. In the early years of the new century, the doctrine was articulated systematically by individuals of such prominence as Coleridge, Wordsworth, Shelley, Byron, Hugo, and Goethe, who investigated the nature of genius as part of a typically modest Romantic effort at self-discovery. By the 1830s and 1840s, one finds repeated references to these generally accepted concepts in Southern popular oratory and the press. The region's infatuation with the Romanticism of Walter Scott and medieval chivalry included as well an enthusiastic embrace of the idea of the genius, who was, after all, merely a specialized sort of Romantic hero. At Southern colleges, for example, it was a favorite topic for student orations, which bore such titles as "Solitude of Genius," "Inefficacy of Genius without Learning," or "Genius: Its Triumph and Its Fate."[20]

The idea of genius was thus readily available to the five Southerners as a mode of social explanation, and they invoked it freely to justify and mitigate their sense of neglect. Hammond's scrapbooks included a collection of clippings on the subject, designed to console the South Carolinian by ensuring him that the "Fate of Genius," as one article proclaimed, was inevitably the "polar blast of envy and the freezing rigidity of neglect."[21]

The educated man of the nineteenth century understood genius to be a biological trait that made an individual both emotionally and intellectually distinctive. A possessor of genius could not help but manifest a series of other qualities which in the nineteenth century appeared to be physiological in origin as was the characteristic of genius itself. The members of the Sacred Circle therefore logically saw their shared emotions and even their common social dilemma as resulting directly from their mental attributes. "There is a native incapacity in the constitutions of the man of genius," Simms believed, "for the just appreciation or enjoyment of the common household privilege of happiness accorded to the hopes of other men." Because he was by definition unlike others, he found himself inevitably isolated from those around him. It seemed unquestionably the "instinct of genius (for I certainly possessed it)" that made Tucker "unfit" for the "society of those whose society is essential to my happiness." Genius had unavoidable social implications that created an unbroken continuity between these thinkers' personal experiences and their intellectual ones; genius was the determining factor in both.[22]

For the modern scholar who tends to accept contemporary divisions between intellectual, social, and psychohistory, the fusion of psychological and social factors made by the Sacred Circle may be instructive. These nineteenth-century men understood that personal attributes and experiences create an individual whose range of choices about the way to lead his life are limited and structured by his inherited capabilities and predilections. What any individual defines as a meaningful and satisfying form of interaction with the world depends largely on personal and social circumstances that have generated his sense of who he is. A man endowed with special intellectual gifts, talents that distinguish—and isolate—him from others even in his earliest years, will tend to confront certain kinds of social difficulties and to make particular kinds of social choices. The members of the Sacred Circle believed that any man's life is in large part determined by a particular mental and psychological constitution that structures his relationship with the larger social world. Few sensitive twentieth-century historians would dispute such a perception.

For the members of the Sacred Circle, this outlook served yet another purpose. The Romantic frame of mind has been regarded by many historians and critics as an effort to discover some sources of stability in a world suddenly engulfed by rapid social and cultural change. The growth of industrialism and democracy threatened existing social relations; the rise of science had begun to challenge traditional bases for belief and sanctions for social order. In the midst of such flux, the determinism of the theory of genius was consoling, for it invoked the traditional religious argument from design as well as accepted scientific canon to guide the Southerners in understanding and directing their lives. In the same way that nineteenth-century social thought maintained that the physiology of women and of blacks had designed them to occupy a particular social place, so Simms, Tucker, Hammond, Holmes, and Ruffin believed that they, too, had a "born allotment," that both God and heredity had formed them for a special calling. In an age increasingly enamored of science, yet tenaciously loyal to its evangelical heritage, the five Southerners turned to hereditarian biology and to enthusiastic religion to legitimate their deviance. The doctrine of genius thus incorporated both religious and scientific justifications for their plight, for it explained their gifts as at once an indisputable physiological reality and a kind of divine grace. The genius was both selected by nature and elected by God.[23]

A BORN ALLOTMENT

Because genius was a hereditary and constitutional trait, it usually appeared in the earliest years of human life. And indeed, the members of the Sacred Circle shared strikingly similar memories of childhood, versions of their origins that stressed the early appearance of their unusual gifts and the experiences of familial rejection they inevitably suffered. Their recollections all seemed fixed upon the high expectations held for them and upon their seeming inability to satisfy these hopes. Each of the five thus found himself imbued with a fervid sense of ambition as well as profound feelings of failure and even rejection for having disappointed both himself and his intimates.

Beverley Tucker clearly believed that he had "been always an alien to my family." While his mother, Frances Bland, was descended from Virginia's oldest and finest blood, Beverley's father, St. George, had arrived from Bermuda just in time to fight in the Revolution and afterward had become a jurist and legal scholar. Tucker's first years passed in what he remembered as idyllic bliss upon his mother's plantation at Matoax. But when Beverley was only four, his mother died and his life was transformed. St. George Tucker lacked the independent means to continue in the life style of the highest Virginia gentry, so he moved his family to Williamsburg where he became a professor of law at William and Mary.[24]

Beverley was evidently a difficult child, for from his earliest years, he explained, "genius" turned my eyes "away from the usual occupations of youth to the highest pinnacles of fame and excellence." His extraordinary gifts made him different from other children and rendered his adjustment to their world problematical. "I had always," he reminisced, "been averse to the winding track along which I was required to climb with other boys. . . . What I should have been if left to myself I know not. But I was whipt on through my school classes without learning anything, but continually aspiring to know things far beyond what my instructors sought to teach me. The moral effect of this was dreadful."[25] Because of what he identified as his genius, Tucker found himself "punished in school and discountenanced at home until I almost learned to hate everyone with whom I had to do." No one, in short, seemed to understand him, so he became "a solitary being. More than half my waking hours were spent in lonely musings, the most dangerous of all occupations to an unformed mind." Still a boy, Tucker found himself prey to a "stupefying melancholy" which encouraged continual reflection on "dark and gloomy subjects" and most often fixated on his mother's untimely death. Her feminine sensitivity might, Tucker believed, have enabled her to understand the analogous sensibility of the genius; she might have mitigated the "severity . . . harshness & . . . oppression" which had so early "warped" and "soured" his mind.[26]

While Frances Bland served as tragic heroine, St. George became the villain in Beverley's scenario of his childhood. The professor was strict with his family, instituting in his Williamsburg house a mock military regime in which he served as commanding officer. But St. George Tucker confronted no easy task in rearing not only his own children, but three stepsons, Beverley's older half brothers, the off-spring of Frances Bland's earlier marriage to John Randolph. In these difficult circumstances, St. George found himself continually embroiled in family quarrels. The Randolph boys, particularly the eccentric John of Roanoke, accused their stepfather of mismanaging their estate during their minority and of mistreating them generally, but concrete evidence of St. George's harshness to his sons is lacking. Eager for his father's affection, young Beverley was also quick to take offense. An occasional delay in correspondence or a paternal suggestion to postpone a proposed marriage seemed to Beverley unquestionable evidence of rejection.[27]

But Beverley's resentment of St. George seems to have arisen less from his father's objective behavior than from a configuration of unfulfilled expectations on the part of both father and son. Beverley was disappointed in his father's inability to maintain him in the life style and social position he had known in his earliest years at Matoax. St. George, in turn, was less than impressed with his son's lackluster performance as a student and his refusal to follow his father's advice about his legal career. But perhaps most important, young Tucker was frustrated by his own failures in school and in the family profession of the law, where unlike his father and successful older brother Henry, Beverley found himself plagued by "cares and doubts about my future success." Genius he might be, but his struggling Southside Virginia law practice gave little indication of it. One year, he complained, his receipts equaled no more than twenty dollars. But Beverley attributed responsibility for this failure to his father's inadequate financial assistance, which he translated into proof of a lack of paternal affection.[28]

The pattern of Beverley's interaction with his father became a kind of prototype; excessive sensitivity to slight characterized and complicated all Beverley's personal relationships, both within and without the family. "Severely humbled as I have been it is no wonder that I have sometimes fancied myself intentionally trod on." And this sense of persecution and unwarranted neglect gave rise to a "surly temper" and a defensive pride that often offended Tucker's associates. A lifelong stammerer, Beverley seemed consistently to undermine his own success. Yet he identified his intellectual constitution as the source of all these difficulties: "there are few in this world qualified to minister to the distempers of a mind like mine. I have always felt myself a stranger in this world, where I have rarely found any who could understand me, and enter into my feelings and keep pace with my thoughts."[29]

But Tucker found one ally within his own family. Salvation from complete despair came in the form of his half brother John Randolph of Roanoke, eleven years his senior. Tucker recognized that Randolph played almost a maternal role in his life. Although not endowed with the peculiarly feminine gifts of understanding, Randolph, Tucker believed, possessed characteristics of genius that enabled him to sympathize with the extraordinary nature of his younger sibling, as well as to share his isolation from St. George. Tucker acknowledged to Randolph that their mother's loss was "irremediable," but, he continued, "I have been most gratefully sensible that as far as it was possible, it had been your study to supply her place."[30]

Randolph supplied Tucker with emotional, intellectual, and financial support and in return received his deepest affection. "Of all that breathes on earth," young Beverley declared, "there is nothing that I love and reverence like brother Jack." And indeed Tucker could find much to admire in his brother, for Randolph of Roanoke was rising to national prominence as a leading conservative congressman and perhaps the most eloquent defender of strict construction of the Constitution. His genius, at least, had found a vehicle for its expression.[31]

Yet the relationship between John and Beverley was tempestuous. Because his aspirations were so high, Tucker chafed as an impecunious rural lawyer, yet despised reliance on others. The "horrors of dependence" weighed heavily upon Beverley and produced not only his difficulties with his father but fostered a growing resentment of Randolph as well. A quarrel ultimately severed relations between the siblings. Although the circumstances are not entirely clear, Beverley seems to have instigated the disagreement as retribution for yet another fancied slight. Randolph, he feared, had aided him only reluctantly over the years. Although Tucker declared himself "incapable of in any wise explaining" their break, he returned most of the lands and other property Randolph had bestowed upon him and in 1815 moved to what he called his "exile" in Missouri. The breach between the two brothers was not healed until Randolph called Tucker to his deathbed in 1832.[32]

As in his early relationships with his father and brother, throughout his life Tucker was quick to perceive hostility and rejection. For example, he readily identified opposition to certain of his judicial views and defeat in congressional elections in Missouri and later in Virginia as mounting evidence of his alienation and persecution. Tucker's childhood experience had led him to expect such treatment; his difficult and overbearing personality encouraged it; and as a result his expectations of rejection became predictably self-fulfilling. But in Tucker's mind all these hardships appeared as merely the natural corollaries of genius, the inevitable problems associated with being an individual of unusual talents in a world reluctant to accommodate the extraordinary.

Like Tucker, Simms was left motherless at an early age and felt, as did the Virginian, that with her death he had lost all hope of worldly contentment. "The extraordinary powers" of the genius, he concluded, might not absolutely "preclude his happiness. But we must allow that they render the work of domestic and social training . . . of immense difficulty and very doubtful result." Only a particularly "noble mother" could "so train a boy of genius as that he shall be strengthened for his peculiar offices, without falling into unnecessary conflicts with society, or perversely forfeiting the delights of his own household. But the chances against such good fortune, to the imaginative nature, are as an hundred to one."[33]

The tragedy of parental death or desertion is a recurrent Romantic theme, and Simms and Tucker merely imitated some of the most prominent poets of their age in their intense concern with personal grief.[34] Simms perhaps had special reason to lament his fate, for as a boy he experienced repeated instances of familial separation and death, which he regarded as profound influences upon his future development. "I had two brothers," he explained, "both dead when I was an infant. I grew up without young associates. I grew *hard* in consequence, hard perhaps of manner—but with a heart craving love beyond all other possessions."[35]

William Gilmore Simms was born in Charleston, South Carolina, to an immigrant Irish merchant and a mother of good Southern family. He described his "immediate ancestors" as "poor," and his father went bankrupt soon after his wife's death. "A discontented forever wandering man," the elder Simms left young Gilmore to the care of a grandmother and set off to seek his fortune in the West. Effectively abandoned by both his parents, Simms was similarly rejected by his peers. Their hostility, he explained, was simply an inability to understand his genius. Years later he recalled his youthful unpopularity in terms which to a considerable degree describe the childhood experiences of pride and rejection common to all members of the Sacred Circle. "Suddenly in the compass of a country village," he reminisced:

a boy springs into sight who claims to be in possession of a secret. He claims to have endowments which are not of ordinary acquisition. His ways are not like those of other boys. He engages in none of their sports. He goes apart from them, loves to muse in secret places and gloats over a book as one suddenly in possession of a great treasure. . . . That he should presume in tastes and pleasures superior to the rest—in which they can neither mingle nor contend—is sufficiently offensive. . . . As they are not willing to believe in his superiority, they set it down for presumption. As he stands alone in his objects he is soon isolated among his associates. This isolation produced gloom, a fervid sense of injustice, a morbid feeling of resentment. . . . This very sacrifice of the usual pleasures of boyhood—the fact that he is shy when they are frank; sad and thoughtful when they are uproarious; solitary when they crowd together, these, alone, should suffice to indicate to any but the willful blind, the imperious exigencies of a peculiar moral constitution, from which the possessor, still striving, still reluctant, is himself unable to get free.[36]

Like Tucker, Simms possessed a highly developed sense of self-esteem together with an extraordinary sensitivity to slight or to any suggestion that his superiority might be overlooked. Thus he developed an assertive, aggressive manner; he would not make it easy, he determined, for others to ignore his genius. "My dear Simms," Hammond gently chided his friend, "You are not modest & delicate in your manners drawing men's loves & sympathies after you. You never meet a man . . . without at once asserting mastery & assaulting him furiously until—unless he turns upon you as I do with clubs & stones & mud—he is obliged to succumb. Do you expect them to go off & call you an angel? . . . You are a tyrant—what can you expect from your victims?"[37]

His abrasive personality tended to transform the rejection Simms had encountered as a child into a paradigmatic experience, and the tragic pattern of familial death continued to plague him as well. His first wife lived only five years after their marriage, and the offspring of his second union seemed similarly fated. Upon the death of his third daughter in 1842, Simms exclaimed, "I have been always . . . in this respect, a marked man—set aside and very much distinguished by the scourge."[38]

Destiny seemed to assume multifarious forms to prey upon and isolate Simms: death repeatedly claimed his nearest kin; genius ren-

NATHANIEL BEVERLEY TUCKER
circa 1847
*Photograph of a portrait by William G.
Brown, courtesy of Dr. Janet
Kimbrough*

GEORGE FREDERICK HOLMES
Courtesy of Duke University Library

WILLIAM GILMORE SIMMS
circa 1859
Courtesy of South Caroliniana Library

dered him difficult and temperamental and alienated him from the world at large. Simms himself perceived a causal relationship between his childhood loneliness and his mature feelings of alienation, and he remarked upon the "isolation in which I found myself at an early age —without father or mother, brother or indeed, kindred of any kind— I was always on the look out for opposition and hostility to those claims of my intellect which I believed to be well founded and which I also well knew, would never be anywhere more jealously resisted, than in a proud wealthy and insulated community such as that in which I was born."[39]

Even marriage to a daughter of the Carolina gentry and residence upon her family plantation at Woodlands did not seem to end his exclusion from this society, and Simms always remained acutely aware that "I . . . occupy no social position myself." Convinced he remained an outsider, Simms complained throughout his adult life of "fits of despondency" and of persistent "Nausea . . . vertigo, languor, indigestion," which he attributed to his gloomy isolation. "As I grow older," he reflected, "I find myself growing more & more jealous of the affections of those I love. I have had so few friends all my life that I feel the necessity more and more daily." Like Tucker, Simms craved both personal intimacy and intellectual approval, and within the Sacred Circle he would seek to satisfy both his "love of fame and [of] human approbation, a terribly large development of which my head possesses."[40]

Although he was born half a world away from Simms and Tucker, George Frederick Holmes manifested the same "depression of spirits" and characterized his personal experiences in similar fashion. Son of an ambitious British civil servant and a woman of the English provincial gentry, Holmes passed the first few years of his life in British Guiana where his father held a series of middle-level administrative positions. But soon young George was separated from his parents and returned to relatives in England to be educated. From the first, George showed considerable promise in school, and his parents determined when he was still quite young that their oldest son should be trained as a civil servant like his father. "Think what a pleasure it would be to Mamma & Papa," Mary Anne Holmes wrote her eight-year-old child, "*if George* could be papa's clerk and save him so much money."[41] But George cherished no such practical ambitions; increasingly he became caught up in abstract and scholarly pursuits, particularly mathematics and classics. Suddenly, however, this impractical bent took on ominous significance, for in 1830, George's father unexpectedly died. To make matters worse, it soon became evident that he had been bankrupt. Mrs. Holmes was "perfectly confounded" by the situation and found herself compelled to turn to the charity of a generous aunt. As the decade wore on Mrs. Holmes became alarmed to note that George was beginning to display striking similarities to his father. Holmes's biographer, Neil Gillespie, has explored these in depth and concluded that "George's boyhood must have been spent in the shadow of his father's memory which provided him with a contradictory model of both excellence and failure," a warning of his own frightening potential for both success and disaster, of his own good and evil genius.[42]

But Mary Anne Holmes was worried above all about her son's manifestations of dangerous—and possibly hereditary—improvidence. When seventeen-year-old George contracted a large debt to buy an expensive set of books, his mother became so angry that George felt compelled to leave England to establish his independence and find his fortune in America. As he later explained to a British friend, he viewed his presence in the New World as a kind of banishment necessitated by his indigence and his mother's rejection. "Poverty," he wrote, "rendered me an exile and still delays my return."[43]

The dedication to letters and the extravagance symbolized by the unfortunate book purchase were to prove a fatal combination in Holmes's life. As a scholar, he never seemed to make enough money to cover his needs, and he was plagued by financial difficulties of such severity that he suffered "the painful anxiety of fearing continually that I might not be able to get bread for my family."[44]

Upon his arrival in America, Holmes stopped briefly in Canada, then moved to South Carolina where he began to read for the bar. Temperamentally unsuited to legal practice, however, Holmes merely bided his time while he sought an academic appointment. But his stint as an Orangeburg lawyer was to be of great importance to him, for it provided an introduction both to many of South Carolina's finest minds and to a young and attractive visitor from Virginia who soon became his wife.

But Holmes's marriage to the daughter of Virginia's Governor John Floyd did not end his monetary troubles. His in-laws were so displeased with their daughter's choice that they placed most of her property legally out of her husband's reach. Lavalette Floyd Holmes was an extravagant woman whose tastes far exceeded the means of a frequently unemployed scholar. Holmes discovered, too, that his wife preferred not to share the boarding-house life that was often his lot. As a result, the two spent many years of their married life apart. Holmes was desolated by these separations which seemed almost a repetition of the experiences of his childhood when his closest relatives were scattered all over the globe. A constant theme in his letters to his wife was the misery of his lonely "exile" from his family. In his commonplace book he transcribed a series of quotations relating to his situation, which he blamed on his destitution and his genius. " 'A man when among his own relations,' " he copied, " 'when afflicted with poverty is as a stranger,' " then quoted Bulwer on a related theme:

> To think is but to learn to groan
> To scorn what all besides adore
> To feel amid the world alone
> An alien on a desert shore.[45]

Holmes's family little appreciated or understood his intellectual labors, and his mother accurately represented their attitude when she bluntly declared, "I wish he would turn his . . . abilities to some better use." This lack of sympathy from his intimates unfortunately was paralleled by a lack of appreciation in the world at large.[46]

In spite of his poverty and his lack of social position, Holmes was a fiercely proud man possessed of what he called a "chilling temperament . . . by nature both cold and dark." His assessment of his own worth was generous, and he did not readily submit to the indignities imposed upon Southern college faculties. Holmes found Richmond College an intellectual backwater and gladly departed in 1846 after a tenure of only a year for William and Mary, which despite its superior reputation proved little more satisfactory. At the time of his arrival the college was embroiled in an administrative furor that resulted in the temporary withdrawal of the entire faculty. Holmes's habitual impatience combined with his pride to prompt him to resign in disgust, proclaiming to the college rector that he declined to associate his reputation with that of a failing institution "for the pittance of 1000 dollars which I could easily make . . . in the poorest region of the globe."[47]

Despite his hasty action, Holmes did find another job, as the first president of the newly established University of Mississippi. With an acute sense of the "injustice" and "indignities" he had suffered in Williamsburg, Holmes departed for Oxford pursued by his creditors. But here, too, failure would haunt him. A refugee in the Mississippi wilderness, Holmes found himself in charge of an institution barely equipped to undertake the tasks of education. The school lacked textbooks; the buildings lacked doors; the students lacked preparation. But Holmes was unyielding in his expectations of his pupils, both as scholars and as gentlemen. His reluctance to police student behavior, however, resulted in massive disorder. After a few months, the trustees took advantage of their president's absence on a trip to Virginia to replace him.[48]

Despite his assertion that he could "easily make" a thousand dollars "in the poorest region of the globe," Holmes found himself in 1849 without employment. Besieged by debts, he retired to live with his wife's family in the Virginia mountains where he devoted himself to writing for periodicals and searching for an academic appointment. The years from 1849 to 1857 were a period of true exile, and he found his "spirits nearly broken" by his lonely experience in a "community which understands little and cares less about . . . abstract investigations."[49]

Inhospitable to Holmes, Virginia appeared equally unappreciative to Edmund Ruffin, even though he was descended from a prominent Virginia family and possessed an objective social and financial security the other members of the Sacred Circle lacked. Although only scanty information exists about Ruffin's childhood, the surviving evidence suggests that the import of his early experiences did not differ substantially from that of the other group members, He, too, lost his mother at an early age and passed a sickly childhood buried in books. Thus even in the first years of life, Ruffin exhibited both his "delicate organization" and his proclivity for intellectual pursuits.[50]

From the time of his early manhood, Ruffin complained of rejection both by his family and society, which regarded him, he feared, with "neglect, slight, and contempt." His entrance into politics in 1823 fortified this conviction; his "views of duty," he discovered, differed so markedly from those of his associates that he could see no hope of appreciation or "reward." His agricultural endeavors, Ruffin complained, were greeted with equal indifference by the Virginia public, despite his conviction that calcareous manures could substantially increase the productivity of eastern Virginia's soils. He felt unloved even by his own children; none, he worried, cared about him or welcomed his visits; he was a man with "no home."[51]

His temperament, Ruffin recognized, was difficult, and his own son had proclaimed him "too sensitive and too suspicious." Like his intellectual friends, Ruffin had an overly excitable sensibility that rendered his always "feeble constitution" painfully subject to derangement by any disturbance. "I have been always," he noted, "very liable to have my nerves . . . agitated & disordered by any vexation or perplexity of mind." He was never far, he confided to his diary, from a "positive state of wretchedness," and he often vented his frustration and unhappiness on others. "It is no wonder," he reflected in his old age, "that I made many enemies & became unpopular with a large portion of the little public around me." Often, he realized, "some remark of censure or sarcasm . . . has been harshly uttered be [sic] me . . . without my thinking." Quite unintentionally he offended and alienated his associates. But his greatest shortcoming, he confessed, was the "vanity and love of notoriety," which caused him to presume a superiority to almost all those around him and to treat with "implacable" resentment any who did not readily acknowledge his claims. So inclined was

EDMUND RUFFIN
in the uniform of the Confederate
Palmetto Guard, 1861
*U.S. Signal Corps photo No. 111-BA-1220 (Brady
Collection) in the National Archives*

he to find evidence of rejection in others' behavior that even a testimonial dinner to honor his agricultural contributions did not diminish Ruffin's sense of neglect. Ruffin apparently was unmoved by this gesture of appreciation, for his only response was to complain that the Virginia press had ignored the event.[52]

Like Ruffin, James Henry Hammond possessed a highly developed sense of self-importance as well as a propensity to feel his talents slighted by others. Indeed, the emotions and dilemmas Hammond described in his extensive and introspective personal papers often seem to be more fully articulated versions of concerns shared by others within the Sacred Circle. Hammond was the son of a New Englander who had migrated to South Carolina in his early youth. After a number of years as a schoolteacher, Elisha Hammond assumed the position of purveyor at South Carolina College, which enabled him to provide for the education of his son, whom he assumed as a matter of course to be "a man of genius." Hammond's aspirations for young James seemed unbounded and apparently varied inversely with his own achievements. As debts crowded in upon him, Elisha envisioned ever more lofty triumphs for his talented offspring. Toward the end of his life, as he confronted bankruptcy and failure, the senior Hammand referred confidently to the manner in which young James would behave "when President of the U.S."[53]

James could not help but be impressed by the overriding importance of his success to his father. "I was," he later recalled, "his pride—his hope. He lived in me & to the very last his heart dwelt on me with the fondest & alas most confident assurances, that I would one day be what he might have been, but for the blast of early hardship." But his father's confidence weighed upon James as an almost unbearable burden of expectation. Endowed with intelligence, a good education, and an impressive appearance, Hammond was made aware at an early age of America's abundant opportunities for success. Yet he recognized the chances of failure in a country where men like his father went bankrupt every day and where only two or three men in every generation became president. In a sense, James Henry Hammond epitomizes the ambitious and conflicted nineteenth-century American confronted by a frightening responsibility for his own condition. Social mobility and social change were forceful realities in the dynamic American society of this period, for the democratization and industrialization of American life had opened unprecedented opportunities for the individual to achieve wealth and power. Traditional controls of church and state had loosened, leaving men without limits upon their achievements—and without certain direction for their lives. To confront such opportunities was exhilarating, but above all terrifying.[54]

JAMES HENRY HAMMOND
in the uniform of the Governor, as
Commander in Chief of the
South Carolina Militia.
*Photograph of a copy of a painting by Gerald Foster,
circa 1842, courtesy of South Caroliniana Library*

The ambivalence of the nineteenth-century Americans about opportunity expressed itself in a number of ways. The pervasive evangelicalism of the age was in one sense an escape from this world of competition and anxiety, for the essence of the evangelical creed was that *any* man had the power to take his freedom and return it to God, to escape from the demands of the aggressive, mundane world into a transcendent kingdom where rules for behavior and belief still were clear.

Yet while he wished to give up the responsibility for achievement, the nineteenth-century man longed for the rewards of success. For James Henry Hammond, this ambivalence provided the motivation for almost every undertaking. Above all, Hammond longed for power, but he could not endure the possibility or responsibility of failure, of proving himself unworthy of his own self-estimation. "What afflicts me," he once explained, "is my perfect conviction that I can never meet any such expectations. It is very painful to know that one *must fail*." In Hammond, one sees most clearly the way in which the doctrine of genius served to lessen individual responsibility and to legitimate worldly failure, thus lightening the burden of talent and opportunity. Although Hammond's life displays this pattern most explicitly, it was a reality for every member of the Sacred Circle; all five intellectuals were forced to deal with both their own and others' expectation of their extraordinary gifts.[55]

Young Hammond seemed well aware of what his father called his "superior talents" and from an early age insisted upon due recognition of them by the world at large. After graduating fourth in his college class, James expected immediately to be welcomed into a position appropriate to his abilities. But prospects for employment did not abound in South Carolina, and Hammond became a teacher at a rural academy. Such a station struck him as entirely unsuitable, and he complained incessantly to his father: "I do not like my present situation because I really *think* & *feel* it is below me. I cannot reconcile it to myself & tho' nothing in the conduct of those around is *meant* to remind me of my situation yet it does seem to me entirely too menial. This is not *pride*. It is nothing but an honest respect to the dignity of my character."[56] Vowing to extricate himself from this degradation, James took up the study of law, a well-traveled road to upward mobility in the Old South. He soon qualified at the bar and entered practice in Columbia, a more congenial environment for his ambition than the Carolina backcountry.

But James's best opportunity for advancement came in a form quite removed from the law, though one successfully exploited by such Southerners as William Gilmore Simms, George Frederick Holmes, and John C. Calhoun. "Never marry," Hammond's father had advised him, "unless a rich . . . woman. . . . Always have an eye to your ways and means." James had listened carefully, and in 1831 he wed a woman who brought him a 7,500-acre plantation staffed with 148 slaves. In retrospect, Hammond acknowledged that his motivations had not been entirely disinterested, but explained how "the extreme difficulties of early life . . . led me to grasp, without sufficient discrimination at means of extrication, not dishonorable . . . but involving still greater ultimate difficulties." Some of the problems he encountered, however, were more proximate than ultimate, for his fiancée's brother had bitterly opposed Hammond's intentions and endeavored to secure his sister's property from the young social climber. A protracted argument ensued over the marriage settlement, which made Hammond painfully aware of his marginality in South Carolina society. "What have I in common with any aristocracy on earth?" he demanded. "What family connections, wealth or rank have I? I spring up among the undistinguished mass of the people." Acquisition of a wife and plantation seemed not to have diminished his feelings of loneliness and alienation, and he set about to make his claims for recognition and acceptance irrefutable.[57]

Hammond's diaries and letters reveal a calculated design for financial, political, social, and intellectual rise; his life became a campaign and his writings a record of his strategic and tactical objectives. His marriage was the first of these and provided both the impetus and the capital for his next endeavor. After acquiring a plantation through his wife, Hammond seemed almost determined to earn it himself, to double its value in order to legitimate it as his own and to prove his independence of his in-laws. Profiting from the financial disruptions of the 1830s and 1840s, Hammond undertook to acquire the land of as many neighbors as he or the sheriff could persuade to sell. Through a series of small purchases, including one in which he bought three hundred acres for five dollars, Hammond succeeded in increasing his holdings by 50 percent in just ten years. An astute businessman, he placed enormous emphasis on financial matters, for they seemed the one area of life where he could assess and control nearly all the variables. "The only thing you can rely on," he once observed, "is money." And in riches he found one sure source of consolation. "It is in the refuge afforded by your wealth," Simms understood, "that you recoil from and suffer disappointment." But while acquisition of property brought a measure of security and some sense of achievement, it did not provide the reputation or acceptance Hammond eagerly sought. Indeed, his financial success won Hammond a certain amount of resentment, expressed in repeated accusations of "avarice" by his contemporaries. Wealth in the mid-nineteenth century did not possess the overwhelming social importance it assumed in the later era of Carnegies and Morgans. In this earlier evangelical age, transcendence still derived from other sorts of achievements, and Hammond set out to pursue these as well. Because, as he confided to his brother, "Reputation is everything," he dedicated himself to what he called a "more elevated ambition" than that of simple monetary gain.[58]

In the course of the next decade, Hammond entered almost every area of public life that might enhance his image. Through participation in local and state societies, he gained a voice in agricultural affairs; he assumed positions of increasing responsibility in the state militia; he impressed his importance on Columbia society by constructing a monumental town house; he began a carefully planned entry into what he called "the literary world" by associating himself with Simms's friends and with professors from South Carolina College. Most important, he entered politics, where he was greeted with almost immediate success by his election in 1834 to the U.S. House of Representatives.[59]

In Congress, Hammond's ambivalence about success appeared in perhaps its most striking manifestations. Upon his arrival in Washington, Hammond thrust himself to the center of the stage, taking up the banner for Southern rights by leading the fight for a gag rule to prevent reception of abolition petitions by the Congress. Suddenly the young legislator found himself "nervous, melancholy, dreadfully dyspeptic," desperately ill with severe pains in stomach and groin. Hammond had few illusions about the cause of his ailment and concluded almost at once that "It is anxiety that has been torturing me & undermining my health." Like other members of the Sacred Circle, he shared the belief that his susceptibility to illness derived from his "nervous disorganization," and this was confirmed by the prominent New York and Philadelphia physicians Hammond consulted. "Your complaints," they concluded, "are dependent on *Functional* not on organic disease." Upon the advice of Dr. Philip Syng Physick, Hammond resigned his seat in Congress at the height of his success and departed for a recuperative tour of Europe.[60]

"Broken down at Twenty Eight . . . one foot in the grave. Dying of decay in the very blossom. . . . Twenty eight. It is young. But I have lived long. . . . Twelve years I have been an invalid—I used to complain—people laughed at me for looking so well and feeling so ill— The world does not see far where it has no interest."[61] Hammond's elegiac self-pity seems almost a caricature of Romantic suffering, and even his friends lacked entire sympathy with his portrayal of himself as a wan and sickly Byronic hero. Unfortunately for his scenario, Hammond gained weight progressively during the ante-bellum period, rendering his associates even more skeptical of his claim to be ever at the point of death. His complaints of illness seemed to evoke little more sympathy than any of his other demands for attention and recognition. This neglect fortified Hammond's already acute sense of exclusion from the social world and enhanced what he called his "contemplative, solitary disposition." His temperament, he found, was as little understood as his physical constitution. "I have always been a shy and sensitive person. . . . I am however generally regarded as a strong example of a confident bold & indifferent person. . . . my sensitiveness has led me to assume as much as possible of the reverse in order to conceal it." Thus, like other members of the Sacred Circle, Hammond appeared—as he described himself—"consummately conceited," "censorious," "peevish, too much inclined to differ & to ridicule men as well as measures . . . say things which I do not wish nor intend." Hammond retreated into the safety of a private self and felt compelled to hide the emotional needs he was convinced others could not understand, just as they were unable to sympathize with his physical weaknesses.[62]

In many ways Hammond's complaints fit neatly within the widely discussed nineteenth-century syndrome of hysteria. At least one of Hammond's friends saw "a good deal of Hysteria" in his constant maladies. Although this ailment has been regarded by physicians of the period and by later historians as "peculiarly relevant to the female experience," the role conflict that has been invoked to explain the feminine nature of the disease need not have been restricted to women. The social dislocation produced by the modernization of American life affected many different sorts of roles and, as I have suggested, weighed particularly heavily upon the intellectual. The thinker's retreat into the realm of "culture" and disinterested truth rendered his concerns very close to those of the century's ideal woman. Indeed, similarly conflicting role prescriptions plagued them both. Like the "true woman," the genius regarded himself as an individual of "rare sensibilities" whose responsibilities were primarily spiritual and transcendent, yet paradoxically required active expression in mundane achievement. Both the nineteenth-century woman and the genius, moreover, were believed to possess a special sensitivity to nervous derangement that made them peculiarly unsuited to the demands of their dynamic and changing world.[63]

While women may have taken to their beds in an effort to restructure their roles and to gain a kind of manipulative power they could not demand overtly, Hammond perhaps invoked his morbid sensitivity to evade the responsibilities of power and achievement. In a sense, his design was so perfect, his strategy for success so all-encompassing that he, like Thomas Sutpen, his Faulknerian counterpart, could not survive as a human being within it. "Oh for a snug little farm," Hammond lamented, "where I could indulge my fondness for the country and for Agriculture without the anxiety created by the idea that the 'main chance' depends on having every screw tight & the whole machinery moving on clock-work principles."[64]

This ambivalence about success continually sabotaged his schemes for advancement. At the very moment of his triumph in Congress, illness forced him into retirement. Eight years later the climax of his successful governorship was marred by a personal scandal which he acknowledged to be "the greatest error of my life." In the fall of 1843, just at the close of his gubernatorial term, Hammond was accused by his wife's brother-in-law, the prominent Wade Hampton, of committing sexual indiscretions with his teen-age daughters, Hammond's own nieces. All his follies, Hammond once explained, arose "mainly from sensibility and passion," the two inescapable liabilities of his genius. While the former characteristic had caused his earlier breakdown, this time the two traits acted in concert. "My morbid & solitary habits engendered by disease, are rendering me keenly alive to every excitement of which I could partake without *immediate* suffering." The event, Hammond lamented, was the inevitable result of the inflexibility of his own design; it was, he declared, "owing to my not having been always able to control myself in every particular." Perhaps he had sought in innocent girlish affection an unquestioning acceptance his ambition prevented him from finding in his more calculated attachments; perhaps these adolescent girls worshiped the presumptions of superiority which mature and ambitious men regarded as arrogance; perhaps Hammond simply found, as he once suggested to his brother, "it is really much easier to cut a figure among women," and even easier among girls.[65]

Because of both Hampton's and Hammond's political prominence, the incident could not remain private, and almost the entire leadership of South Carolina felt compelled to take sides. "An unfortunate rupture with Hampton," Hammond confided to his diary, "terminated my relations with him and his whole family including Manning and the Prestons. They pursued and are pursuing me with the bitterest persecution. This event . . . will embarrass me through life. I have been wrong in the matter—the result of impulse not design." Although Hammond attended the inauguration of his successor as governor in fear of a "direct attack after the ceremony" from Hampton or his henchmen, retribution was to be more protracted. The ultimate result of the incident was Hammond's effective exclusion from an active role in South Carolina politics for more than a decade, for Hampton implacably and successfully opposed every suggestion of Hammond for office. The retirement into agriculture for which a part of Hammond had longed was forced upon him. Yet he complained bitterly of the injustice of his destiny.[66]

Already convinced of his alienation, Hammond developed a sense of real martyrdom in the mid-1840s. He had behaved, he insisted, no worse than many other men who had not been similarly chastened in consequence. Because he was "personally not popular," the fateful incident had provided jealous enemies with a convenient and long-sought justification to banish him. "Did you ever feel a 'cold Shoulder?' " he demanded. "Ah it is icy. The Arctic seas have nothing that so freezes up the *heart*. And yet to be expecting and suspecting cold shoulders is even worse than touching them. That," he concluded with a metaphor that may have revealed more about his self-image than he intended, "is Promethean agony." The causes of this hatred, he felt, were his lowly origin, his difficult disposition, and his extraordinary gifts, all conditions of his birth—of his genius—for which he held no responsibility. With satisfaction, Hammond clipped an article about himself from a newspaper. "He is of that class of minds," it declared, "which nature seems to have condemned to be solitary that the world might be peopled with ideas."[67]

The members of the Sacred Circle thus discovered in their lives the basis for strong psychological as well as professional bonds. Even though the details of their biographies differed, they found that the configuration of their experiences as human beings and men of genius had equivalent emotional import and had structured their relationships with the world in comparable ways. Objective social position and actual social experience were not the significant or determining factor in the lives of these men; Hammond, for example, continued to feel himself a failure and a pariah even after he had been elected governor and had amassed one of the largest fortunes in South Carolina. His behavior in the Hampton incident almost seems to have been designed to prevent him from having to relinquish this cherished self-image, and perhaps Tucker's stutter and Holmes's extravagance functioned in somewhat the same way.

Although the social positions of all five men were in some ways insecure and uncertain, their status did not in an objective sense justify their intense and persistent complaints of social exclusion and exile. The deep feelings of isolation and marginality expressed by the members of the group make sense only if we recognize that to a considerable extent these arose from subjective factors, from the *combination* of psychological with social insecurity, which they explained in terms of their defining attribute of genius. As they implied by their insistence upon the inseparability of personal and social experience, the significance of social facts lies in the interpretations individuals give them. Men's definitions of social situations are as much a function of their own predilections and of the vocabulary made available by their age as of the reality to which they respond. An individual calculates his choices and actions in accordance with the significance he imparts to his world; a study of his social behavior must, therefore, portray his experience in the terms he perceives it, by encompassing and explaining the personal and cultural as well as the social factors that simultaneously influence his choices. As Max Weber understood more than half a century ago, to study society is to explore "all human behavior when and insofar as the acting individual attaches a subjective meaning to it."[68]

These five Southerners all explained their persistent feelings of isolation and depression by portraying their lives as dramas of Romantic alienation. All were proud and defensive men who cherished a profound sense of their own superiority and desperately sought to explain why they were denied comparable recognition from others, for acceptance was all-important to them. "Everything with me," Tucker proclaimed, "depends upon the estimation in which I may be held." But they complained not simply of public neglect nor required public approval. All felt intense personal loneliness, for their childhood experiences and their difficult temperaments had combined to distance them from family and isolate them from immediate associates. Their desire for fame and their lofty ambitions were all part of a more general need for recognition that generated an intense craving for personal acceptance and intimacy. As Hammond succinctly explained to his diary in 1841, "I want a friend."[69]

Thus the Sacred Circle was designated to provide both intellectual and emotional reassurance. Simms wanted Tucker's letters to represent both his "mind & heart" and urged, "Let me hear from you soon and *lovingly*—for . . . this sort of nourishment is . . . ever necessary, to the intellect as well as the affections." Those within the group would serve as surrogate family members; they characterized themselves as each others' brothers, fathers, and sons, and Simms even named one of his children Beverley Hammond. These thinkers' emotions and intellectual predilections were so similar, Tucker remarked, that it was almost as if they "had suckled at the same breast." Indeed, it seemed that in a sense they suckled one another. "Your letters," Hammond wrote Tucker, "are a part of my sustenance," to which Tucker replied, "yours are meat, drink and clothing to me."[70]

Genius, these thinkers believed, endowed them with a capacity for friendship and a need for intimacy that only others of equally extraordinary gifts could satisfy. Their sensibility rendered them susceptible to unusually intense emotional attachments. Thus the genius surrounded himself with individuals of like temperament who were his peers in both mental and emotional capabilities, for without such associates, he was doomed to perpetual isolation in a world of philistines.[71] The network in itself would supply the personal intimacy they craved and would serve at the same time as a vehicle through which to explore the positive functions of genius and to seek the public recognition they all desired. The emotional sustenance provided by their interaction would endow them with the strength to assert their intellectual and professional claims; it would enable them to minimize the debilitating depression and loneliness of genius in order to maximize its achievements.

The sensitivity—and superiority—of genius in the past almost always had implied emotional and social exile; yet the members of the network recognized they would be able to satisfy their ambition only by transforming this pattern. Since the nature of the genius was fixed by birth, it was not he, but the world about him that had to change, to learn to welcome and cherish this difficult but elevated being. Because society had failed to provide a role appropriate to the configuration of values and emotional needs of these men, they joined in insisting that it create one. Fortified by their professional and personal interaction within the group, the members of the Sacred Circle set out to define the positive prescriptions for the social role of the intellectual, to explore the "true business of genius."[72]

THREE

The True Business of Genius

efore an assemblage of South Carolinians mourning the brilliant Calhoun, James Henry Hammond explained his conception of the rightful place for the man of genius. Human beings "who have received from heaven an extraordinary endowment of intellect and virtue," he proposed, should be "adored" by the less gifted members of their species. Just as men should show reverence for their maker, so they should worship "the attributes of God as manifested through his favorite Creations. . . . those great minds that have been appointed to shed light and truth upon the world." The vocation of the man of knowledge, he proclaimed, was a holy one, and the thinker was divinely inspired. All the members of the group agreed that the "intellectual man" bore the "characteristics of his race in the highest perfection" and served as a "seer," the "mortal manifestation of the Godhead." Nevertheless, they lamented, the world too often failed to recognize God's favorite creatures or to heed their inspired messages.[1]

A SACRED VOCATION

Convinced they had been divinely appointed, the members of the Sacred Circle endeavored to define the purpose of their mission and to place it within a context of beliefs that would sustain them in spite of their presumed mistreatment by the less gifted majority. Every social role requires a general configuration of values to give it meaning and to provide the emotional and cognitive satisfaction necessary to ensure its continued performance. These systems of role prescriptions often appear self-serving; indeed they are designed to convince individuals that their particular social duties are necessary and valuable. But this element of self-interest, even self-adulation, does not necessarily diminish the sincerity with which the beliefs are held, nor does it undermine their influence over behavior. Beverley Tucker thought it genuinely remarkable how "my ambition and my convictions coincide."[2]

In the search for a vocabulary to explain their dilemma, the group seized upon the terminology of traditional Christianity both to understand and to direct their lives. Enthusiastic religion was entirely consistent with their Romantic outlook and served both to supplement and to reinforce the more secular component of their world view. By drawing an analogy between themselves and religious figures, they hoped to demonstrate their earthly role and to evoke the values of Christianity as both justification and explanation of their self-image. Theirs was, as Holmes put it, "a sacred vocation," and their function could be easily defined in Christian terms. Human beings communicate by placing an event or a sentiment in a category that identifies or explains it in terms others can understand. Indeed, the essence of any culture is a repertoire of shared categories. For the American, and especially the Southerner of the mid-nineteenth century, many of the most powerful and recurrent symbols had biblical origins. The use of biblical referents to provide meaning and transcendence for contemporary events was not just a product of the century's evangelistic fervor, although this no doubt strengthened the disposition to perceive events in terms of religious archetypes. From the time of their arrival in the New World, Americans had tended to think of themselves as a chosen people and to lament their failings in terms borrowed from Old Testament prophets bewailing the sins of Israel. Among New England Puritans these recurrent evocations of doom and decline became conventionalized as the jeremiad, at once, as Perry Miller has noted, a literary form and a mode of perceiving the world.[3]

For the five Southerners, the jeremiad provided a meaningful framework in which to express and legitimate their dissatisfaction with the South and their place as thinkers within it. Biblical metaphors therefore appeared throughout their lamentations about the region. In an article on "Southern Agriculture" in 1842, Simms recited the traditional Protestant prayer for absolution, with its "mournful language of scriptural self-chiding"; Beverley Tucker demanded to know if, like Egypt, "Are we not warned?"; Holmes, who continually sought historical archetypes to explain his own age, discovered remarkable parallels between his world and that of Jeremiah. "Out of the north evil shall break forth upon all the inhabitants of the land," the prophet had warned the people of Judah, and so the literal-minded Holmes prudently set aside a category in his commonplace book for notes on "Hordes from the North." Like the people of Judah, the faithless Southerners would be chastened. The fate of Sodom "is upon us," Tucker warned; the South, Simms feared, was "ripe for the destroyer."[4]

The jeremiad was a part of the Southerner's Christian as well as his American heritage and thus a doubly appropriate formula to describe the decline he perceived all around him. As David Bertelson and others have suggested, Puritans were not the only Americans to embrace the jeremiad: the writings of eighteenth-century Virginians Robert Beverley and William Byrd might be seen to fit this formula, as can proclamations of nineteenth-century men such as those within the Sacred Circle. What made these lamentations of decline meaningful for Americans of such widely different regions and periods? Perhaps Perry Miller has best explained the jeremiad's purposes, for he recognized that the metaphors a civilization embraces to describe its experiences have a more than figurative significance; they often take on a life of their own, molding as well as describing perceptions and sentiments. The jeremiads, he wrote, "constitute a chapter in the emergence of the capitalist mentality, showing how intelligence copes with—or more cogently, how it fails to cope with—a change it simultaneously desires and abhors." For Miller's Puritans, as for these Southerners, the jeremiad was a means to express and thereby to blunt their ambivalence about change, an effort to temper anxiety about the future by paying obeisance to the values of the past. While the five bemoaned the abandonment of the old virtues, they sought eagerly to satisfy their ambition within the new social world emerging about them.[5]

But the jeremiad was not simply a literary form for lamenting social decline or a device for resolving ambivalence about change. Holmes, Tucker, Hammond, Ruffin, and Simms found a special emotional resonance in the image of themselves as Jeremiahs—as prophets without honor speaking truth to an unheeding world. This conception seemed to explain and justify the sense of social neglect that suffused their lives. As Simms explained, genius craved "consideration. Possessed of great truths, its first and only care is to procure a hearing. It demands an audience, attention, appreciation." But the man of mind rarely was accorded the deference he sought, and so he developed a different relationship to his society. "Denied to be a teacher, he becomes a prophet and . . . denounces the wrath of heaven upon the blind and bigoted generations which refuse to hear." Like the Romantic artist, the genius retreats into the realm of the transcendent.[6]

Such a self-conception provided the Southerners with both an explanation of their social alienation and specific normative implications for their identity and role. Like his biblical counterparts, the man of mind was selected by God; his vocation was not his own choice, but a divine calling. Providence, Simms declared, "has fitted . . . us for a special and peculiar labor." While the "youth may choose to be a lawyer, a doctor, or a merchant or a soldier," the genius "is called, as Samuel was in the night-time, by a voice whose summons he does not understand, but dares not disobey." In this divine inspiration lay seemingly indisputable evidence of what Simms called the "legitimacy" of the intellectual and his product.[7]

The concept of calling implied an obligation. Although the chosen might not always be eager to follow his inspiration, Hammond warned of God's "severe condemnation of the servant who did not make profitable use of his talent." Special gifts ordained special duties—a kind of intellectual *noblesse oblige*—and might prescribe special suffering as well. Hammond saw in his poor health, political failures, and social ostracism evidence that his "mission is doubtless to be broken on the wheel as a warning to the rest." To be elected by God might mean to be set apart like Job: first as the recipient of special favors, but then of plague and misfortune.[8]

The intellectuals' failure seemed to underscore the transcendence of their mission. Because the man of knowledge "comes in the name of a prophet," Holmes explained, "he must expect 'A prophet's reward'—in disbelief, dishonor, outrage, contempt, persecution." But this was of little consequence, for he was vindicated by his election to a "heavenly function" and consoled by the awareness that his "capacities and power are providentially bestowed."[9]

The intellectual's alienation was, in fact, a positive good, for it both enabled and encouraged him to transcend his society. Just as his rewards were not to be found in the present, neither were his true concerns. Hammond reassured Simms, "I have long seen that you were not 'honored in your own country.' What prophet is? . . . You must live *in* as well as for the future." Hammond promised Simms "the unbounded realm of ages to come over which to reign."[10]

To the network of Southerners, the essential characteristic of the intellectual appeared to be his ability and determination to escape "the bondage of the present" in the two senses Hammond described—by living both "for" and "in" the future. The first and to them the most pressing issue was to satisfy their desire for fame by assuring one another that time would recognize their achievements. Turn your "back on the nineteenth century," Hammond urged Simms, and think instead of the "twentieth & twenty thousandth century. Damn the age & the men of the age." After all, Hammond modestly reminded his friend, Christ had been rejected by his contemporaries.[11]

Ruffin shared Simms's feelings of futility, and Hammond consoled the Virginian in nearly identical terms. The failure of the South to heed Ruffin's ideas was only temporary, Hammond insisted: "For such labors as yours you cannot expect instantaneous general appreciation. The great body of the people do not comprehend them & most of the rest are mere politicians full of their own intrigues. Time must therefore elapse before your services in the cause of agriculture will be generally understood & your fame duly established."[12] Tucker addressed his students at William and Mary on the same point, urging them to calculate their success in eternal terms. Even though his lessons might be "most unfavorable to popularity and advancement," he reminded them that *the end is not yet. We do not live for ourselves, nor even for our contemporaries alone . . . fame is immortal.*" Thus the five were consoled in their lack of present gratification, for, they assured themselves, they, too, would be recognized one day. The career of the intellectual, like the Christian life of ascetic self-denial, should be undertaken in view of an eternal reward. By conceiving of themselves as prophets, they transformed their social isolation from a sign of rejection into evidence of their moral and intellectual superiority.[13]

But in his prescription for the man of knowledge, Hammond insisted not just that he defer his rewards and exist "for the future"; he must live "in" the future as well. The Carolinian intended the intellectual's thought and concerns to transcend his particular mundane situation. Just as he was to seek eternal rather than immediate renown, so he ought to devote himself to the solution of eternal and universal rather than immediate problems. Instead of simply accepting his society's priorities, he ought, Simms advocated, to "discover that which is hidden from all other eyes—which other minds have not conjectured—which other persons have not sought." Mundane "events should always be made subservient" to general principles in philosophical contemplation of the world; present "convention," Simms emphasized, "is always the foe to truth."[14]

In the effort to describe their concerns as intellectuals, the five resorted repeatedly to words like "truth," "principle," "universal," "eternal," "philosophical," and "sacred," which they felt captured the essence of their search for the transcendent. The vagueness of these terms perhaps manifested the uncertainty that characterized the world view of this period. But the phrases succeeded in expressing the sense all five shared of the remoteness of their ultimate interests from the affairs of the world around them, an intellectual separation analogous to their own distance from their society. The contrast between immediate and ultimate concerns that characterized these Southerners' perception of reality stemmed directly from the Christian world view and was reinforced by the Romantic contrast of real and ideal. Intellectual, like both Romantic and Christian concerns, were essentially outside of time.[15]

But the group's allegiance to these concepts served another purpose as well, gaining for them a kind of legitimacy and a sense of self-righteousness. "Truth" and "sacred principle"—whatever their particular connotations—were ideas the nineteenth century could not reject easily. If no more specific values could be salvaged from the cultural upheaval of the era, it was perhaps best to settle for at least some ethical precepts on which there could be general agreement.

The contexts in which these phrases recur, however, reveal at least a part of the meaning with which they were infused. When Ruffin stated, "My object is to find truth, & not to warp facts to suit a favourite hypothesis," he indicated the importance of disinterestedness to "philosophical" inquiry. This emphasis was central to the belief system of the group. In a personal notebook, Tucker proclaimed a commitment to advancing his "own principles," not himself. Like his cousin Ruffin, he found selflessness essential to the quest for truth. Ambition, the clamors of faction, the desire for power, Tucker warned, were hostile to "the discovery of truth." The pursuit of a "philosophical aim," Holmes agreed, required the avoidance of all "spiteful polemic."[16]

The attainment of wisdom, therefore, would be impossible until men reached a moral state in which selflessness and disinterestedness prevailed. Truth would gain its rightful ascendancy only when mankind had been "regenerated" and "disenthralled." The devotion of the genius to the pursuit of knowledge implied an obligation to promote "moral progress" and "to perfect and prepare the races of men for a more perfect organization and superior conditions"—to make them, in other words, more like himself.[17]

The genius was thus to serve as a model for the rest of humanity. His exemplary qualities and generalized superiority made him a kind of Romantic hero, destined to provide the world, as Simms described, with "its inspiration, when it would acknowledge a higher appetite than is ever provoked by gain."[18] The endeavors of the man of mind, like those of the hero, always had a spiritual purpose, for intellectual and moral tasks were inseparable. "It is thus," Simms explained, "that the poet ministers to religion." The pursuit of truth was like the quest for the Holy Grail; only the pure and regenerate could find success.[19]

Hammond traced this conjunction of intellect and morality to the very structure of the human mind. "The thinking and Impelling portion of the Human organism" was its "Mind—Soul—Spirit—Intellect." To Hammond the four terms seemed essentially interchangeable. "All men," he proclaimed, "are inspired more or less according to their intellectual endowments." Immortality characterized the intellect as well as the soul. The gift of mind was not simply reason or cognition, but a kind of divine inspiration, a blessing from God analogous to the grace that was indispensable to the evangelicalism of the age. Simms explained to Tucker that when he spoke of mind, "I do not mean the activity of the reasoning faculties simply," for he found himself "more & more suspicious" of rationalism. As a man of genius,

Simms was himself concerned above all with "the profounder moral nature which . . . elevates the mind with a spiritual atmosphere which we cannot define."[20]

The man of mind was thus a kind of incarnation of divine law, a human antenna especially designed to appreciate the "latent and the spiritual" in all forms in which they appeared. "His life is . . . one continued gauge for the offices and instincts of the moral nature." His mission was to apply his special sensitivities to every area of knowledge that might be productive of truth, to evaluate every facet of life around him.[21]

All areas of human activity and speculation were of potential interest to every intellectual, for each topic had an inherent moral lesson which the man of knowledge was obligated to elucidate. In the first issue of his *Southern Magazine*, Ruffin examined the "moral" influences of banks and paper money. Tucker found that the study of national law was "more a *moral* than a *legal* science," and he outlined for his class the just causes of war and the duties of men to others, as individuals and as groups. "What is all this but morality?" he asked. The study of politics was simply the examination of other men's actions under a "moral microscope" with the purpose of deriving lessons for future conduct. The "science of civil polity and jurisprudence is a branch of that great system of moral government by which the author of all things rules the universe." Thus the study of politics was but the "performance of a holy function," part of a much larger religious task. Discovering truth and its moral implications appeared the ultimate purpose of the group and the underlying justification for any intellectual endeavor on which the men of mind embarked.[22]

Clearly, Hammond, Tucker, Simms, Ruffin, and Holmes shared what the historian Charles C. Cole described as the propensity of their age to transpose all issues into the "moralistic octave." All knowledge was united simply because all learning was designed to inculcate morality. In essence, this outlook was the logical product of the educational system of the early and mid-nineteenth century, which offered as its capstone the senior course in moral philosophy, taught by the college president and designed to draw all higher learning together into a didactic whole. Universities were the pre-eminent—one might argue the only—institutions of intellectual life in the Old South, and it is therefore not surprising that their codification of human knowledge should be accepted by the members of the network. As students, professors, and visiting lecturers, all five were socialized in the collegiate world view, and the sources of their exposure to moral philosophy are not hard to trace. As early as 1824, Hammond had copied into his moral philosophy notebook at South Carolina College a firm resolution of his own commitment to this science of "what ought to be."[23]

The ideological and emotional context of moral philosophy had a particular appeal for these men because of its relevance to many of their own concerns and predispositions. D. H. Meyer has suggested in *The Instructed Conscience* that the configuration of beliefs that made up moral philosophy was peculiarly functional for many nineteenth-century Americans. Rapid social change, increasing wealth, and the democratization of life in the new nation had challenged traditional sources of terrestrial authority. "The American Revolution, the Steam Engine . . . the Locomotive," had, as Hammond recognized, "changed the face of human affairs." At the same time, the transition in American religion from an emphasis on piety to an overwhelming concern with moralism had mitigated fear of God's wrath. The consequent insistence of the age upon God's benevolence undermined divine sanctions over human behavior as well.[24]

As deference to earthly and celestial masters diminished, thoughtful Americans sought to justify the new social order, yet simultaneously to preserve the most cherished of traditional beliefs. In Meyer's view, moral philosophy served as the answer to this need, as the means of maintaining a "dual commitment to the values of the past and the promise of the future."[25]

Nineteenth-century moral philosophers offered a systematic justification for replacing the authority of church and Scripture with private conscience, which would rule men both individually and as groups. Francis Wayland, author of the textbook on moral philosophy used most widely in ante-bellum America, advocated that conscience reign sovereign within each man and that men of conscience rule the world; the human microcosm would reproduce the hierarchical cosmos. Serving as what Norman Fiering has called a "semi-secular way station" between a world of faith and one of science, moral philosophy endeavored to demonstrate the unity of truth and the compatibility of reason and religion by marshaling science in support of morality. Based on the analysis of duty—those duties men owed to God and to their fellow men—moral philosophy sought to internalize social control in every individual.[26]

Like the moral philosophers, Hammond, Holmes, Tucker, Ruffin and Simms considered social order and amelioration as the ethical responsibility of the individual; duty would serve as an instrument of personal and therefore of social restraint. The Southerners' warnings about the dominance of faction in politics and the overriding importance of wealth in America echoed the moral philosophy texts. The men of mind felt, too, that the most threatening aspect of change in their world was the decline of virtue that seemed to accompany social evolution. Civilization appeared to Holmes "menaced with utter annihilation in the wild conflict of selfish interests, the rejection of fixed

principles of morality, and the destructive fury of uncontrolled passions." Simms emphasized that it was imperative to devote intellect
to establishing "sure pledges for security in a time of great popular
commotion."[27]

Dedicated to the improvement of their race, the five Southerners
enshrined the concept of duty as the overriding principle both motivating and unifying all their endeavors. Tucker viewed his studies of politics
as the analysis of the "duty we owe to government, considered as a part of
man's social duty to his fellows." He organized his course on law in much
the same way Wayland had structured his textbook on moral science,
with sections devoted to duties to oneself and duties to others. The study
of law appeared as but a specific aspect of the more general subject of
morality. Hammond informed Ruffin that his interest in agricultural
improvement derived from a "sense of duty," while in a letter to Hammond, Simms affirmed that the "laws of duty" constituted "the essential
religion." The concept of moral obligation would replace piety as the
force that ordered man's life.[28]

But all five acknowledged that the nature of man's duties was not
entirely clear. Only inspired investigation by individuals of special
talent could illuminate the true nature of moral obligation. Unusually
gifted men would reform the study of virtue, transform it into a
science, and codify ethical precepts for the unenlightened. Because
the members of the group believed that spiritual and intellectual
excellence were so closely related as to be almost synonymous, they
did not question their own fitness for this role. Their moral sensitivities
particularly suited them to serve as the public conscience—just as
Wayland had prescribed.

Thus, while they perceived themselves as prophets, ostracized by
their world, and legitimated by scorn, paradoxically they defined the
nature of their sacred vocation as moral stewardship, the practical
guidance of a society in need of their spiritual leadership. "Duty,"
Tucker proclaimed, demanded that he act as a "safe guide to blind
but honest ignorance." God had deemed "the great ones of the earth
the stewards of his bounty, & will call them to a strict account of their
stewardship." Simms agreed that the genius's "Superior endowments
were specially conferred by Providence" for the "tuition and patriarchal guardianship" of the rest of the human family. "The true business
of genius is to lift and guide a race."[29]

The role of the prophet provided consolation, but it failed to satisfy
the five Southerners' ambition or blunt their awareness of living in "a
Practical Age." Genius had to be relevant as well as transcendent; the
man of mind had to find a social place for himself and for the products
of his intellect. These thinkers therefore craved to be, as Hammond
explained, the "guides and guardians" of others. The man of knowl-

edge, Simms recognized, always sought "domination. To govern human sympathies, to control men's minds, win their affections, fashion their tastes." Genius, he found, "is not less a reformer than a discoverer." The intellectual could not restrict his concern to empyrean realms of contemplation; he could not retreat entirely into the realm of "culture," but needed to exert his control over the popular mind and serve as an instrument of God, as Tucker exhorted, "in his great work—the MORAL GOVERNMENT OF MAN."[30]

Only individuals of special intellectual and spiritual worth could point the human race toward truth and virtue. "How many men," Tucker demanded of Hammond, "are capable . . . to form themselves any code of principles, or even to understand such a code?" Clearly, mental superiors were needed to establish proper standards for belief and behavior. The development of an appreciation for things of the mind, Simms explained, "must necessarily tend to humanize and to elevate mankind." In this, he concluded, lay "the best guarantees for the popular conduct," and therefore for social order.[31]

A prime duty of the man of mind, these five Southerners agreed, was to control others, for all legitimate authority derived from moral superiority. The genius, Simms had observed, sought domination; Hammond agreed that knowledge was synonymous with power; Tucker found that "all the authority to which man is made subject on earth is God's instrument for the accomplishment of his great work in the regeneration of his fallen nature." Such a conception of their own gifts dictated that these five Southerners act as moral stewards, leaders in their society. Here once again, as Beverley Tucker had remarked so artlessly, their convictions as well as their ambition seemed to coincide.[32]

The members of the group legitimated their intellectual concerns as an effort to establish a science of morals, a firm new foundation to replace the eroded bases of social authority. In an analogous manner, they justified their desire for social and political prominence as part of a religious obligation to "lift and guide" the human race. The men of mind thus paradoxically employed older, spiritual values as an avenue of access to the wealth and status they claimed to disdain. If they could convince their society that homage was due to intellectual talent and moral superiority, then they would ascend to the positions of eminence they coveted. To establish a recognized place for the man of knowledge in the South was to create a social role that would satisfy both their ambition and their principles. Moral and intellectual values could lead to worldly success. But if they should fail in their effort to accomplish such change, if they never should attain recognition in this life, their ultimate achievement was secure, for the genius expected his true reward, they assured themselves, only in another realm.

Earthly failure was no longer frightening for it was simply evidence of gratification deferred, the emblem of transcendence.

Hammond, Ruffin, Tucker, Holmes, and Simms thus developed out of their conception of the sacred role of genius two seemingly inconsistent images of the worldly position of the intellectual. He was at once a prophet, rejected by his society, and a moral steward sent from heaven to dominate and reform it. Both these images served important functions for the men who embraced them. The metaphor of the prophet captured the emotional significance of their common plight and acted as a consolation to them in their exile. "Was it for the encouragement of the future prophet," Simms wondered, "that we are left to fancy that, having done his work, the seer was caught instantly up to heaven?" The metaphor of stewardship, by contrast, was intended to be normative; this was the role the five Southerners thought should be theirs; this was how they planned to achieve their common purpose, to find a social expression for their intellectuality. Thus they transformed their ambivalence about worldly success into a fundamental characteristic of the intellectual role.[33]

THE DILEMMA OF THOUGHT AND ACTION

The members of the Circle were well aware of the paradox inherent in this conception of their sacred duty. Should the ultimate commitment of the genius, they wondered, be to thought or to action, to the ideal or the real, to the philosophical or the practical? Was it possible to compromise between these extremes, to "combine society & study"? Because of what the members of the network described as a constitutional predisposition toward ambition, these questions had personal as well as social import and were especially difficult to resolve.[34]

This dilemma was explored incisively by James Henry Hammond in an address at South Carolina College in 1849. Hammond characterized the nineteenth century as "a Practical Age: an Age of Action—fact & common sense: one in which metaphysical discussion is despised and theory held up to scorn." But, he warned, anyone seeking to understand his own time "must not limit his observation to passing events & the practical experiments or the plausible theories of his own day."[35]

Jeremy Bentham and "the whole school of plodding utilitarians" dominating contemporary philosophy had been so preoccupied with mundane cares that they had not recognized that "Action is in the main the result of thought." This "excited age," Hammond lamented, had failed to recognize the value of contemplation, or of those devoted to it: "Wealth & Office are the only sources of Power that are generally acknowledged & we are strenuously taught by precept & example, from our cradles up to clutch at gold & cater for popularity. . . . The Spirit of the Age prescribes these courses, & the noblest intellects & proudest spirits too often unable to break from the bondage of custom & opinion, succumb and fall beneath it." But the social pressure upon the man of genius to cultivate popularity by dedicating himself to practical concerns and his own advancement ultimately frustrated his intellect and inhibited the progress of his society. By lowering himself to "such vulgar uses," Hammond warned, he inevitably encountered "the sorest trials & bitterest disappointments."[36]

Because he sought relevance in an era he recognized to be devoted to "practical" concerns, Hammond attempted to broaden the definition of this "watchword" of the age. Practical, he insisted, must mean not just that which was immediately useful, but should encompass considerations of the welfare of mankind and society over the long run. Thus he concluded that many individuals currently considered "practical" more accurately would be labeled "successful," for their achievements were, in an ultimate sense, more harmful than beneficial. Mundane success was often, he pointed out, the result of self-seeking ambition and greed. The "life of man," he observed: "is so short & truth & virtue bear fruits so slowly, that great immediate results are rarely achieved but by a violation of their precepts. Intrigue, corruption, & force are the usual means by which our practical men on a large scale advance themselves at the expense of others." Worldly success, he concluded, could be achieved only "by dint of energetic selfishness."

Hammond suggested an alternative definition for what he considered the "truly practical man," an individual like Socrates, Archimedes, or Bacon. "To profound knowledge he adds well directed energy & works earnestly manfully & hopefully for high & noble ends with little thought for consequences to himself." In essence this described the disinterestedness and transcendence which the members of the network attributd to genius and by implication to themselves. Even though such men "were regarded by most of their contemporaries as visionaries—as enthusiasts & dreamers," Hammond found in their speculations the possibility of "the only true & lasting progress of our Race." Thus contemplation was eminently useful and the man of knowledge indispensable to society.[37]

Through this effort to redefine practicality and utility, Hammond sought to resolve the conflict in the role prescriptions for the man of mind. The concerns of the genius could be simultaneously transcendent and relevant if only the rest of the world would recognize the importance of universal questions to particular situations, of thought to action. In his oration, as in many other endeavors during his life, Hammond sought to educate the South on this point, to convince them of the importance of intellectual issues to the daily operations of their world. At the end of his address, he specified how his audience, made up of highly educated Southerners, might aid him in his evangelical task. Men of mind should participate, he advised, in the practical affairs of the world, using social institutions with which they were associated as instruments to channel the beneficent products of knowledge into their society. Just as agricultural reform served a larger purpose of moral improvement, other social actions might promote cultural ends. Practical acts could be undertaken with a view to advancing universal knowledge and truth. For example, political "office might be a convenient fulcrum" for genius, for "knowledge is the sole lever with which . . . [to] put the world in motion." Knowledge might also be transmitted through the "Public Press," which would serve the man of genius as "a tripod from which he may give utterance to his oracles." Thus, Hammond concluded, the man of mind could be both transcendent and relevant, serve both the present and posterity, be both a prophet and a reformer.[38]

The dilemma he explored in this oration troubled all the members of the network. Tucker was deeply moved by his friend's formulation of the problem and reviewed the address enthusiastically for the *Southern Quarterly Review* in April of 1850. Applauding Hammond's exposure of the selfishness of utilitarianism, Tucker emphasized the importance of convincing the world that the ideal was relevant to the real. Simms agreed as well on the necessity of redefining utility in order to make his own work appear socially relevant. He hoped that "a new experience of what is useful and needful will dawn upon our national consciousness." With this discovery, he was certain literature would acquire "the dignity of a profession. . . . There is a utilitarianism in art and fiction," he noted, "as well as in politics and trade." Simms returned frequently to this theme and delivered an entire lecture on the relationship of "Poetry and the Practical." Today's abstract idea, he insisted, would become practical tomorrow. "The *usefulness of art*," he wrote in a review article on "Southern Literature," "is the grand lesson which must be taught to the young." He urged Southerners to "put down as teachers, that class of men, misnamed utilitarians, who test the value of all pursuits, only by the money profits." Only the "Genius of the moral world can . . . sway the tempest." Therefore, Simms urged, "we must teach the worship of that Genius . . . of the *Ideal*, as a corrective agent against the dangers of the *Real*." Once again Simms evoked religious imagery to impress upon the South the importance of the man of knowledge and his product.[39]

In the series of letters to Simms which Holmes published in the *Southern Literary Messenger* of 1844, the younger scholar expressed similar concern about the relationship of practical and intellectual issues. Holmes believed that "the author and the public reciprocally act and react without intermission" even when they were unaware of their effects upon each other. He explicitly recognized, as had Hammond, the pressure on the man of letters to gain social recognition for the importance of his product. "Authors," Holmes wrote, "are gods easily drawn down from the realms of the pure empyrean when their votaries desire it; if they be neglected for their too great elevation, they are sure to descend to that platform where there is the most certain chance of adoration, that they may not be deprived of sacrifice, honor and homage." The ambition of the man of mind made it impossible for him to defer his need for fame, or, therefore, to ignore the demands of his audience.[40]

Like Simms, Holmes recognized the need for a social movement to convince the South of the worth of intellectual endeavor, and he discussed with the older author how they might together "facilitate or hasten" the approach of this "brightening prospect for literature." Holmes believed that educational institutions were the most promising means of disseminating his message, but he found that the nature of schooling was particularly important. In a discussion in the *Southern Quarterly Review*, Holmes applied Simms's categories of practical and theoretical to the educational process itself, criticizing the idea of narrowly vocational training. "In our day," he wrote, "a practical education . . . is generally preferred . . . to a liberal one. And yet, if we abandon the ordinary loose and cloudy habits of thought and speech, we shall soon discover that a liberal education is essential to a really practical one." Like Hammond and Simms, Holmes viewed the question of utility as essentially a problem of semantics, and in his inaugural address as the president of the University of Mississippi, he stated this explicitly. "The belief that there is a distinction, or even an opposition between the highest intellectual desires and the practical wants of men is a popular fallacy very current in the present day." In reality, he concluded elsewhere, "literature does not impede but assists the active energies of practical life." To Southerners avidly engaged in the political questions of the moment, he suggested that learning might indeed "furnish the Statesman and the combatant in the arena of politics with the brightest and keenest weapon in his armoury."[41]

Thus the members of the group endeavored to reconcile the disinterestedness required for true intellectual labor with the need—which thy readily attributed to their ambition—to play an important and recognized social role. By redefining utility and broadening its meaning, they hoped to include themselves and their work within its compass. In the effort to find a mundane "business" for the transcendent genius, they developed the general prescriptions for their role which this chapter has described.

But these general principles had more specific implications as well, for they structured the manner in which the men viewed their whole lives. The effort to reconcile thought and action, to make the ideal socially relevant, was to be a major preoccupation in every project they undertook. These precepts about the role of knowledge and of the intellectual dictated not so much specific social actions, but the spirit with which any endeavor should be infused.

Because moral philosophy enjoyed such wide currency among educated Americans in the nineteenth century, it provided a framework through which the five Southerners could enhance the significance both of themselves and their role. Moral science stressed that sacred principles should direct all human actions, and thus it rendered thought relevant to every human undertaking. Holmes, Hammond, Ruffin, Tucker, and Simms approached the mundane aspects of their lives—agriculture, politics, literature, law, publishing, and so forth—as particular embodiments of moral axioms and as opportunities to instruct others in the performance of their earthly duty; so, too, they sought social positions that would enable them to institutionalize their theory of stewardship, the guidance of the human race in the interest of virtue.

But they found it far easier to assert the social necessity of moral speculation than either to convince the public of this relevance or to work out the conflict between mundane and transcendent ambition within their own lives. Like many other Romantics, each member of the Sacred Circle found himself continually torn between involvement in the real world of affairs and periodic withdrawal into a more ideal, more elevated—and less demanding—realm; at Hammond's Silver Bluff, for example, high above the Savannah, or at Ruffin's Marlbourne on a ridge overlooking the surrounding Virginia countryside.

Any attempted resolution of the dilemma of thought versus action was inevitably a compromise. From the repertoire of ideas available in their culture, the men of mind had fashioned a conception of their role designed simultaneously to reflect their actual situation, to provide personal meaning and emotional satisfaction, to affirm their social importance, and to direct their future actions. Created both to mitigate reality and to conquer it, this system of beliefs inevitably was riddled with inconsistency. Nevertheless, the justifications and formulas the Southerners had borrowed from Christianity, Romanticism, moral philosophy, and nineteenth-century science assumed a life of their own and became active influences over the intellectuals' existence. The contradictions in the Southerners' thought did not simply reflect, but ultimately reinforced, the paradoxes of their lives. When the five tried to apply the precepts Hammond had promulgated in his oration, they found—as indeed he had warned—that even the noblest spirits would "fall beneath" the pressure of a crass society. As they endeavored to implement their ideals, the members of the group discovered that it was very difficult, as Simms phrased it, to maintain "the whiteness of one's soul."[42]

FOUR

A *Novum Organum:*

REFORMING THE WORKS
OF MIND

ntellectual and social historians often have depicted mid-nineteenth-century America as a culture beset by spiritual crisis. The bustling optimism of the Jacksonian era, its burgeoning population, and its rapid economic expansion masked deep-rooted insecurities. The passing of the New England theology had removed the image of an all-powerful predestining God from the center of the universe and transferred to man responsibility for the condition of both his soul and his world. While this new sense of man's power to shape his destiny served as a source of confidence, it proved profoundly disturbing as well. A God more benevolent than fearsome was not a firm sanction for social order. Moreover, the emphasis on man's ability to discern religious truth led to a seemingly unprecedented proliferation of sects and creeds. To many Americans, it seemed clear that these religious deviants were misguided, for surely truth could not come in so many varieties. But how could men distinguish divine will from the erroneous products of human invention?[1]

To complicate this unstable situation, an increasing awareness of the practical and theoretical achievements of science produced additional questions about the criteria for knowledge. Were scientific and religious truth analogous and complementary, and, if not, how could they be reconciled? Educated Americans recognized that these problems ultimately were rooted in the epistemological questions that had generated and structured two centuries of European philosophical debate. Yet Locke, Berkeley, Hobbes, and Hume had provided no answers satisfactory to articulate and critical Americans eager to dismiss unyielding philosophical dilemmas and concentrate on the more immediate business of the new nation. Locke had failed to explain the nature of the relationship between ideas and reality; Berkeley had denied the existence of matter, Hume of belief, and Hobbes of morality. How could man function in a world that relied on such intellectual systems for guidance?

Many educated Americans thus turned with relief to Scottish common-sense philosophy. Here was a philosophical system that rendered the activities of mind both relevant and reliable. By-passing questions about the certainty of human knowledge, the Scottish thinkers invested man with the ability to establish operational hypotheses concerning the world and his place within it. What man's consciousness discerned was real, the Scots declared. Scientific empiricism and moral intuitionism were equally valid; the mind, they affirmed, could recognize both material and spiritual reality.[2]

But as Daniel Walker Howe has suggested, the Scots were in a sense only "shrinking back from the abyss." The widespread acceptance of common-sense philosophy in the United States only smoothed over growing doubts about the compatibility of reason and revelation, the legitimacy of religious and moral truths. These questions ultimately lay unanswered and continued to distress Americans who believed philosophical and religious uncertainty to be the source of social disorder and upheaval that were becoming endemic in American life.[3]

Holmes, Tucker, Ruffin, Simms, and Hammond were all deeply affected by the intellectual confusion of their age. Each of the five was personally dissatisfied with religion as he knew it, and each sought a faith that was at once epistemologically sound and emotionally meaningful. On a more general social level, they bemoaned the religious sectarianism of their age, which they saw as the equivalent of political factionalism. Founded in selfishness, it detracted from the discovery of the single, unified, and guiding truth in which all men might unite. The most pernicious consequence of this confusion of belief, however, was the social and intellectual upheaval it had produced. No one could agree, it seemed, about what constituted either truth or virtue. Without such consensus, there could be no firm basis for social order.

The Southerners' conception of themselves as individuals of special intellectual and spiritual insight rested on the conviction that men were capable of intellectual knowledge and moral certainty. But in an era that had not recovered from the impact of Hume's skepticism and Hobbes's cynicism, the existence of such human abilities was subject to considerable doubt. If the five were to gain recognition for what they considered their distinctive gifts, they had to convince their society that they had access to indisputable truths. In order to find a social place for themselves, therefore, the men of mind had to develop a system of knowledge and belief that seemed intellectually sound and convincing, as well as socially relevant.

George Frederick Holmes was certain that there existed a direct

correlation between society's chaotic state and the intellectual confusion he saw around him. "All the heresies and distempers of the
day, religious, social, political and intellectual," he declared, "have
their roots in unsound philosophy and inadequate logic." His duty,
Holmes believed, was to build new foundations for intellectual, and
consequently for social order, to end this "lamentable anarchy" by discovering the "true laws of social organization, with the design of
thence descending to the amelioration of the social distemper of the
times." Without a firm basis for knowledge and belief, there could be
no foundation for morality. "Without any fixed standard" to regulate
his conduct, man was unable to decide the right way to behave. Such
"enervation of consistent principle" produced the "ascendency of avaricious aims" which constituted the "greatest source of present evil in
American life."[4]

Because social stability depended directly upon intellectual order,
the works of mind appeared to Holmes as the most appropriate initial
focus for the reformist spirit of the age. "A new revolution is even
now in progress," he declared, "a renovation not merely of one particular branch or department of knowledge, but of the whole domain of
intellect." Because social disorder seemed acute, Holmes prescribed
the application of "medicaments to the mental and moral elements of
the body politic . . . to chill the revolutionary tendencies by eradicating
from the minds of the people the habitudes which produce an appe-
tency for revolution." The symptoms were social, but the disease and
its remedy were both essentially intellectual.[5]

In an earlier, less secular age, man had lived within a web of sacred
meaning that had influenced every aspect of his life. But the emergence of conflict between reason and revelation had undermined not
only the integrity of this earlier conceptual world but the legitimacy
of all knowledge. Holmes proposed to re-establish "an entire harmony
between the speculative and active life" of man by reconciling science
and religion. In this manner, he hoped to find the foundation for a
"practical and operative belief" that would demonstrate that philosophical speculation remained essential in guiding men and society
and would satisfy his own longing for religious certainty.[6]

More than any other member of the network, Holmes was obsessed
with the need to find a plausible personal religion. The period of his
association with Simms, Tucker, and the others in the 1840s and early
1850s was just the beginning of his quest, but at this time Holmes first
confronted issues that were to trouble him until his death in 1897, a
half-century later. During these years, Holmes evolved from what
might almost be characterized as a deistic rationalism to a recognition of his own and his society's desperate need to discover new foundations for both sacred and profane knowledge. Although Holmes was

a more abstract thinker than were his associates within the Sacred Circle, most of the problems he formulated during the forties and fifties articulated general concerns shared by others in the network. But because the scholarly Holmes was by far the best read, he tended most explicitly to locate these dilemmas within the context of the philosophical tendencies of the age. He therefore indicated most specifically the way in which the interests of the Sacred Circle reflected the search for certainty that preoccupied the wider intellectual world and has been seen as a defining trait of the Victorian frame of mind.[7]

Although he had been raised an Anglican, Holmes began in his early twenties to express grave doubts about organized Christianity. He wrote so critically about religion and the Bible at this time that after his return to faith years later, he destroyed his youthful musings because of their "impropriety and infidelity." Holmes's questions about the nature of religious truth led him to embrace a philosophy of extreme empiricism that denied the usefulness of trying to go beyond the realm of immediate experience. Although he acknowledged the inadequacy of the epistemological efforts of Locke, Hume, and Berkeley, Holmes advised humbly confessing "ignorance of all concerning . . . [mind] except its phenomena . . . instead of blindly groping into the regions of imagination. . . . The facts," he concluded, "are all we know."[8]

Yet even in his early period of confidence in man's cognitive powers, Holmes recognized the need for a renovation "of the whole domain of intellect" to re-establish the social importance of the products of mind. Therefore, Holmes urged, empirical methods must be applied to the study of society, to reveal social laws analogous to the scientific truths produced by experiemental investigation in the course of the last two centuries. For the materials from which to create this new social science, Holmes turned to the record of social facts—history.

As he became increasingly preoccupied with these problems during the 1840s, Holmes began to recognize that he had erred in confidently dismissing all epistemological difficulties. If he hoped to establish a valid system of knowledge that would appear meaningful to his society, he could not continue simply to assume the compatibility of science and religion. In a series of letters to Simms published in the *Southern Literary Messenger*, Holmes confessed deep concern about the intellectual problems in which they both took such great interest. The need to reform thought was much greater, he observed, than the pace at which it was being accomplished. By the end of the decade, Holmes had come to recognize that a completely new metaphysics was required to reconcile science with religion and to provide the foundation for a return to social harmony.[9]

In 1848, the same year that the European revolutions underscored for Holmes the critical condition of contemporary society, the young scholar discovered the work of Auguste Comte. Like Holmes, Comte hoped to use scientific history as the foundation for an objective science of society, and he, too, believed the reform of mind essential to the preservation of order in the world. Holmes found Comte's thought "so congenial . . . to the temper of the current age that it cannot be prudently disregarded." Yet while it promised the "greatest benefits," Comtean Positivism also threatened the "most pernicious consequences," for it directly challenged religious faith; Comte viewed religion as an outmoded conceptual system soon to be replaced in the march of progress by pure science. But Holmes insisted that world order could be maintained only by a code of belief that affirmed both religious and scientific truth. Thus it seemed to the young scholar that Positivism articulated a large proportion of the evils of the day and embodied the rest. It was a tantalizing half-solution, the reformulation of a question, not its resolution.[10]

From this time on, the issues involved in the survival of mind and belief as ordering principles in the modern world were clearly defined in Holmes's mind. Primary among these was always the conciliation of science and religion, a goal he hoped to achieve through what he called his Philosophy of Faith. "The duty of every man who is unwilling to renounce his Christian convictions is clear and obvious," Holmes explained. "He must strain every nerve" to reconcile religion and philosophy, and he must begin by determining "the origin or mode of human knowledge." While in the early 1840s epistemology had seemed profitless, Holmes soon came to consider its issues inescapable. Behind man's belief in the ability of his intellect to discern scientific truth, Holmes asserted, lay a faith in the power of reason that attested to the existence of another kind of unverifiable yet undeniable knowledge. Thus man could discover truth by means of two kinds of faith, both of them logically unjustifiable. Faith in the senses as interpreters of the scientific world was paralleled by faith in "something beyond the grasp of human reason which constitutes the basis of our certitude and knowledge" of religious and moral truths. Therefore, Holmes concluded, faith in religion was no less reasonable than faith in science. One could be empirically demonstrated and the other could not; this was their only difference.[11]

Holmes's effort to reconcile science and religion demonstrated a certain lack of philosophical depth and a considerable degree of intellectual naiveté. In a sense, his solution was alarmingly Humean, for while he demonstrated the equivalence of two kinds of faith, he proved only that both were equally uncertain. Yet, at the same time, Holmes's position was not unlike that of the Scottish philosophers, who thought that in dealing with ontology they might avoid the question of certainty altogether. In place of common sense, however, Holmes suggested that men rely on faith.

This ingenuously optimistic attempt to solve his generation's most pressing philosophical dilemma permitted Holmes temporarily to proceed with the effort to make belief "operative." Eagerly, he returned to investigation of the social questions he judged to be the immediate product of this intellectual upheaval. The need to validate the sources of human knowledge nevertheless arose again and again in the course of his career, and he devoted most of the rest of his life to the development of a science of society and of an epistemological foundation on which it might rest.

The evolution of Holmes's thought during the 1840s and early 1850s was closely related to his personal experiences and to his own growing need for religious consolation. During the decade, Holmes experienced a number of professional setbacks, including the loss of his professorship at William and Mary and of the presidency of the University of Mississippi. From 1849 until he joined the faculty at the University of Virginia in 1856, Holmes remained unemployed. Personal frustration thus reinforced his conviction that the spirit of the age was not properly receptive to the kind of intellectual endeavor he practiced and represented. In his family life as well, Holmes experienced a number of crises, including the birth of a retarded daughter and the death of his only son. These tragedies and his marriage to a devout Catholic made religion increasingly important in Holmes's life. His sister-in-law attributed to him a "naturally . . . religious" inclination, evidenced by the "bump of *reverence* upon that little head of yours." But whatever the causes, by the 1850s Holmes was actively pious, and his personal notebooks and journals indicate that for the rest of the life he was engaged in an intense search for sacred truth. Philosophical and scholarly questions assumed enormous personal importance.[12]

Holmes did indeed have a significant stake in his intellectual explorations, for the legitimacy of his own identity as both Christian and man of mind depended upon the establishment of the validity of human knowledge and of religious truth. If knowledge and morality had no firm basis, his role in providing ethical and intellectual guidance to the less gifted members of humanity was useless if not fraudulent.

The same personal imperative that motivated Holmes's search for belief influenced other members of the network. All were dissatisfied with the conventional churches in which they had been reared, and all experimented with a variety of other religious systems. Simms explained to Hammond that his "original thinking . . . seperates [sic] me from all the Churches." Yet he found that "My mind has always . . .

been governed by an earnestness of tendency approaching to Religion." He explained in the mid-fifties that his desire for firm and substantiated belief attracted him to spiritualism. By communicating with his dead children, he believed he discovered empirical evidence for the existence of God, "substituting," he explained, "my own certainty for the alleged experiences of other people."[13]

Hammond shared Simms's interest in spiritualism and flirted with a number of other religious movements popular during the nineteenth century, including mesmerism and metempsychosis. In 1856, Hammond sent Simms a list of questions to ask a medium in New York. The two Southerners found in direct, verifiable communication with spiritual beings the unification of science and religion that they eagerly sought. The testimony of those who had communicated with spirits appeared to Hammond to provide new certainty "far stronger than any which the Bible offers us to prove that its teachings are revelations from God."[14]

Like Holmes, Hammond longed for the personal consolation of deep religious faith. "I desire to believe," he stated simply. But existing churches seemed preoccupied with useless theological squabbles. "I am inclined," Hammond wrote a friend, "to think we want another religious revival. . . . It will build up on the ruins of the miserable *sects*, whose bigoted & ignorant selfishness is the curse of our day. We want an universal religion."

Society seemed to Hammond to "require supernatural sanction." Established churches served an important function in controlling men's behavior by cultivating an abhorrence of sin. But while he professed loyalty to the Christian faith because of the "general disorganization of all civil & moral establishments" that would result from its demise, Hammond admitted, "I never knew anyone who had a free, lively, intelligent & thorough belief in even the essentials of Christianity." Like Holmes, Hammond found that the failure of modern churches to satisfy either man's spirit or his intellect undermined their social utility. Existing religion appeared to Hammond entirely inadequate. "Who believes it?" he demanded.[15]

The problem of conciliating religion and science, of establishing a firm foundation for faith, seemed to Hammond inseparable from the epistemological conflict between idealism and empiricism which he had outlined in his South Carolina College address. Perhaps, he had concluded hopefully, man might gain knowledge through action, faith through works, and thus prove the unity of truth. In this formulation, Hammond equated the nineteenth-century religious dilemma of faith versus reason both with the ancient philosophical problem of idealism versus empiricism and with the conflict between thought and action that characterized his own life. His problems as man of mind seemed simply a microcosmic representation of the greatest philosophical issues of his century.[16]

Beverley Tucker agreed wholeheartedly with Hammond's analysis in a review of his friend's oration. Indeed, Hammond's suggestion that "the truly wise" endeavor to conjoin religion and science, "to perfect faith by works," appealed to Tucker as "the only true light for the only true Philosophy."[17]

Tucker, however, was less troubled than many of his contemporaries about the conflict between faith and reason. He did not doubt that man's religious insights could be empirically justified or that idealist and empiricist knowledge reinforced each other. The coming of Christ had made such a view indisputable, for Jesus provided *experimental proof* that the conclusions drawn from the workings of the mind and the aspirations of the heart were true." From that time forward, man's instincts, "his native sense of right and wrong—his impulses and desires," were firmly established as "facts to reason from." The conflict of idealism and empiricism, Tucker concluded, had arisen from the empiricists' failure to acknowledge the existence of internal as well as external senses. While Holmes had resolved the dilemma by positing two kinds of faith, Tucker took the opposite approach and asserted that there were two kinds of senses or of empirically verifiable facts. The friends agreed, however, that man could be both intellectual and moral, for they shared the comforting assumption—which many Americans later in the nineteenth century would find unfounded—that the truths of religion and those of science were essentially harmonious.[18]

Tucker had confronted the problem of reconciling religious and scientific truth as early as the second decade of the century, when he first encountered the work of Thomas Chalmers, a widely revered Scottish theologian who insisted that the discoveries of modern astronomy verified the glory of God. In this early period, too, Tucker had deplored the fanatic sectarianism of American religion, bemoaning the fact that "so many are wandering in serpentines and by paths of their own tracing, which they erroneously call the way of holiness." Tucker himself felt at ease in none of these churches. "My opinions on most subjects are original, perhaps peculiar, . . . but the practical results of the manner in which the gospel is preached are not such as to show that there is no better way."[19]

Chaos seemed to predominate in religion as it did in society at large; the divine symmetry of nature was not reproduced in the lives of men. "In the moral world alone do we find disorder, embarrassment & confusion." Order appeared to Tucker as evidence of God's design, and, conversely, social and spiritual conflict implied a lack of righteousness and a need for moral reform. Tucker began writing extensively on religious subjects in the mid-twenties and even described himself as a would-be George Whitefield, eager to convert others to his own beliefs.[20]

Like Hammond, Holmes, and Simms, however, Tucker was not a sophisticated philosopher, and, not surprisingly, failed to resolve dilemmas that had confounded the greatest minds of his age. Tucker accepted Hammond's formulation of the issues, in particular the need to reconcile science and religion, reason and revelation, empiricism and idealism. To Tucker, however, these problems appeared by the 1840s personally far less pressing than they seemed to certain other members of the network. A generation older than Simms, Hammond, and Holmes, Tucker had experienced his personal crisis of belief in the 1820s. By the forties, he had returned docilely to the Episcopal church. Although he appreciated the issues his friends raised, Tucker believed that his conception of two kinds of senses at least blunted the immediacy of these philosophical dilemmas. Perhaps because he recognized that his life was nearing an end, Tucker was far more concerned with the practical manifestations of these dilemmas in his own time. The problem of relating thought to action in the Old South—the need to encourage conduct based on calculations of truth instead of interest—seemed to him far more important than to reconcile Berkeley and Locke. Having accepted his own resolution of the conflict of science and reason, Tucker devoted himself to communicating the news of their compatibility to the people of his society; the South had to be convinced that morality and intellect retained ultimate legitimacy. Tucker hoped to impress the Southern mind with the immediate truths of ethics and politics rather than those of abstract epistemology.

Edmund Ruffin was nearer to Tucker in age than were Holmes, Hammond, and Simms, and he also was closer to his fellow Virginian in religious and philosophical outlook. Like the other four men of mind, Ruffin felt the need to reform thinking, for he found that many of the social ills of the day arose from "erroneous deductions from true principles and sound propositions." These misperceptions and misunderstandings were in part secular, but they pervaded religion as well. Ruffin thought the proliferation of sects was certain proof of error; men who fought single-mindedly about how to reach God never would find him.[21]

Although they differed in the extent of their involvement with formal epistemological issues, all five Southerners insisted upon the close relationship between the social upheavals of their time and the need for a reform in thinking. Mind and society appeared to them to be in direct and constant interaction, and thus they believed intellectual questions had an immediate relevance to the social world. But men could not be expected to revere intellect when it continually produced what Ruffin labeled "erroneous deductions." By rehabilitating thought and then demonstrating its value to society at large, the five Southerners believed they would contribute to the solution of the social dislocations of the day, as well as to the improvement of their own status.

While members of the network agreed on the need for the reform of mind, they were not all involved to the same extent or in the same manner. Holmes perceived the problem in more personal and more philosophical depth than did the others. He indeed saw it as central to his effort to find a place for himself in the world. Hammond and Simms shared to some degree Holmes's personal desire for religious certainty, and thus they, too, were emotionally as well as intellectually involved in the effort to reconcile reason and revelation. But Simms and Hammond did not share Holmes's philosophical sophistication— Holmes, for example, found spiritualism naive and absurd. Hammond and Simms, moreover, were content to smooth over questions to which Holmes repeatedly returned. Tucker acknowledged the importance of reaffirming the compatibility of science and religion, but by the forties, he felt he had managed to do this in a fashion satisfactory at least to himself. By that time the Virginian had passed beyond the personal crisis of belief that provided the emotional motivation for deep involvement in this issue. Ruffin was more removed from nineteenth-century philosophical disputes than the others and did not view the problem of the failure of mind in the same far-reaching terms. He nevertheless shared their belief in the need for a reform of intellect that would provide convincing foundations for both sacred and profane knowledge. In commonly accepted truth lay the only bases for social order.

Many nineteenth-century Americans were confident that the Baconian empiricism of contemporary science represented the most systematic approach to truth ever devised by man. In view of the general esteem in which the seventeenth-century English philosopher was held, it is not surprising that several of these Southern men of knowledge endeavored to legitimate their demands for intellectual change by phrasing them in Baconian terms. Holmes asserted that the world needed "an intellectual reformation analogous to the Instauratio Magna of Lord Bacon."[22]

In his Novum Organum, Bacon had sought to replace sterile Aristotelian abstractions with a philosophy that rendered thought relevant to everyday life. For this reason, he was a particularly significant intellectual model for the five Southerners. Holmes praised the philosopher for recognizing that "moral political and social amelioration" could come only "as the consequence of an improved logical method." The major promise of the Baconian inspiration appeared to Holmes to lie in the development of a systematic approach for understanding the social world—one paralleling the methods of natural science. The seventeenth century had explained physical laws, but the disorders and upheavals of the nineteenth century demonstrated the need for an analogous science of society. A new Bacon, Holmes proclaimed, must aim as had his predecessor centuries before to redress "the contemporary disorganization of society" and must "propose the revivification of moral sentiments" by means of a "more correct and enlarged determination of the principles and laws of all valid reasoning."[23]

As the member of the network most involved in the study of philosophy, Holmes wrote most extensively about Bacon and even excused himself to Simms for "so frequently employing Baconian terms." He also completed a draft of a biography that demonstrated his interest both in Bacon's intellectual search for the foundations of knowledge and in his social role as a scholar in British politics. But Holmes was not the only member of the network to regard Bacon's achievement as a model for contemporary times. Tucker frequently invoked the English thinker and Hammond anticipated a new "Baconian era in moral science & in morals."[24]

Baconianism was so pervasive in force in nineteenth-century American philosophy and science that its influence upon these Southerners is not at all surprising. Perhaps more interesting is the commitment of Hammond, Holmes, and Tucker to *reinterpreting* Bacon for their time and demonstrating what they conceived to be the nineteenth century's limited and even erroneous understanding of his thought. While many of their contemporaries invoked Bacon as the legitimation for materialism, Hammond, Holmes, and Tucker emphasized the spiritual and idealist aspects of his philosophy, which they insisted were logically inseparable from his empiricism. One way of reforming mind, they perceived, was to accept the prevailing Baconianism but to redefine its essence to support their own views. Bacon could serve as a useful lever for intellectual change.

By its exclusive occupation with his empericism, the nineteenth century had, in Holmes's view, "mutilated" Baconian philosophy, which

has been accepted and construed in a much narrower spirit than that which animated its great founder, and has been dwarfed into a mean and beggarly limitation to things sensible and material, to the exclusion of its aptitudes for higher thoughts, feelings and objects. Man, matter and money—an ominous alliteration—have been venerated as the triune divinity of the nineteenth century, and conceived to be the legitimate idol set up by Lord Bacon. The experimental philosophy has been the only part of his labours that has been cordially accepted, and the Baconian instauration, thus shrunk and withered has been made at once the tool and the divinity of the age.[25]

Tucker agreed with Holmes that the age had erred in promoting Bacon as the "authority for a low, grovelling sensual earthly system 'the Gospel of enlightened selfishness.'" This perversion of Bacon's intentions for the utilitarian ends of personal gain appeared to Hammond, Tucker, and Holmes as a flagrant manifestation of the intellectual and moral corruption of their age. Bacon had not, they insisted, been a forerunner for despised utilitarianism. The seventeenth-century philosopher, they emphasized, had been committed to disinterested intellectual inquiry and to the discovery of moral truth as well as to the principles of physical science. They did not deny that empiricism was enormously important. But, as Hammond explained in his college oration, it was but a *part* of the Baconian system and had to be understood within its larger context. Bacon had seen himself as a participant in the long human quest—of which Hammond also felt himself to be a part—to establish firm foundations for both sacred and profane truth. Knowledge gained from experiment and observation, the Southerners concluded, complemented, but did not contradict, the truths of revelation or religion.[26]

Understood within this broad metaphysical framework, however, the inductive method had enormous potential for promoting "human improvement." Although they continued to insist upon the validity of religious truth, the members of the network could not help but recognize that their contemporaries were likely to be more receptive to empirical evidence than to knowledge acquired in a suprarational manner. In their youth both Holmes and Hammond had expressed a reluctance to undertake metaphysical inquiries, for, as Holmes explained, they were "sceptical" of their "utility." Even after their recognition of the importance of epistemology to the intellectual crisis of the age, both men seemed eager to handle these abstractions quickly and to return to consideration of their implications for social life.[27]

Holmes continually stressed the need for an "operative" belief, a species of thought that would impel men to action. Aware that the Philosophy of Faith he promulgated in the early fifties did not endow human knowledge with certainty, Holmes declared human beings presumptuous to expect absolute self-assurance. "What is conviction," he demanded: "We are able to arrive at certainty sufficient, if not for our intellectual satisfaction, at least for our wants; and we do entertain convictions, whether we admit or deny their theoretical validity."[28] Dedicated from the outset of his career to making knowledge useful to society, Holmes grew impatient with epistemological issues that did not relate to practical questions. Holmes found Bacon an inspiration because the English philosopher's "harmonious reconstruction of all speculation" was designed specifically as a "preparation for a more enlightened, efficient, and successful practical procedure."[29]

Holmes was unable to demonstrate the ultimate validity of discoveries of the human mind and thereby gain unassailable legitimacy for intellectual products and the intellectual role. Nevertheless, having arrived at what he characterized as "sufficient certainty," he eagerly proceeded in his effort to convince society of the importance of truths that transcended present social circumstances. The consideration of epistemology was but one part of an effort to make the works of mind appear meaningful and reliable. Because the members of the network felt ill at ease with metaphysics and recognized the abstruseness of such inquiry in the eyes of society, they chose to emphasize other fields of intellectual endeavor in their attempt to demonstrate the relevance of speculative inquiry to social life.

Thus motivated, the five eagerly embraced the concept of a new social science, designed to illuminate transcendent moral and social laws that simultaneously would prescribe and foretell the future course of society. The foundation of this science was to be the study of history, for in the records of past events lay the empirical data for the derivation of social laws. "The past," Holmes wrote, "may prophecy to us of what the future should accomplish. And . . . we may make the prophecy the instrument of its own fulfillment." The conception of themselves as prophets and as stewards required an intellectual product that would serve the functions of prediction and guidance such a self-image required. If only they could communicate to the Southern people the social and moral truths of their condition and the laws that should direct them, the five men were convinced they would succeed in alleviating the social disorders of their time.[30]

PHILOSOPHY TEACHING BY EXAMPLE

With these ends in view, Holmes, Hammond, Ruffin, Tucker, and Simms turned to the study of history. "A necessary preparation for a complete . . . Renovation of Knowledge," Holmes proclaimed, "would be a Philosophical History of the Intellectual, Moral, Social and Political Progress of mankind." History appeared to the five Southerners as "philosophy teaching by example," a record of social and moral phenomena awaiting Baconian perusal for the revelation of its general truths; it was, Tucker and Hammond agreed, simply the record of "a series of Experiments" from which man might select "the principles that have been found to be based on truth."[31]

The members of the network were committed to what they called the "philosophical study" of the past, to discovering and elucidating general principles by means of specific details, and to "placing History on its true platform as a moral science." Contemporary moral philosophy had failed to replace corruption with virtue, Holmes believed, because it lacked a firm and convincing scientific foundation. Although the group insisted on the validity of perceptions of the moral sense, they recognized that moral laws might be illustrated more persuasively through history. If morality were transformed into an empirical science, perhaps it would reclaim its ascendance in human affairs.[32]

Their interest thus centered on the didactic potential of historical writing. History, declared Tucker in a review of Macauley, was "instruction" designed to impart "a high moral lesson." In an article on William H. Prescott, Simms explained that a philosophical historian was "not so much after details as principles. He . . . is better prepared with a speculation than a fact. . . . He corrects the morals of history." Judge and steward of the past, the historian was scholarly evangelist offering guidance for present and future action. The success of historical writing, Simms, declared, could be measured "in proportion as it makes favourably for the cause of humanity and virtue."[33]

By examining the growth and decline of societies through the ages, the man of knowledge could discern the character of social and moral progress. With the perspective provided by time, he could, according to Hammond, see facts in their "true as distinct from their obvious tendency" and generalize them into laws. By uniting man with eternity, history provided a kind of transcendence, and this, combined with its implicit moral lessons, promised to establish it as a surrogate religion for an age confronting a crisis of belief.[34]

The special intellectual and moral insight of the genius particularly suited him to the historian's calling and at the same time permitted him considerable freedom with historical fact; he was superior to the mundane realities not just of the present but of the past as well. This view of the historian's role was by no means limited to the members of the Sacred Circle. Such eminent nineteenth-century scholars as George Bancroft and Jared Sparks felt free to alter quotations to suit their own literary tastes and even, on occasion, their political inclinations. The genius, Simms explained, must be accorded "liberties of conjecture," for "it is the artist only who is the true historian. It is he who gives shape to the unknown fact—who yields relation to the scattered fragments, who . . . endows, with life and action, the otherwise motionless automata of history." Even though "the facts may not be truly set down," Tucker explained that the "high moral lesson" the historian "finds is worth more than the truth he misses."[35]

For Simms, these general prescriptions assumed a very practical purpose, justifying his exercise of increasing liberty with the facts of the regional past as the sectional crisis intensified. A new 1860 edition of his *History of South Carolina*, originally published in 1840, sought to establish the early origin of sectional differences and to prove Southern responsibility for Revolutionary victory and American independence.[36]

Simms had begun this distinctly partisan use of history as early as the late forties, and on 15 December 1848 wrote to Hammond, "By the way, read an article in the July no. of the Southern Quarterly entitled 'South Carolina in the Revolution' if you would see how I have carried the war into Yankeedom & furnished an argument, much needed, to our politicians." When he set out on a historical lecture tour of the North in the mid-fifties, the Carolinian certainly seemed to be provoking ideological warfare between the sections. His audiences were so outraged by his politicization of the past that he was forced to retreat to his own side of the Mason-Dixon line after only a few appearances. This reception bewildered Simms, for he did not understand that what he viewed as creative history appeared to Northerners as bias and polemic. By the 1850s, Simms's fiction and historical writings were directed at essentially the same goal and, to a large extent, employed the same methods. "My novels," he explained to the editor of the *Southern Literary Messenger* in 1856, "aim at something more than the story. I am really . . . revising history."[37]

The five men of mind did not recognize that their desire to establish history as a science had specific implications for the way they should approach the study of the past. Instead, they established goals and criteria for historical writing identical with those they applied to other forms of literature. All works of mind should be dedicated to discovering and communicating moral truth, for this was the legitimating purpose of the intellectual.

While their almost total lack of detachment rendered their "creative" history considerably less than scientific, it was, by this very fact, particularly revealing of the Southerners' values and of their attitude toward the world around them. The specific historical periods and the moral lessons the members of the network chose to illustrate tell more about their own world than about any past society.

Simms's chief concern was the Revolution, for he hoped that in demonstrating "the glory of our ancestors," men such as Francis Marion and Nathaniel Greene, he might encourage the South to "assert her character—to reassert her history." The virtues of bygone days lay dormant in South Carolinians, but once reminded of their heritage, they would rediscover their inherent nobility and behave in the same glorious manner as had their historic forebears.[38]

The Revolutionary spirit seemed to Simms analogous to the Southern nationalism he was encouraging and gave him a prototype for his own role as an intellectual gadfly, urging the people to assert their national autonomy. The Revolutionary movement, he declared, had "originated with the native intellect of the country. . . . It was a revolt of the domestic genius." The struggle for American independence, Simms believed, had been in essence a movement of mind, much like the one he sought to create in the Old South.[39]

Ruffin shared Simms's interest in the Revolution and wrote a chronicle of one of his ancestors entitled "The Blackwater Guerilla." The members of the network seem to have had a peculiar interest in the figure of the partisan, the individual able to use his distance and isolation from society to make a significant impact upon it. Simms, for example, studied Marion and Chevalier Bayard, whom he described in these terms, and Tucker wrote a novel entitled *The Partisan Leader.* Perhaps the partisan appeared as a kind of military analogue of the role they themselves hoped to play. Simms even described Marion as a social "reformer," suggesting his own identification with the Revolutionary hero.[40]

Holmes, understandably, was not particularly interested in the American Revolution. Born an Englishmen, he did not share his friends' enthusiasm for the revolt of the colonies, but instead found an earlier period more instructive. Because Holmes had read extensively in the philosophy of history and was familiar with the works of Vico, Michelet, Herder, and Schlegel, his understanding of the uses of the past was far more self-conscious than that of the other members of the network. Under Vico's influence, Holmes viewed the course of history as a spiral. "The peoples of the earth . . . all pass through a career analogous to that with their predecessors. . . . all follow in the same path." Holmes proclaimed "a direct parallelism" between present and past. The contemporary American experience was both "anticipated" and "illustrated" by the history of Rome between Caesar and Justinian. The Roman past had special relevance for Americans in an age of growing materialism, corruption, and social disorder, for it portrayed:

the intimate connection between social progress and social disorganization, between material wealth and popular distress, between national aggrandizement and political corruption, between the decline of religious faith and the destruction of all the elements of permanent national vitality. . . . A diligent examination of these times also conveys the important lesson that germs of new life are always to be discovered among the debris of ancient organizations. . . . that we must look in the chambers of the dead and dying for the budding signs of a coming resurrection.

The study of Rome would reveal principles on which to base the intellectual and moral reformation of the nineteenth century. Failure to heed the lessons of antiquity to elevate the Southern spirit threatened to produce the same invasion of "Hordes from the North" that had devastated the ancient city. Holmes's conception of time as a spiral made history a study of typologies.[41]

While other members of the group devoted themselves to the American and the Classical past, Tucker and Ruffin turned to an era usually considered beyond the purview of the historian. In keeping with their prophetic self-conception, both men undertook to compose histories of the future. Ruffin's explicitly didactic creation was entitled *Anticipations of the Future to Serve as Lessons for the Present Time*. Organized as a series of letters, the volume was designed to demonstrate to the South the folly of remaining within the Union. Beverley Tucker's *Partisan Leader*, originally published in 1836, was later taken by Northerners as direct evidence of a Southern conspiracy for independence dating back to the time of nullification. Tucker himself declared the work to be a "true history" of the causes of Southern secession, which he predicted would occur before 1850.[42]

In searching for present lessons in past experience, however, the members of the network found that the traditional emphasis on political and diplomatic events provided insufficient information about many of the issues on which they most desired instruction. Because they conceived of themselves as men of knowledge, they sought historical understanding of the role of mind and of belief, as Simms demonstrated when he traced the Revolution to the rise of "domestic genius." In their search for this ideational component of the past, for an elusive characteristic they sometimes described as "spirit," the five intellectuals inevitably became involved in social and cultural history. Tucker insisted that men must understand all parts of the past—not just wars and diplomacy—if it was to serve as a guide for the present. Simms, too, emphasized the spiritual and intellectual effect of a people's total social experience. The Revolution might be studied profitably, he advised, through an investigation of the "family fireside" and in the "domestic life of a people," for from this background emerged the character of a nation, its morals, and its spirit. In an enthusiastic review of a history of Ellet's *The Women of the American Revolution*, Simms advocated historical inquiries that "would undertake faithfully to ascertain, to what degree the action of the political world was influenced by the emotions of the social." In his own studies of the Revolution, Simms minimized the influence of taxes and incompetent British rulers. Social progress, such as the growth of population and the "unfolding resources" of America, had brought changing allegiances and the growth of an American national spirit, which had served as the motive force behind the conflict.[43]

Through study of the morals of a society, a historian might arrive at what Tucker called the "inner life" and Holmes described as the "intellectual spirit" of a civilization. This effort to elucidate a *Zeitgeist*, to understand the intellectual and spiritual motivations of figures in the past, made biography an important historical mode, expecially for Simms. "One of the most instructive forms for the preparation of history," biography was particularly suited to inculcate moral lessons, for it provided this age of hero-worshipers with models for emulation.

Tucker recognized this purpose in his review of Sparks's *Life of Washington,* observing that the volume would inspire Americans "to mould ourselves by his precepts and example." In four full-length biographies and countless other essays and reviews, Simms continually drew analogies between past and present for the instruction of his contemporaries and, frequently, for the consolation of his fellow intellectuals. Simms believed that Captain John Smith had exemplified the qualities of selflessness and virtue the Southerner perceived as the essence of greatness, but, like other men of genius, Smith had been greeted with scorn. He "pined with denial, while he beheld others grow prosperous and insolent in the wages of his adventure and the spoils that should have rewarded his genius only." Smith, Simms concluded, had "shared the fate of merit," for he had "died in obscurity . . . neglected after the completion of his tasks." But failure to gain recognition in his own time would "not lessen the value of his performance in the regards of posterity." As a genius neglected by his own age, Simms was gratified to note the fame Smith had been accorded after his death.[44]

In a similar manner, Chevalier Bayard had suffered during his lifetime because of his selflessness, "his utter disinterestedness." He had been born into an era preoccupied with the "grossest passions," when chivalry and virtue were at their "lowest condition." Nonetheless, Bayard stood as an exemplar of morality. "His simple rule was to sacrifice himself always—his interests, his rights, his vanity, his ambition, to his duties." And like all men of virtue and genius, Bayard also suffered from dedicating himself to principle rather than to personal advancement. "That he never received the baton of Marshal of France is due rather to the fact that he lacked the arts of the favorite . . . was too great a lover of truth to possess any of the expertness of the courtier." To portray the extent of Bayard's virtue, Simms invoked an image he often used to describe his own struggle against a materialistic world; the chevalier, he declared, had "kept the whiteness of his soul free from spot in spite of the contagion in which he lived." Simms could not avoid identifying with those whose lives he recounted, and his histories thus became a kind of autobiography. His concern about his own relevance as a man of special gifts was projected onto his historical inquiries, and in this sense historical exploration assumed the form of a search for legitimacy. Just as one era was parallel to its predecessors, men's lives seemed to repeat themselves as well.[45]

Through biography Simms hoped not just to derive lessons from a single life, but to approach the spirit of a people and to define the relationship between the extraordinary individual and his time. Tortured by the need to find his own place, Simms sought to explore the problem historically. Great men, he concluded, "represent the moods as well as the necessities of a race"; they were the supreme expression of the spirit of the people. In an age that increasingly recognized the masses as the ultimate source of all wisdom, the members of the Sacred Circle sought convincing legitimation for the authority of the few. The genius, they suggested, should be recognized as superior to the people simply because he was the quintessential emanation of them; he understood them better, Holmes suggested, than they did themselves.[46]

Biography was useful, therefore, as an instrument to approach "the moods as well as the necessities of a race," to endeavor, in other words, to understand national character, for this was the overriding purpose of historical inquiry. The belief in a moral and intellectual spirit peculiar to a nation was central to the conception these Southerners shared about the study of the past. In the conventions of nineteenth-century Romanticism, "nation" had come to mean not as much a political entity as a people or race, which was the source of national character and the determining force of history. A race, as Simms had explained, had certain "necessities," certain peculiar characteristics that controlled its experience and could be understood by the historian as rules governing its development. Simms subscribed to the widely held belief in the importance of Anglo-Saxon blood to the origins and maintenance of parliamentary republicanism. This "Teutonic origins" theory, as it came to be known, was embraced by many prominent nineteenth-century scholars, including, for example, George Bancroft, who like Simms was convinced that the success of British and American government arose from the "sagacious instincts of the Anglo-Saxon nature" and the "inherent virtues of the Anglo-Saxon stock."[47]

"In our day," Holmes agreed, "the distinct functions of different races in the onward march of human progress promise to be recognized as the principal axiom of historical science." The influence of racial attributes on history seemed to Holmes most clearly illustrated in Roman national character, which he portrayed as distinguished by innate greed. Like the concept of genius, race or national character seemed biological in origin, but spiritual in expression.[48]

The importance accorded the role of national character in shaping history thus implied a pessimism about the nature of man, an awareness of biological constraints that limited his moral as well as his physical and intellectual achievements. By recognizing his predestined nature, man might structure his life and society to restrain the evil and encourage the positive qualities. The vices of individual humans were the cause of the social disorders of the time. "The burthen of complaint," Holmes explained, "must be charged upon the nature of man and the constitution of the universe; it cannot be avoided by

socialistic or other schemes; it must always be borne, though it may
be very materially mitigated by prudent ameliorations, and by the
wide dissemination and encouragement of human charities." Thus
history became the study of man's limitations and imperfections, a
chronicle of his failures and successes designed to clarify his options
in charting the future.[49]

THE NATURAL AND HEALTHY COURSE
OF IMPROVEMENT

Human beings appeared to these Southerners not essentially virtuous, but corrupt and self-seeking. The great miscarriage of nineteenth-century reform, they therefore concluded, arose from its failure
to recognize the truths of human nature and history. Hammond found
men to be "fools . . . knaves & often devils," all possessed of an "evil
genius"; Holmes in turn insisted, "We cannot join the new faith: we
do not live in Utopia; . . . we cannot shake off our conviction of the
imperfection, the frailty, the folly, the frequent iniquity of men."
Structural reform would not improve society, for it was not social
institutions but the men within them that were corrupt.[50]

Reform, however badly needed by the nineteenth century, could
not "proceed in entire ignorance or disregard of the laws of human
nature" and consequently "impede the natural and healthy course of
improvement by leading it astray into devious paths and impracticable
short cuts." Reformers should abandon their preoccupation with the
increase and distribution of material wealth, for obsession with goods
and money represented the greatest wickedness of the age. "The true
object," Simms believed, was not " 'the happiness of the greatest number' nor the promotion of a vulgar prosperity, founded in the wealth,
the public improvements, or the industry of the nation." Instead,
reform must endeavor to "re-erect the fallen spirit,—arouse the dormant moral energies, and dignify the character of man." Until personal avarice was suppressed and a sense of transcendent duty was
restored as the motivating principle for human behavior, public disorder and corruption would prevail. Thus reform should be directed
not as much at social questions as toward the spiritual elevation of
individual human beings.[51]

Pessimism about Northern utopian schemes did not however, imply
a total rejection of the idea of progress or a desire to cling uncritically
to the past. The Sacred Circle insisted that they objected to the particular nature of Northern designs for social amelioration rather than
to change itself. Because the human spirit determined the nature of
social evolution, all real progress had to originate in the hearts and
minds of men. Thus true reform could not move faster than intellectual and moral progress. If human interference forced social forms to

develop more rapidly than the principles and ideas on which their orderly operation depended, social upheaval would ensue.

Reform, Hammond insisted to Tucker, was but a means and should not be worshipped as an end in itself. "It must not . . . be supposed that I am opposed to 'progress and improvement' in human affairs." He was, he proclaimed, "a decided and zealous advocate of progressive and continual improvement. But it is improvement based upon the revealed Will of our Creator." Elsewhere he warned that serious dangers lurked in any ill-considered reform effort, which might at any moment "degenerate into that wild and reckless spirit of innovation wh. delights to break up established forms merely because they are old." Ruffin agreed upon the importance of placing prudent limits on change. Even "the wisest and purest of reformers," he observed, "by the heat of their zeal to oppose evil are often urged to press their doctrines beyond the proper limits that both truth and expediency would prescribe."[52]

But it was often difficult to determine exactly how to moderate reform. While it was important not to succumb to the extravagant and delusive schemes of socialists and other radicals, Holmes emphasized the dangers that would ensue if thinking men retreated entirely from promoting human improvement through carefully directed social change. By dedicating themselves to bettering their world, men would resist "being tempted into the blind retrogressive policy of those whose only idea of amelioration, is a return to the usages of feudalism and the thirteenth century." At the same time, a commitment to active reform could avert "that imprudent temporizing with incipient perils which canonizes the present and leaves time and accident to heal, prevent or aggravate the imminent calamities of the future." Even though man was predestined by the necessities of his biological and racial heritage, he could develop a program of improvement informed by an awareness of the historical and genetic limitations upon both himself and his society. Through proper employment of the products of mind, he might exercise considerable control over his own future and that of his world.[53]

Even Beverley Tucker, the senior member of the network, acknowledged the necessity of carefully considered social change. By the time of his close association with Simms, Hammond, and the others, Tucker was an old man and a conservative renowned for his devotion to the ideals of Revolutionary Virginia. Yet the nostalgia he displayed for a mythic squirearchy of republican virtue underlay what was in certain respects a dynamic social philosophy, oriented toward the future and toward reforming Southern civilization. Is order to reinstate the old principles and the former moral excellence of the South, Tucker was amenable to proposals for change in his own world.

Profoundly influenced by his half brother, John Randolph of Roanoke, Tucker embraced many of the congressman's conservative views on the limited role of government, the pre-eminence of the states in the federal union, and the importance of aristocracy to society. But Tucker did not display a blind allegiance to his brother's position. The two quarreled bitterly on several issues, and Tucker rejected many of his sibling's beliefs. As a young man, Tucker had been far more radical than his brother and admitted that at one point his views had been thoroughly democratic. The greatest influence Randolph wielded over Tucker was on the question of states' rights, and to these principles Tucker always remained firmly dedicated. In the realm of more general social thought, however, Tucker felt free to differ occasionally from his eccentric brother, as, for example, in his vigorous support for slavery. Tucker recognized, moreover, that the clock could not be turned back to the eighteenth century, and that the rise of the common man could not be reversed entirely. Tucker's remedy for the sordid level of political life and public morality was to accept social change, but endeavor to retain the old cultural standards. The principles and the virtue of the early republic could be preserved if the common man could be transformed into a gentleman, a chivalrous and honorable country squire. Such a man, Tucker explained, "scorns what is base, and detests what is brutal." But an individual could attain this exalted standing "either by nature or by training." Thus "from this aristocracy, as they are pleased to call it, none are shut out but by their own fault." Tucker sought a nobility of achievement not ascription; his ideal was an aristocracy of merit and of virtue.[54]

In a lecture to students at William and Mary, Tucker applauded the abolition of primogeniture and entail in Virginia—a reform his brother had deplored. Tucker even urged the further division of landholdings in the state so that a society of truly equal men—a republic of all white males—might flourish. With an underclass of blacks to perform all distasteful work, in time whites might all be squires. In such a society, Tucker believed, the great force of avarice would be minimized, for every man would have all the wealth he could reasonably desire. Relieved of the need to compete for personal gain, men would be able to devote themselves to perfecting their virtues, for these would be criteria for leadership and the means of gaining social place. In such a world, Tucker believed, disinterested virtue and selfless devotion to duty once again might prevail.

Tucker continued his lecture on the problems of social amelioration with some significant observations about the nature of reform and of social change. From a theoretical point of view, he noted, the county court system in Virginia appeared decidedly unfair. Endowed with the right to appoint its own members, the court seemed to institutionalize a self-perpetuating elite. But, he urged, before Virginians rushed to abolish it because its structure seemed inconsistent with republican principles, they should examine its actual operation. In fact, Tucker contended, the system had worked well. Virtuous men had run the courts which, in consequence, had dispensed justice to all. Until Virginians were sure they had an institutional arrangement that would work better in practice—not in theory—than the existing system, they must not meddle with it.

Tucker conceived of the social world as an intricate structure. Sweeping theories about natural law and natural rights appeared meaningless in face of the complex customs and interrelationships that had evolved over centuries to constitute contemporary society. Through the inductive study of all these specific social phenomena, men might approach an understanding of social law that never could be derived through deductive reasoning from abstract "first principles." To Tucker, society appeared an organism in which many separate parts united to make a whole greater than any simple aggregate of its elements. Changing slowly over time, every culture developed through its own historical experience a particular character and particular needs. "There is no best in government," Tucker declared. "That which is best for one people is not best for another." The gradualness of this evolution implied to Tucker the futility—and the danger—of intrusive reform efforts aimed at immediate social amelioration. The county court system worked, Tucker believed, not because of its theoretical perfection. Rather, a sense of duty and a commitment to justice had evolved over time, and these principles made the institution operate fairly and efficiently. Because tradition played a determining role in the life of any society, reformers could not ignore the influence of past experience on present social institutions and phenomena.[55]

The conception of society as an integrated organism that had evolved over time was shared not just by the members of the Sacred Circle, but by many Southerners in the ante-bellum period. In a recent article in the *Journal of Southern History*, Theodore D. Bozeman has shown how Joseph LeConte's naturalistic world view made him particularly receptive to the social organicism prevalent during the late 1850s in the intellectual community around Columbia. In the same way the young scientist's naturalistic outlook made him receptive to the organic social imagery, the deep-rooted historicism of the five members of the network predisposed them to similar social views.[56]

Society appeared a natural phenomenon, an organism, in the sense that its course of development was determined by a set of constituent elements with which it initially was endowed. Because history was the study of this unfolding potential, a kind of social embryology, it drew attention to the interrelation of different time periods, to the fundamental and persistent unity of any society. The members of the network found in their historical explorations no record of men establishing social compacts, as Locke had suggested. Human beings, they concluded, never had existed independent of societies; they were born into a social state and from the first were linked with those around them by ties of custom and tradition. Men did not possess natural rights, but instincts like "ambition, avarice, lust" which they had an inescapable duty to control. Because they viewed men as inherently evil and morally frail, the five Southerners could not imagine them independent of social restraints. Freedom was not a right but a privilege man earned by demonstrating himself able to suppress the "profound corruption" that was the essence of human nature. One should receive, Simms declared, only "such liberty as becomes ones moral condition." Tucker admitted that his idea of government was "at variance with all the theories of the social compact which have been put forth." But the Virginian found that these theories were in turn "at variance with all we know of the early history of the human races." He could not bring himself to "reject the testimony of history," and thus he found himself compelled "to doubt the justice" of concepts of natural law. In the empirical study of the past, he had discovered truths which deductive and theoretical reasoning had obscured.[57]

The writings and pronouncements of these five thinkers were filled with testimonies to their social organicism. Perhaps the most common example was their recurrent references to the diseased nature of society and the need for appropriate remedies. Like an individual being, the social organism could malfunction and require medication. The men of mind constantly anthropomorphized society, assigning to it a national character, a soul, and a moral sense.

Holmes was so struck by the analogy beteen the growth of societies and that of organisms that under the heading "Illustrations of Historical Law and Development" in his notebook he included two full pages of quotations from Matthias Schleiden's treatise on botany. By carefully comparing modern societies with civilizations of the past, Holmes believed he might predict certain conditions of their growth and change. He likewise seemed to assume that the laws of development that applied to plants could be extrapolated to the growth of social organisms. The study of the natural world promised to produce important insights for the social scientist. In their eagerness to adapt the methods of natural science to the study of the social world, Holmes and the other members of the network incorporated within their world view much of its vocabulary and many of its conclusions.[58]

Emphasis on the organic nature of society was a logical corollary of the efforts by the members of the network to transform history into a science and to enhance the importance of their observations by arraying them in scientific language. In the same way that the evocation of

Bacon elicited the respect of most educated men of the nineteenth century, natural history was associated in the public mind with certain knowledge and with the potential for human improvement attributed to modern science. Thus the Southern intellectuals hoped to appropriate for their own ideas a portion of this legitimacy. But the organic conception of society, with the almost reverential respect it implied for the processes of history, served yet another purpose within the world view of the group. Because society appeared as a manifestation of the operation of historical and scientific law through the ages, it had a kind of transcendence of its own; because the past determined the present and future, because a social entity was a complex web of custom and tradition, man's ability to intervene positively in social processes was severely limited.

The belief in the determining force of the past and the inherent baseness of most men provided Simms, Ruffin, Tucker, Holmes, and Hammond with two justifications for opposing indiscriminate meddling with the intricate workings of society. But the members of the network resisted the conclusion that societies were entirely predestined by their past or men entirely predetermined by their evil nature. Individuals might reform themselves, recognize the necessities of their nature, and overcome—or at least control—their inherent evil. So, in an identical manner, societies might come to understand their historic character and, within limits, guide their own future. But because they were both organisms, men and societies were constrained by their heredity.

This understanding of the world performed yet another useful function for these men of knowledge. Because the only power a society could wield over its future derived from its understanding of the meaning inherent in its past, men with special insight into the laws of historical development seemed destined to be the teachers and the guides for others. Similarly, men with special moral insight and virtue would be most qualified to direct the reformation of individuals who had not approached equal excellence. Hammond explained the structural implications of this view to his friend Simms: "While mankind remain without the endowment of perfect knowledge for this world at least, & have sentiments, passions, appetites & Wants, they cannot be let alone. . . . The Many will be compelled to deposit in the hands of a few ample powers to control & regulate the whole—to repress Evil and promote Good: to prevent, to compensate & to enforce, as well as to 'restrain.' " Thus on both an individual and a group level men must be directed by the special insights of the genius, whose superior knowledge and virtue enabled him to help others discover the constraints built into their lives, and thus gain understanding of their potentialities.[59]

Obsessed by the need to establish a place for themselves, the Southern men of knowledge set out to rehabilitate the works of mind to make them appear philosophically more sound and thus more dependable and useful to the rest of the world. Accepting the prevailing Baconianism, they carefully redefined it to incorporate their antimaterialistic values and to support their belief in the importance of intellect and spirit to society. Similarly, the members of the network embraced the concept and the vocabulary of evangelical reform, a configuration of beliefs that in a general way had become a part of the Southern as well as the Northern world view and had evolved into a normative reality throughout nineteenth-century America. But, in the same way they had reinterpreted Baconianism, the five Southerners redefined the meaning of reform, placing limits upon the way in which it might be undertaken and insisting that it had to be directed by individuals with the intellectual and moral insight to ensure its beneficial outcome.

Thus the renovation of knowledge the men advocated was a decidedly self-interested effort at change. Finding a social place for themselves was central to these thinkers' lives, and they could not help but interject their personal concerns into their intellectual and spiritual endeavors. The essence of the reformed works of mind was their didacticism. History, literature, and art all were designed to teach others, and the man of mind, by implication, was to be the guide and director of the human race. Great men, to paraphrase Simms, had been placed on earth to tutor their contemporaries.[60]

FIVE

Uniting Our Minds and Energies:

THE PRACTICE OF STEWARDSHIP

eforming the works of mind, however, was but a part of the effort to make thought "operative"—as Holmes put it—and the thinker relevant in society. Because the true business of genius was to teach and to lead, his work was by definition didactic and therefore required an audience receptive to his evangelical appeal. Since they believed that all social change originated in the spirit and intellect, the five Southerners assumed that men's minds and souls were the primary focus for any efforts at improvement. "The first step in this reform movement," Simms declared, was to "dispossess our people of their old convictions." An unenlightened public, Holmes warned, "exercises an influence adverse to the growth of intellectual eminence." The South's benighted moral state, he feared, would prevent the elevation of men of knowledge to their deserved importance and would impede regional progress toward spiritual excellence. As Simms explained in the *Magnolia,* the destiny of the South, as well as the future of the man of genius, depended upon increasing "the intellectual appetite among our people."[1]

The members of the network therefore dedicated themselves to improving the mental and moral condition of what they described as the great undifferentiated mass of the Southern people. Only the conversion of ordinary men, the uplift of the "domestic mind" shared by the population generally, could ensure a continually deepening commitment to truth and to the disinterested inquiry upon which truth depended. Only by developing the moral courage that arose from intellectual independence could the people resist Northern efforts to dominate them economically, politically, and culturally. Southerners, Simms emphasized, had to be encouraged "to believe more in one another and in themselves—to give their full faith to the genius of the community in which they live, and to foster it with all their most favouring affections. Their life is in their genius."[2]

For Simms, genius had a dual meaning; it implied special spiritual qualities distributed among all the people as well as the particular individual who, like Simms himself, possessed an unusually rich intellectual and moral endowment. In the relationship between these two aspects of the definition, Simms found direct implications for his own social role. As the supreme embodiment of these transcendent characteristics, the man of mind was a highly concentrated incarnation of the spirit of which all others partook. "The man of genius," Simms explained, "is the offspring of the popular impulses." Thus the South Carolinian envisioned a spiritual and intellectual unity of Southerners under the guidance of the man of mind, who represented and incorporated the finest attributes of the people from whom he arose, the qualities upon which their social survival depended.[3]

Like evangelical reformers throughout the nation, these five thinkers saw in moral leadership the opportunity simultaneously to institutionalize the rule of virtue and of themselves. Their language and objectives were strikingly similar to those of such British and American social thinkers as Ralph Waldo Emerson, Francis Bowen, Francis Wayland, Matthew Arnold, and Thomas Carlyle, who decried the ascendance of materialism in modern life and sought to replace it with their own spiritual hegemony.[4]

The mass of the people, Simms hoped, might be fashioned into a moral counterweight to the factions of selfish politicians and office seekers presently controlling American life. As Simms explained to Hammond, he harbored an evangelical faith in a potential for holiness and spiritual improvement within every human. If only the proper means could be discovered to evoke this, every individual might come to embrace moral—and thus political—truth. Simms's belief in democracy, he explained, was therefore more a "religious sentiment than a principle in politics" and consisted above all in the conviction that all men must be elevated to "responsibility and trust." Under the influence and control of the genius, whom they would recognize as the supreme expression of themselves, the people would be transformed into allies for the cause of mind and morality. This belief in the people was not meant to be radical or revolutionary; it arose, Simms reassured Tucker, from the conviction of their ultimate conservatism. Once properly enlightened and converted, the people would readily acknowledge the transcendence of the genius and the importance of his concerns. After all, Simms explained, he conceived of "Jesus Christ as being the first exponent" of these principles and thus the ultimate source of all efforts of social or political improvement. Evangelical reform was simply a mode of Christian duty.[5]

The members of the Sacred Circle therefore devoted a considerable portion of their efforts as a group to evangelizing the South and to institutionalizing the right they had claimed to judge and direct their society. As Hammond explained, the men of mind needed to narrow the gap that separated them and their sacred concerns from the world; they ought to demonstrate the mundane relevance of their transcendent gifts and interests. By "uniting" their "minds . . . and energies" with those of all Southerners, they could uplift the region as a whole —and at the same time establish their own place within it. The members of the network viewed the creation of unity—unanimity of opinion and support for the goals of the man of mind—as their essential purpose. Like seventeenth-century Puritans or nineteenth-century utopian communitarians, these intellectual Southerners intended their society to serve as a model for the amelioration of the entire human race. A reformed South would be a plantation set upon a hill.[6]

The concerns of these five Southerners echo the tenets of an evangelical and reformist ideology that too often has been considered predominantly Northern in character. A sense of America's transcendent mission infused the entire nation, and similar fears of degeneration from this divine purpose are evident in the jeremiads that issued from both North and South in this period, as indeed they had for two centuries. An underlying motive of all nineteenth-century evangelical endeavor was the effort to retain an equilibrium between moral change and social and economic progress; to render virtue continually relevant within a changing complexion of mundane affairs; to retain standards for human conduct within a drastically altered social environment. These dilemmas were every bit as real in the South as in the North; the cotton region harbored no immunity from the "social distempers of the times," as the multifarious lamentations of the Sacred Circle clearly demonstrate.[7]

While the existence of a basically religious orientation toward life throughout the nation is in one sense witness to the cultural similarity of the sections, Southern reformism was idiosyncratic. While Northerners and Southerners agreed upon the importance of individual moral uplift to general social improvement, most Southerners remained strongly tied to what they called their "peculiar institutions" and to a largely organic view of social order and processes. Their reformist tendencies therefore never assumed the hostility to traditional institutional forms which scholars from Ralph Waldo Emerson to Stanley Elkins have described as characteristic of Northern Transcendental efforts at improvement. Southerners seemed to have considerably less faith in the ability of the individual entirely to overcome his own imperfections or to intervene effectively to improve long-standing social arrangements; they were acutely aware of social and historical constraints upon both individuals and institutions. But with their organic social views, these Southerners certainly had counterparts among the more conservative Northern advocates of improvement—among, for example, those Northern clergymen who supported a theocratic ideal or sought to serve as their "brothers' keepers." And as for many Northern reformers of both conservative and more radical leanings, education, individual enlightenment, and uplift seemed to the members of the Sacred Circle the most obvious "engine of modern improvement."[8]

But the reform endeavor in the region was inevitably shaped by the South's particular configuration of institutions and intellectual resources. The principal vehicle available to the advocates of improvement seemed to be the "public press," and, most specifically, the review, that medium of enlightenment and communication which became so influential in both England and America during the late eighteenth and early nineteenth centuries. In an era of alarmingly rapid change, the review served as a highly efficient instrument for intellectual socialization and modernization. Confronted by a new social world, the American could find advice and etiquette books to direct everything from his sex life to his table manners; similarly, he could turn to the review to learn—in predigested form—the proper way to think within an environment of constantly shifting beliefs and values. In the South, the review had a particularly important mission. One of the few "sources of popular tuition," as Simms phrased it, the review became the premier embodiment of the intellectual role, reflecting the values and many of the confusions of the man of knowledge, uniting him with other thinkers, and providing him with a way to reach out to his society.[9]

Hammond, Holmes, Ruffin, Tucker, and Simms all were involved with the press—and particularly with reviews—as editors and contributors, and these ventures served as a major focus of their interaction. Simms began his journalistic career at the age of nineteen and remained an editor for most of his adult life. During the forties, however, he dedicated himself with particular intensity to cultivating the Southern mind through the creation of a thriving periodical literature. In 1842–43, he edited the *Magnolia;* between January and December 1845, the *Southern and Western Monthly Magazine,* also known as *Simms' Magazine,* until it merged with the *Southern Literary Messenger;* and from 1849 to 1855, the *Southern Quarterly Review,* which was the leading regional publication of the era.[10]

Hammond had become involved in publishing at almost as early an age as Simms, for in 1830 he assumed editorship of the *Southern Times,* a news publication with a decidedly "literary character." Apparently, too few South Carolinians demonstrated the necessary interest in this endeavor, for after five years, the *Times* failed, abandoning "its humble efforts" for the "improvement of the age." Convinced that "others, my inferiors had swept the real honors of life from me" while he had wasted his energy on the *Times,* Hammond never again took an editorial position, although on several occasions he discussed with Ruffin the joint sponsorship of an agricultural paper. Hammond did not doubt the importance of reviews to the "domestic mind" of the South. Urging others to employ the public press in the cause of human improvement, he planned and produced articles of his own which he offered to Simms for publication.[11]

George Frederick Holmes first encountered Simms when the older author was soliciting contributions for the *Magnolia.* Throughout the ante-bellum period, Holmes derived a major portion of his income from periodicals, and from 1849 to 1856 depended upon magazine writing entirely. Holmes served as an associate editor of the *Southern Quarterly Review* from 1842 to 1843 and contributed extensively as well to the *Southern Literary Messenger, Methodist Quarterly,* and later, *DeBow's Review.*

Ruffin's initial effort in publishing was the *Farmers' Register* (1833–42), which he dedicated to the cause of agricultural reform and general Southern improvement. Scientific and scholarly in its tone, the *Register* was acclaimed by leaders of the agricultural press as the premier organ of its type. By 1842, however, Ruffin had begun to use his journal to attack the banks, and consequently he neglected questions of husbandry. Many subscribers canceled, complaining that the *Register* had abandoned agriculture for political diatribes. Ruffin thereupon founded the *Bank Reformer,* which was short-lived, and then a publication of broader appeal titled the *Southern Magazine.* Tucker, who had been a major contributor to the *Southern Literary Messenger* throughout the thirties, was Ruffin's chief ally in this endeavor, and indeed, as Ruffin explained, Tucker's "fellow feeling" had encouraged him "to make the venture." But Ruffin was unable to find enough supporters to enable the magazine to survive more than two volumes. Thomas Roderick Dew and others had promised assistance, but found themselves too busy to provide the help Ruffin required. Despite this discouragement, Tucker and Ruffin continued to write for publications managed by others. A number of Ruffin's pieces, more scientific than literary in character, appeared in DeBow's commercially oriented *Review,* while many of Tucker's productions were published in Simms's various magazines.[12]

Writing for the public press was a major occupation for every member of the network, and all dedicated considerable energy to establishing reviews that would, as Simms described, "give to Southern opinion that tone and character which it is so desirable for the independence

of the intellectual character of the country that it should possess."
Hammond, Holmes, Simms, Ruffin, and Tucker shared a very specific
conception of the goals of a review and of the values it should embody.
Because it was designed to institutionalize the role of mind, the members of the group believed it should be governed by the same principles that motivated all intellectual endeavor. Like the man of knowledge himself, the review would serve as steward of public morality
and intellect. Through the *Southern Magazine,* Ruffin hoped that the
people of the region might be "organized and disciplined." Intended
to "direct and control . . . opinions" and to "maintain truth," the review
was to be the means through which the intellectual exercised his "dignified authority."[13]

The concerns of the review were moral as well as intellectual, and
the periodicals assumed a kind of ethical mission. Holmes explained
that "our imperative duty, as Reviewers," was "to denounce and rebuke
immorality." Ruffin agreed that his *Southern Magazine* must rally both
the "moral and intellectual forces" of the people. Such a goal dictated
that the reviewer maintain above all a "dignified attitude," for as
moral philosopher, he must not, Hammond cautioned Simms, stoop to
the level of "controversialist." In a letter to his brother, Hammond
urged him to "Remember in writing for a Review that you must not
take *one* side. . . . You must shew both sides fairly & then give a dig-
nificed preponderance—as by mere force of reason to the one you
lean to. You must *judge;* not *advocate.*" Judgment implied truth; advo-
cacy suggested factionalism. A review, Ruffin emphasized, should be
"free from all adherence to either of the existing political parties."
Like the intellectual himself, a review must be disinterested and
"philosophical."[14]

But just as the man of knowledge in his role as historian had found
it difficult to avoid incorporating sectionalist sentiments into his work,
as reviewer, he did not long remain aloof from questions of political
and social controversy. In the same way the man of mind paradoxically identified himself as both prophet and steward, so he intended
the review both to illuminate transcendent truth and to create a distinctively Southern mind and character; he did not recognize that the
universalism of the first goal might conradict the particularism of the
second.

As embodiment of the intellectual's role, the review manifested his
conflicts and his ambivalence. Would reviews be dedicated to truly
significant intellectual inquiry, which undoubtedly would render them
beyond the comprehension of the general public, or should they
embrace less lofty standards in order to gain greater social influence?
To what extent should reviews express timeless intellectual and moral
concerns or, conversely, dedicate themselves to serving the South, as

Simms urged, in the "defence of our Institutions, and the exhibition of our character"? Tucker specifically stressed the need to make reviews socially relevant. Periodical literature should, he declared, "efface the impression made by ruder minds" on the people and "stamp its own instead." The man of knowledge must attempt in the review to "commune with the minds of living men."[15]

Reviews insisted upon their abhorrence of partisanship, but regarded the defense of the South as a primary goal. An 1847 editorial in the *Southern Quarterly* strikingly illustrated this contradiction. The *Review*, its editors proclaimed, aimed to "arouse and animate to active exertion the Southern intellect and Southern learning." Dedicated to "that most glorious and noble of all pursuits, the pursuit of knowledge," the journal hoped to divert the people "from the too eager chase of the fleeting honors of political life, to the more permanent distinctions of literature and science." But this admirable goal was only the

first great object of the Review. There are other purposes, collateral and incidental, but deeply important, which it will not fail to subserve. The people of the Southern states are so far a peculiar people, that . . . we are arraigned before the bar of Christendom for alleged wrong-doing. . . . We will not stand mute. . . . The calm, temperate, thorough discussion of the question of slavery will therefore occupy no inconsiderable portion of the Southern Review.

The essay vigorously defended slavery and free trade, then concluded by declaring its devotion to the "cultivation of genius, the vindication of moral and religious truth."[16]

This editorial embodied the conflict between universalism and particularism, transcendence and partisanship, that characterized both the Southern intellectual and the vehicle he created for the dissemination of his views. Convinced of his righteousness and the validity of his intellectual insights, he allowed himself "liberties of conjecture" both as historian and as reviewer that gave free rein to his own subjectivity. He could and often did choose to discuss extremely controversial works—such as *Uncle Tom's Cabin* or Harriet Martineau's attack on slavery. Every member of the network published one or more defenses of the peculiar institution in Southern periodicals. Despite avowals of disinterestedness, both the intellectual and his journals became increasingly partisan as the public upon which their survival depended grew more hostile to the North. Southerners thus endowed these periodicals with a curious and even inconsistent dual purpose, "the vindication of their rights and the development of their intellectual resources."[17]

The man of knowledge believed that elevating the domestic mind simultaneously implied raising the general level of intellect and advancing the individual man of genius to a position of deserved esteem. Because of the close correspondence the five Southerners had established between—as Tucker put it—their ambition and their convictions, they regarded the fate of the Southern mind as inseparable from the personal destiny of the intellectual. Designed to serve both these causes, the review reflected a conflict of practical and transcendent loyalties that undermined its credibility with the Southern public. The repeated financial failures of Southern periodicals undoubtedly represented the effects of this inconsistency of purpose as well as the South's unreceptiveness to endeavors of the mind.

Despite numerous setbacks, however, Simms and the other members of the group continued their efforts to make reviews into institutions for Southern intellectual life. Even though the review often became a source of "pain, disquiet and the most unintermitted mental drudgery" to its sponsors, it remained the Southern writer's best hope of advancing both himself and his work. Simms intended to use periodicals to widen the circle of men of knowledge within the South, to enlist individuals throughout the region into the vanguard of the movement for intellectual and spiritual reform. At the same time, he hoped that reviews would enhance intellectual communication and provide the mental stimulation that was nearly nonexistent in the rural South because of the "very sparseness of our population." Periodicals did establish contacts among men of mind, as, for example, between Simms and Holmes, and provided opportunities as well for the thinkers to "puff" each other's work. Simms urged Hammond to assess Ruffin's *Essay on Calcareous Manures* for the *Southern Quarterly* and thereby "give him a good lift." Hammond could, Simms explained, simultaneously "do a good thing for me, for Ruffin & the State and . . . for yourself."[18]

By institutionalizing the functions of the intellectual in periodical publications, these Southerners were in part endeavoring to elevate learning into an occupation of acknowledged importance, worthy of a fixed place in society. Simms felt writing for reviews was a "professional duty," an obligation that arose from his desire to establish intellectuals as an indispensable social class. By creating channels of communication among thinkers and between them and the rest of their world, reviews might provide a formal structure for the activities of the Southern mind.[19]

Because reviews were the premier organ of the intellectual class in the South, their contents indicate a great deal about the concerns of men of knowledge and the substantive social and intellectual problems in terms of which they expressed their conception of their role. As indicated in the last chapter, the discussion of history and philosophy occupied a considerable proportion of their interest, but they also became involved in more concrete social issues. Because reviews were intended to reflect the union of practical and theoretical concerns that characterized the intellectual's role, articles often dealt in a "philosophic" manner with issues of immediate social interest, such as agriculture, banking, or slavery. By examining a contemporary issue within a historical context, the reviewers believed, they broadened the intellectual and moral scope of their undertaking and rebutted in advance any charges of polemicism or partisanship that might be leveled against them. Thus, for example, Holmes discussed Aristotle's views of slavery, and Simms examined the agricultural attitudes of the ancients. While the men of mind discussed and theorized about social problems in periodicals, in their own lives they embarked on less speculative efforts at reforms. The reviews were aimed chiefly at "Uniting our minds," as Hammond phrased it, but the five intellectuals undertook a number of other projects with the more tangible goal of "uniting our . . . energies."

Like most Southerners, the members of the group did not question "the great and primary value" of agriculture "in affecting the condition of the human family, and conserving the social harmonies, and promoting and sustaining the moral basis." The soil appeared the source of social morality, and the "bald and sterile fields" of the eastern South became a symbol for the general degeneration of Southern civilization. Because of this special spiritual—as well as its crucial economic—significance, agriculture served as a primary focus of the intellectuals' reformist concern.[20]

In review articles and public addresses, the members of the Sacred Circle continually stressed the importance of bringing "thought" and intellect "to bear upon our agriculture," for they never doubted that every reform depended ultimately upon the power of mind. Hammond bemoaned the fact that "There is & has long been a strong prejudice against 'book farmers.'" The "leading and intellectual men," Simms agreed, should transform agriculture into a science. Holmes wistfully longed for a day "when the tillers of the ground are all informed—philosophers expending their genius in discovering more profitable modes of culture." Ruffin published "An Apology for Book Farmers" and emphasized that reformers would be able to induce improved agricultural practice only by "teaching the theory and rationale" behind new methods. Thus their practical efforts at agricultural reform all centered around elevating the intellectual level of the farmer.[21]

The men of knowledge endeavored to institutionalize the role of mind in the management of agriculture through a number of different methods, of which the publication of agricultural essays and periodicals such as the *Farmers' Register* is but an example. Simms, Hammond, and Ruffin hoped to establish their own plantations as models, practical examples of theoretical principles, in the "exhibitory" mode of improvement widely advocated by Northern reformer Horace Mann. "I have laid off some experimental acres along the public road," Hammond explained to Ruffin, "and put up sign boards so as to *force* all who are not blind to see. I am running 'Marl' against 'Nothing' & 'Marl & Cotton Seed' against 'Cotton Seed' & every man who goes up to town *shall know* which beats." Hammond, Simms, and Ruffin experimented extensively with this limelike substance, which was designed to rejuvenate the soil by reducing its acidity and thus rendering it more receptive to the beneficial effects of animal manures. Use of such calcareous materials was the essence of Ruffin's agricultural philosophy, and the other members of the network hoped to assist in convincing the South of the importance of his speculations. Hammond also experimented with other agricultural innovations in an effort to demonstrate the practicality of crop diversification. When cotton prices fell in the forties, he quickly recognized the economic danger of South Carolina's almost exclusive reliance upon cotton and rice. For that reason he tested a number of new crops for market production, including a species of sugar cane called imphee, which proved unsuccessful, as well as silkworms and wine grapes.[22]

Declining soil productivity had influenced many Carolinians to move westward, thus disrupting the ties of organic community upon which the Sacred Circle believed the social order rested. Hammond proposed to alleviate this social and moral problem by increasing the land available for cultivation within the state, both by rejuvenating exhausted fields and by creating new ones. Like the Romantic prototype of all frustrated intellectuals, Goethe's Faust, Hammond set about reclaiming swamp lands through elaborate drainage schemes, applying engineering calculations to the improvement of agriculture.[23]

But the men of mind were not content to educate the South through the example of their own experiments. Hammond and Ruffin were eager to increase available knowledge of agriculture and thereby to strengthen the case for heeding scientific wisdom. During almost a year of traveling about South Carolina on behalf of the agricultural survey for which Hammond had selected him, Ruffin gathered data and appeared before groups of farmers to explain the "social and moral benefits" of marl. As a result of this experience, Ruffin decided that a regular lyceum, a series of agricultural lectures given throughout Virginia and South Carolina, might permanently establish the importance of knowledge to the practice of farming. But Hammond feared such a plan never would meet with success among his benighted countrymen. As a less ambitious venture, Hammond suggested instead that Ruffin aid him in the establishment of an agricultural paper for South Carolina and even purchased from the Virginian a second-hand printing press. But Hammond was hardly less utopian than his Virginian friend and soon had forgotten plans for a paper in the excitement of what he described as another "visionary scheme" for agricultural improvement:

Why could I not build a Brick Laboratory here on this healthy ridge—a decent wooden cottage for a Professor—a Boarding House & outhouse to accommodate 50 young men & have a College for Agricultural sciences? . . . If we could turn out annually 50 young men who have learned these things so as to be able to think, reason & act in farming as professional men in their callings . . . what a country we might have in 50 years. . . . Not one Agriculturalist in 100,000 knows the least thing of Botany, geology, mineralogy, or chemistry, all of which sciences are essential to his knowing what he is about every day of his life. His whole occupation is one of unmixed quackery.

Agriculture, Hammond insisted, must be transformed into a profession requiring prescribed intellectual training and standards; mind must exert its influence over the primary economic activity of the South.[24]

Ruffin never created his lyceum nor Hammond his agricultural college, but other schemes proved more fruitful. Ruffin, Hammond, and Simms were active in the formation of local farmers' organizations and state agricultural societies. Hammond wrote proudly to Ruffin of his role in founding the "ABC Farmers Club" near Beech Island, South Carolina, which required each member to subscribe to one agricultural paper and undertake one farming experiment annually. Hammond seemed naturally to assume the dominant role in the group and discoursed to his neighbors on such uplifting topics as Cato's views on manure. Simms and Hammond had served as delegates to an agricultural convention in 1839 which created the State Agricultural Society, and Simms was chosen a member of the committee that planned the details of its constitution. Both men remained active within the organization, with Hammond participating during the forties on committees on hogs and marl, while Simms restricted his involvement to the somewhat more poetic endeavors of encouraging wine and silk production. Hammond assumed a leadership role from the first and was elected to deliver the anniversay oration in 1841, when he urged the assembled farmers to adopt "manuring, contracted planting, drainage," and "book learning."[25]

Dedicated to ameliorating agriculture through advancing knowledge, the society reflected the same Idealist conception of reform as did the members of the network. There was little effort to provide legislative incentives to encourage or require crop diversification, for these South Carolinians thought that to try to alter practice without reforming belief would be useless. The proposals adopted by the society reflect its conviction that the only way to begin agricultural change was to transform minds through education. At one meeting Simms recommended establishing agricultural schools, equipped with farming implements and livestock, for the poor boys of each district. Undoubtedly this suggestion appeared too ambitious to the society, for it was tabled, but the members unanimously passed a resolution urging the trustees of South Carolina College to add agricultural chemistry to the curriculum. As a result of his work as South Carolina's agricultural surveyor, Ruffin participated in the state society and sponsored an award for the Carolina farm using marl most effectively.[26]

While Ruffin was working with Simms and Hammond for agricultural reform in South Carolina, he actively urged similar improvements in his own state. He was a major force behind the establishment of the Virginia State Board of Agriculture in 1841 and was elected corresponding secretary at its first meeting. He proposed a detailed plan of action that included dividing the state into eight districts with a board member to supervise each. As Ruffin's biographer Avery Craven described, "It was a dream come true—the agricultural leader recognized and official aid given to the cause." But Ruffin was soon disappointed, for his proposal was bypassed and what he saw as a "parsimonious & totally inefficient plan" put in its place.[27]

But Ruffin did not give up entirely on agricultural societies, even though he declined the presidency of the Virginia organization when it was offered to him in 1845. When in 1850 he was invited to address the agricultural clubs on Maryland's Eastern Shore, he composed an oration "written to condemn what I deemed the usual wrong procedure of agricultural societies." Like so many other Southern institutions, he asserted, they had been copied blindly from their counterparts in the North, where a different type of farming with different goals and different problems predominated. Ruffin denounced this "misplaced deference" and "humble imitation" of the North. Southerners had to develop an independent character and a domestic mind aware of its section's peculiar needs and virtues. When the Virginia State Agricultural Society was reorganized in 1851 in accordance with many of his suggestions, Ruffin was delighted. He became president and dedicated the organization to "agricultural instruction and improvement."[28]

The intellectual's perception of the agricultural problem could not be separated from his dedication to regional autonomy. Staple crop farming, the Sacred Circle believed, had rendered the section dangerously dependent on the fluctuations of the world cotton market, as the depression of the forties had demonstrated forcefully. At the same time, the failure to grow necessary foodstuffs had enslaved the South to Northern and Western grain producers. In an address before the State Agricultural Society in 1841, Hammond warned of both moral and economic effects of such dependence, and Simms emphasized the "*dishonouring* business of importing from other and rival nations their breadstuffs and provisions." To break the force of this hegemony, the South needed to develop agricultural principles and methods suited to its own particular situation. "We need an agricultural literature peculiarly our own, based upon scientific theories & experiments made on the spot," Hammond declared to Ruffin. Perhaps the creation of an independent literature would encourage the reorganization of all agricultural societies and of the practice of farming as a whole to serve the special needs of the South—to enhance rather than undermine her peculiar character. Hammond found that the decline of Southern agriculture had left the region "utterly impoverished & as an almost necessary consequence utterly degraded." Simms cited an ominous historical parallel:

We may date the real beginning of the decline and down fall of the Roman Empire from that period when they became habitually dependent for their supplies of grain, on the conquered provinces. There is no truth less questionable, and none should be more emphatically impressed upon the minds of our statesmen than that which teaches that a nation is never in greater danger of subversion and shame, than when, through a base neglect of its own resources, and a disregard of its becoming industry, it is reduced to the necessity of sending to other countries for its supplies of food.

Economic dependence, the men of knowledge feared, created intellectual servility and consequently corrupted national spirit and morality.[29]

Their conviction of the need for self-sufficiency influenced several members of the network to involve themselves in another reform of Southern society: the promotion of industry. Just as the South should not depend on others for her foodstuffs, they believed, she should demonstrate her cultural maturity by developing manufactures capable at least of supplying her own necessities. Such diversification was a major object even of the South Carolina State Agricultural Society, which resolved that "a combined system of Agriculture, Manufactures and Commerce, are essential in promoting the prosperity and happiness of a community." The reform of agriculture, Hammond emphasized in an 1849 oration, was only a first step. In addition, "some new element must be introduced into our industrial system. Some pursuit diversifying our labour & calling into action fresh energies & opening up a wider field for the creation of common intellect must arouse & enlist the interest of our people." Diversity in society would encourage and support endeavors of the mind. Any single economic pursuit could not "furnish scope enough for the infinite variety of gifts which it has pleased God to bestow upon man." Hammond urged the South to take advantage of the availability of cheap labor, its mild climate, and rich resources of water power to establish cotton factories. But he recognized that "traditional forms of thought and habits of action" posed enormous obstacles "of a moral character" to such an undertaking. But manufacturing was not, he insisted, "uncreative . . . and devoted to petty details." In fact, the mechanic arts could make an important contribution to "the training of the mind," and this enhancement of the domestic genius was the goal he envisioned when he urged industrial development upon his region. "It must not be supposed," he reassured conservatives, "that in thus advocating the encouragement of the mechanic arts & extensive manufacturing among us . . . that I look upon them in any other light than as means—not ends." Hammond was convinced that industry would contribute to the achievement of transcendent aims, for "occupations of utility & necessity ultimately terminate in the pursuit of the beautiful & true."[30]

Simms agreed that manufacturing would encourage spiritual advancement in the South. In an article in the *Southern Quarterly Review,* he equated industrial and moral backwardness. Manufacturing, he explained, was the practical application of human genius. Any people who wished to be favorably regarded by history were required to "do something more than provide a raw material." They ought, Simms insisted, "to provide the Genius also, which shall work the material up into forms and fabrics equally beautiful and valuable." But, he lamented, "This duty has been neglected by the South, abandoned to her enemies," and, as a result, the region as a whole exhibited "a slavish deference to the will, the wit, the wisdom, the art and ingenuity of the people to whom we yield our manufactures."[31]

Through their interest in promoting industry, Simms and Hammond became friends of William Gregg, who had established a successful textile factory at Graniteville in 1845 under a state charter which Simms had supported during his service in the legislature. In 1847, Hammond and his brother discussed purchasing the factory from Gregg or entering into partnership with the more experienced businessman. Two years later, Simms and Hammond visited Graniteville together, while Hammond studied the operation for ideas he might use to convince his district agricultural club to establish its own cotton mill.[32]

None of these projects materialized, but Hammond's interest in manufacturing soon involved him in another problem, the battle against the state bank, for its conservative investment policies, he believed, inhibited the growth of industry in South Carolina. As one manufacturer explained to Hammond, "The bank is in the way of our introduction of machinery, and this must be got rid of before the least thing can be done." Hammond was convinced that the old South Carolina aristocracy had turned to the bank as a means of security after the abolition of primogeniture in 1790. "When the Bank was established the more ready of them took possession of that. That has kept them up," he declared. The old "Hunkers" were now uniting with young hotbloods, such as Robert Barnwell Rhett, in an effort to maintain oligarchic control and to retard all progress within the state. It was the "traditional ideas" of these men that had to be combated, for until the people of the state could free themselves from the political and spiritual domination of this faction, the state was doomed to decline.[33]

As part of his campaign for industry, therefore, Hammond attacked the bank, first from his position as governor, then through a series of essays published in the Charleston *Mercury* during 1846 under the pseudonym "Anti Debt." Only when the bank was destroyed, Hammond insisted, would the independent spirit of the people of the state emerge from thralldom.

In the effort to promote economic diversification in South Carolina, members of the Sacred Circle became involved in creation of what Simms called a "Mechanical Conventicle," a spiritual union to uplift the South through the introduction of manufacturing. Amidst hostility he viewed as equivalent to that experienced by the first conventicles of Christians in heathen Rome, Simms sought to form a cell to evangelize on behalf of Southern industry. The South Carolina Institute for the Promotion of Art, Mechanical Ingenuity and Industry was founded officially in 1849, with Hammond delivering the inaugural address. His election to this honor was carefully calculated by the proponents of industrialization, for Hammond's well-known hostility to the protective tariff made his Southern loyalties unquestionable and thus rendered him the perfect individual to overcome "doubt and serious opposition" to the "introduction of manufactures among us." He "was the very person to make the necessary distinctions" between judicious economic diversification and slavish imitation of the industrializing North. Organized in accordance with the same didactic purposes that motivated the agricultural society, the institute encouraged industry by offering prizes and sponsoring fairs where everything from "specimens of plumbing" to racing sculls, mill machinery, printing and binding, and daguerrotypes were exhibited.[34]

In Virginia, Ruffin shared Hammond and Simms's conviction that industrial development and regional self-sufficiency were essential to the advancement of Southern genius and moral character. "No correct thinker," he declared, "will deny the benefits of the home markets, built up by the establishment of manufactures and trade." Farmers as well as industrialists would enjoy "the benefits of the existence in the same vicinity of the several interests of agriculture, mechanic arts, manufactures, commerce and navigation." Holmes concurred in "condemning uniform and exclusive" dedication to agriculture. "We agree," he declared, "in desiring a variety and sufficiency of manufactures for domestic consumption," for without such independence, a nation was likely to perish, morally and politically, as well as economically.[35]

Even Tucker supported the diversification of economic pursuits in the South. Despite his idealization of the Virginia squirearchy, he made no protest against the industrial schemes of his friend Hammond, and replied enthusiastically when the South Carolinian sent him drafts of two speeches that articulated the need to introduce manufacturing into the Southern economy. Tucker also discussed with Hammond his support for the extension of railroads from Virginia to the West, and he bewailed the corruption that had retarded such endeavors. Tucker thought that introducing diversity into the Southern economy by increasing trade and manufacturing would bring many benefits to the South. Commerce, he declared, "is not merely the handmaid of benevolent enterprise. She is herself the great apostle of civilization to the whole human race." Trade, Tucker emphasized, would not be restricted to goods, but, more important, would include commerce of ideas. Diversity would promote knowledge and intellectual endeavor, for "knowledge is the guide of enterprise" and the "most precious article in the merchant's assortment." Tucker regarded the promotion of railroads as an evangelical "duty" which Virginia "owes to herself, the World and the Creator of the World."[36]

The society of the Old South long has been considered essentially agrarian and rigidly anti-industrial. Vigorous support for economic diversification by such notorious advocates of Southern sectionalism as Simms, Hammond, and Ruffin seems somewhat surprising. Even Tucker and Holmes, who traditionally have been portrayed as emphatic opponents of manufacturing, were in fact sympathetic to the creation of regional self-sufficiency. It is important to recognize, however, exactly why the members of the network were interested in industry and what they hoped it would accomplish. They did not want to make the South over in the image of the North or nineteenth-century Britain. Industry promised to provide a means of achieving Southern economic, and, consequently, intellectual and spiritual independence. Through carefully monitored social change, the men of mind hoped to preserve the old values and ethos of Southern life. As Hammond reassured Tucker, "The thing is to reconcile . . . industry with free trade, slave labour, agricultural advancement & Southern tone." Holmes, too, emphasized that diversification of the economy must not undermine the essence of the Southern world view, nor result in the establishment of Mammon as the god of Southern civilization. By adopting manufactures "with moderation and discretion" the South would "continue to be prosperous and enlightened, and increase in both respects." But, Holmes continued, if she were to change "with avidity" and compete with the North in trade and manufactures, "the South will become the North," a thought he could not abide. Manufacturing should be introduced only with careful regard "to the moral and social effects on the community." But if Southern planters did not "do the job," Tucker warned, "the Yankeys will."[37]

The members of the network did not advocate radical, disruptive change in the Southern way of life, but they did launch an assault upon what Hammond called "traditional forms of thought & habits of action." The men of mind shared a conception of a mythic South that had been ruled by truth and disinterested virtue. Change that would reinstate these values would be acceptable, even though it might produce a social and economic structure different from anything the South previously had supported.[38]

In a sense, these intellectuals' endeavors to reform their society were all educational efforts, for persuasion, not institutional alterations, they believed, was the basis for social change. It is therefore not surprising that improvement of the system of schools and colleges in the South was a central concern for the Sacred Circle as indeed it was for increasing numbers of Southerners during this period. In the last years of the ante-bellum era and particularly in the decade before the Civil War, interest in educational reform and improvement sprang up among a variety of social classes in a number of regions throughout the South. At least in part, this concern reflected a self-conscious effort to strengthen the region against Northern ideological as well as political hegemony, but the movement cannot be attributed entirely to such narrow motivations. Petitions demanding educational improvement flowed into the South Carolina legislature from grand juries throughout the state; school systems, particularly in Southern cities like Charleston and New Orleans, were drastically overhauled; periodicals from the *Southern Literary Messenger* in Richmond to *DeBow's Review* in New Orleans were filled with articles demanding Southern textbooks and schooling for Southrons, as well as less polemical essays suggesting teacher training, establishment of common schools, more generous funding for universities, and widespread instruction for women. As intellectuals, the members of the Sacred Circle long had been concerned about the status of education, for they well understood how closely it affected their own standing in society. But education, they believed, was of transcendent importance for the entire social and moral order as well as for their larger evangelical purpose.[39]

During his term as governor, Hammond took special interest in the institutions of public education in the state, for he believed learning was "by far the most important matter of Temporal concern—nay of Immortal, for it is the larger part of and everywhere claims a place by the side of Religion." South Carolina, he asserted, had a duty to educate its citizens, for "the establishment of a State at all presupposes intelligence—intellectual cultivation." Mental training would produce the morality essential to social order. In the most practical sense, Hammond explained to Simms, education was the way to undermine the efforts of corrupt and degenerate demagogues by raising the mind of the people above the level of their base appeals.[40]

The existing system of public instruction appeared to Governor Hammond "a disgrace to an enlightened people." If, as he maintained, the world was to be "mainly governed by the force of intellect," then a state had an especial obligation to the "mental culture" of its inhabitants. "Every dollar which can be spared from the absolute wants of the State" should be first offered to education, Hammond declared in his first governor's message. "Ignorance and free institutions cannot coexist," for where there are no institutional restraints, men must be taught to exercise vigilance over themselves: "They must guard against their own prejudices and passions; against local and narrow views; against party spirit, against their proverbial love of change; in short they must guard against their own ignorance, which is the fruitful parent of all these dangers." Educational reform was essential to the maintenance of social order. Thus Hammond proposed to the legislature the establishment of academies in every district of the state to generate an adequate supply of teachers and advocated a special school of science to meet the state's technological and agrarian needs.[41]

From his editorial chair, Simms vigorously supported Hammond's schemes as well as the more general cause of educational improvement. Having written a history text, Simms was particularly interested in the books used in Southern schools and in the *Magnolia* urged his compatriots to abandon Northern publications, which he believed encouraged the slavish dependency of the Southern mind. Simms insisted on "the necessity,—which has not been often apparent to the Southern people themselves—of preparing the lessons at home which are to inform the minds of our children."[42]

Holmes agreed with Simms and Hammond about the importance of introducing a distinctively sectional education. Southerners must not be permitted to "imbibe at the North delusive views which will infect their minds during their whole life." He continually stressed the central role of learning and the "especial necessity for its diffusion in consequence of the peculiar requirements of the present times"; education would elevate Southerners to the level of moral excellence necessary for their sectional redemption.[43]

While Holmes and Tucker actively contributed to the cause of education through their positions as college professors, the other members of the Sacred Circle participated in the movement for educational improvement in different ways. Hammond served as a trustee of South Carolina College; Simms acted as a free school commissioner for

Barnwell District; Ruffin worked "in a faithful & laborious service of six years as one of the Visitors of William and Mary College," where, he stated proudly, "I moved and carried important reforms" including raising faculty salaries to a level more befitting the deserved status of the man of mind.[44]

While the amelioration of the Southern system of schools and colleges was an obvious focus for the intellectual's effort to uplift the Southern mind, it was an endeavor designed to produce results over the long run, rather than in the immediate future. The beneficiaries of improved primary and secondary schools, and even of universities, would not be fully functioning members of society for a number of years. As the ante-bellum period advanced and the necessity of Southern uplift and solidarity began to seem more pressing, the members of the Sacred Circle turned increasingly to another area of Southern life that offered the possibility of more direct action and, they hoped, more rapid improvement.

Politics was the aspect of Southern civilization in which corruption seemed to rule unassailed. Here despised demagogues and factions vied for popular favor; here an abject servility to the North manifested itself most concretely. Yet, ironically, politics also offered the most logical opportunity for the exercise of stewardship. What was government but the institutionalization of leadership and the recognition of the superiority, or at least power, of some men over others? Political involvement appeared to Beverley Tucker as "being called" to work with God in his great design, "the moral government of man." Ideally, to lead or to govern was to serve as a divine representative, for "all the authority to which man is made subject on earth is God's instrument for the accomplishment of his great work in the regeneration of his fallen nature." Tucker sternly warned his charges, "whosoever resisteth the salutary restraints of social order and discipline resisteth God."[45]

But Southern as well as national politics seemed to have abandoned dedication to principle for the advancement of personal interests. "For what is all this waste of time," Tucker demanded, "this waste of substance, and, worst of all, this waste of excitement, which, once spent, leaves the mind unfit for action? For what is it but to dance around a *hickory pole,* or to celebrate . . . a *log cabin,* or to rally to some symbol, no matter what, of a man like themselves, the idol of the moment . . . pledged to no right, consecrated to no principle?" Ruffin summarized the outlook of the group when he chose as the motto for his *Southern Magazine,* "Party spirit, the madness of the many for the gain of the few."[46]

Disdain for political factionalism, selfish office seekers, and ambitious politicians had been commonplace throughout the nation in the pre-

Jacksonian period. Virginia's "gentleman freeholders" and the advocates of the "country ideology" who had dominated South Carolina
politics through the Revolution were particularly strongly committed
to a vision of politics as a rational process of selecting the best men
to rule. By the early nineteenth century such attitudes had been
enshrined as basic tenets of most moral philosophy texts, and they persisted especially strongly among those individuals inclined to style
themselves as a moral or intellectual elite, above the selfish, mundane
interests of the mob.[47]

Opposition to the concept of faction dictated that the five thinkers
stand aloof from both Whigs and Democrats. They disapproved heart-
ily of both organizations, citing the centralist tendencies of the former
and the mobbism of the latter. "I can," Tucker declared, "act with no
party." The members of the network were united in their opposition
to the new nature of American political life, the extension of participation in government, and the consequent lowering of political
purposes and tone. But the five claimed to lament not as much the
changing locus of political power as the moral and intellectual degeneration that accompanied it. The danger of democracy seemed to lie
primarily, Simms believed, in its threat to the most fundamental
beliefs of society, to all that was "sacred and hallowing."[48]

In the evolution of the group's ideas about politics, their feelings
crystallized around John C. Calhoun; his fate seemed to represent the
tragedy of public life. Residents of a state dominated for decades by
this "Cast-Iron Man," Simms and Hammond of necessity had to deal
with the implications of his pre-eminence for their society, as well as
for their own ambition. For the other members of the Sacred Circle,
Calhoun was of both immediate and symbolic importance. Undoubtedly,
much of the group's hostility to Calhoun arose from their jealousy of
his success. But, characteristically, they translated their dislike into
the terms of the dilemma they themselves faced as intellectuals. Calhoun served as a tragic example of the fate of a man of talent and
intellect forced by circumstances to abandon principle for expediency.
The politician's "intense passion for the Presidency," Simms explained,
had "warped his better mind and baffled his own purposes." Calhoun's "vacillations and changes," Holmes concluded, were simply the
result of the dilemma of a "great mind" in a mediocre world.[49]

Yet Hammond identified with Calhoun even as he criticized, for
the two had much in common. Of undistinguished origins, both had
married into South Carolina's planter aristocracy and had aspired
to political power. Calhoun, Hammond observed, had been "often
denounced for his ambition, but . . . 'Ambition is,' as Mr. Burke justly
said, 'the malady of every extensive genius.'" Hammond recognized
that Calhoun had been produced by a Southern culture that sanctioned

and even encouraged greed, ambition, and political machination. In his diary, Hammond reflected,

How often do we see men, misplaced in this world. . . . It is always a melancholy thing to contemplate. . . . Mr. Calhoun was a striking instance of it. Destined in this country to incessant disappointments. Thwarted, defeated, in a manner crushed by those who were vastly his inferiors in all respects. . . . But what could such a man do in a nation of Demagogues . . . where practically none but an Arch-Demagogue could exercise power for even a limited period.[50]

But such conditions had to be changed. The involvement of the intellectual in politics ought to have two closely related purposes: to free the Southern mind from the domination of corrupt demagogues, both Northern and Southern, and to replace their leadership with that of the spiritually elect. This moral elite would release Southerners from a reign of political corruption by subjecting them to the principles of truth in which alone man might find true freedom. "In the thoughtful wisdom of those who have leisure to think wisely, and no temptation to think wrong . . . in these is your best defence."[51]

Like every other issue they confronted, politics appeared to the men of knowledge as a problem of spirit and of intellect. The "prowess of the leader" lay "in the mind," and his office was to prevent "tumultuary insurrection." Freedom, Tucker believed, manifested itself in peace and social order, and these flourished only when men attained the proper level of reverence and understanding for their government and its principles. Thus, as he explained, "it hardly seems too much to pronounce, as a political, as well as a moral truth, 'That the seat of freedom is in the mind.'" Correct thinking produced an orderly world in which liberty might thrive: "It is his [God's] decree that self-control is the inseparable condition of political freedom; and that they who, being free, refuse to put moral chains on their own appetites, shall establish over themselves a master, who shall load them with fetters of iron. . . . It *is* the will of Heaven that passion shall be submitted to the dominion of reason." Government in its ideal form would be simultaneously an instrument of control and of moral and intellectual education; it would be by its very nature evangelical.[52]

But as it existed both North and South in the mid-nineteenth century, government did not seem to meet these high standards. Politics was not an arena for the practice of stewardship, but of demagoguery. Politicians endeavored to control the masses for personal advantage, not for improvement of the race. Too wise to submit completely to this unprincipled leadership, the people remained uncontrolled, and social disorder prevailed. The only hope for harmony, Tucker explained, lay in re-establishing the rule of "those who have the leisure to think wisely"; in "making the seat of intellect the seat of power."[53]

The members of the Sacred Circle therefore eagerly sought what they considered their rightful political positions. But they soon recognized that the South was not ready to defer to the rule of intellect in government. Their political involvement, therefore, was as marginal men, as individuals seemingly designed to lead a society they had yet to create. Tucker warned his students that "the discreet and conscientious are condemned by bigots and system makers of all parties." Factionalism ensured "the blundering misrule of the rash and unscrupulous, while the men most competent to manage . . . are condemned to inaction and obscurity." But, Tucker declared, he would dedicate himself as a teacher to increasing the number of these misfits, for "it is not my business to study popularity but truth."[54]

Political involvement was thus the supreme expression of the five Southerners' effort to establish themselves as enlightened and disinterested stewards, God's earthly representatives. But they soon discovered that they could not achieve success as politicians without abandoning the values they had established as integral to their position as men of special spiritual and intellectual gifts. Thus they set about to reform political life to coincide with their convictions. Like the concept of utility with which their more speculative endeavors had been concerned, political expediency needed to be redefined, transformed into "that . . . which is determined by an enlarged and enlightened view of the permanent interests of the whole community."[55]

Although politics was the field in which Hammond gained his greatest prominence, he never lost his profound ambivalence about the life of public affairs. From the time of his first term in Congress, he concluded that "Talent, virtue acquirement are all obscured . . . by overwhelming party intrigue, bluster and blackguardism." Throughout his career, Hammond refused to campaign for office, insisting in the tradition of South Carolina's "country ideology" that he intended to be sought out by those who understood his merits. Looking back over his life, he announced in an 1858 speech to the people of his district that he was proud of "having never been a mere party politician, intriguing and wire pulling to advance myself and others." The Savannah *Republican* admired Hammond's scruples, describing him in an article he clipped for his scrapbook as one of those rare politicians whose "ambition is the country's good and not its office." Hammond, they declared, was "our leader in the work of reform, the dedemagogizing of Southern politics."[56]

Hammond's refusal actively to seek office or to admit his political ambitions led to long periods of enforced retirement during his political career and rendered him incapable of responding effectively to the indirect attacks made upon him by Wade Hampton after their quarrel in 1843. Hammond's reluctance to be considered a campaigner influenced him not to combat Hampton's opposition, and thus Hammond remained outside of South Carolina politics for well over a decade. During this time, however, his compatriots repeatedly proposed him for the frequent vacancies in the state's delegation to the U.S. Senate. Hammond's ambivalence about political life manifested itself most clearly in the protestations of indifference about the outcome that filled his correspondence each time the state legislature considered his name and the obvious pain and disappointment that pervaded his expressions of relief when he was informed of his defeats. Although he insisted that he preferred to remain a private citizen, Hammond showed that these failures were desolating. When at last sent to the Senate in the late 1850s, he clearly was excited to be returning to the "Arena," as he called it, and he reported to Simms with pride the frequent mention of his name as a possible presidential candidate in in 1860. But he could not admit even to his dear friend that he himself entertained ambitions beyond his senatorship. His health, he insisted as he had steadily since 1834, would not permit him to continue in public life. In his moralistic view of politics Hammond found an ideological framework within which to justify his own emotional reluctance to commit himself to relentless pursuit of the main chance. By regarding politics as a form of moral stewardship, Hammond could in part surrender the responsibility and burden of his career to God.[57]

Hammond shared his proclivity for political independence—or perhaps self-destructiveness—with other members of the group and encouraged his friend Simms to join him in many of his unpopular positions. Despite their support for slavery, Hammond and Simms opposed the formation of a newspaper or a political party designed specifically to defend the peculiar institution. Such "agitation" and politicization of the issue, they feared, would lead the South to support slavery for reasons of self-interest rather than because it was morally right. "It is mean and contemptible," Hammond wrote Simms, "to think of going to the ballot box with the fanatics on such a question." Hammond urged that they appeal to Southerners "as freemen, not as partisans" and defend slavery on a philosophic rather than a purely political basis.[58]

Although no other member of the network was as intensely involved in politics as was Hammond, all experienced to a lesser extent the political failure that plagued his life. Their lack of success, they agreed, arose from their commitment to politics as a moral force, intended to disseminate and institutionalize truth in society. Politics was a vehicle for uplifting and reforming the Southern people. Because of this evangelical potential, it belonged rightfully to the man of mind, who alone could comprehend the broader social and moral issues it encompassed. Simms informed Tucker that the only hope for the South lay in "taking

the affairs out of the hands of professional politicians" and replacing
private interest with public welfare. "To do this," he continued, "we
must appeal directly to the people. We must take the stump for it."
But Simms insisted to Hammond he desired political office only as a
means of achieving the broader goals he had established for himself
as a part of his transcendent calling. He did not want "political place
except as affording a field in which I may work according to my vocation—and, as I believe—according to my destiny."[59]

Simms served one term in the South Carolina legislature, but lost his
bid for re-election in 1846, a humiliation he attributed to his intellectuality. The "novelist," he declared, "hurts the politician." South Carolinians perceived an antagonism, he believed, between the goals of the
man of knowledge and the nature of politics as they had come to
understand it. Hammond wrote bitterly to Tucker of the reasons for
Simms's political failures: "Having like yourself raised a literary reputation, the street corner politicians cannot conceive how he should
know anything of statesmanship which comes altogether from reading
newspapers & discussing mares' nests in the thoroughfares."[60]

Ruffin shared Hammond and Simms's aversion to the methods of
nineteenth-century politics and experienced the same lack of success in
public life. Ruffin first had become politically active upon his election
to the Virginia senate in 1823, but before his term expired, he resigned
and returned to his plantation. "My views of duty," he explained,
"were very different from those usually acted upon by other representatives." He quickly recognized that "for conforming to mine, I should
be like to have no reward, save the approbation of my own conscience."
Unlike others around him, Ruffin did not advance "personal and private interests" and discovered that these scruples alienated him within
the political world. Nearly three decades later, he tried once again to
return to public life, but found that neither his values nor the criteria
for political success had changed. "I was much too honest to long
retain—popular favor," he observed bitterly. In 1850 he lost an election as an independent candidate for the Virginia state constitutional
convention because, as he explained, he opposed "caucus organization
dictation and rule."[61]

Virginia was equally unkind to Beverley Tucker, who conceived of
politics as a kind of mission. Defeated in an attempt to secure office
during his residence in Missouri, Tucker lost an election for Congress
soon after his return to his native state in 1834. Effective political
action, he concluded, required man to tolerate "measures which his
judgment condemns." The pursuit of truth was antagonistic to the
cultivation of popularity. For these reasons, Tucker held no elected
political office between the time of his 1834 defeat and his membership
in the 1850 Nashville Convention just before his death. Instead, he

endeavored to educate his students at William and Mary to reform the practice of politics in the South by imbuing it with the idealism he had tried to cultivate in them. As Tucker explained to Hammond,

My great aim is to supply materials for the reconstruction of the States Right party, and I rejoice in the belief that I have done something towards it. You may have seen that old hunkers, as they are called, have lost much of their power in Virginia, and the work has been chiefly that of my pupils. I have never endeavored to influence their choice between men and factions. I have told them plainly that it was a choice of evils, of which each, according to his own notions, should choose the least.[62]

But Tucker lamented that the honorable art of statesmanship should have become a sordid undertaking. Politics, he asserted, should be the communal discovery of God's will, and government the institutionalization of his leadership on earth. Social order and morality could be restored only if politics were reformed to serve this transcendent function, only if the spiritually and intellectually gifted, "the MIND of the community," were accorded their "just supremacy." Ideally, government was the practice of stewardship—moral reform and social restraint. "Society cannot exist," Tucker affirmed, "unless a controlling power upon will and appetite be placed somewhere, *and the less of it there is within, the more there must be without*." For these Southerners, the concept of "order" had a dual meaning, implying both social hierarchy and public tranquillity. But these separate definitions had a close semantic relationship. Like many educated individuals of the nineteenth century, the members of the network believed that until all men attained moral excellence, only the maintenance of the first sort of order—that of rank—could preserve the latter—social peace. External, political, and social freedom could flourish only insofar as it was complemented by internal restraint.[63]

The men of mind thus considered it their duty to serve as agents of external control at the same time they worked to inculcate ethical principles in the population generally. Genius, as Simms had explained, was no less a reformer than a discoverer. Spiritual and intellectual superiority, they insisted, required that they direct their multifaceted talents toward transcendent purposes: maintaining terrestrial order and elevating the human race. Stewardship was thus the overriding motivation and justification for every mundane undertaking, for their role was inescapably evangelical. This outlook imparted a unity of purpose and meaning to their existence at the same time it legitimated their unbounded social ambitions. In politics, in agriculture, in every human endeavor, the members of the group believed God had intended them to show the Southern people the way of light and to compel them to follow its path.[64]

SIX

A Sacred Duty:

THE PROSLAVERY ARGUMENT

n the proslavery argument, Hammond, Holmes, Ruffin, Tucker, and Simms made their most concerted attempt to reconcile transcendent with practical aims, spiritual conviction with mundane ambition. To the twentieth century, such application of intellect in the service of human exploitation may appear incomprehensible, even unforgivable. Yet the five Southerners found in the defense of slavery a logical—and in some ways necessary—culmination of their endeavors to institutionalize moral stewardship and thus establish a recognized place for mind in their society. Ironically, they were to invoke timeless intellectual values and nationally shared evangelical commitments to justify the South's peculiar institution.

Historians long have regarded the elaboration of the proslavery argument in the years before the Civil War as "puzzling," its motivation and purpose difficult to understand. Scholars have agreed that the defense of slavery could not be what it initially seemed, and they have found no rational explanation for the tedious repetition of the same ideas over a period of more than three decades. Yet if one thinks of their ideas not exclusively in the context of the slavery controversy, but in terms of their meaning to the men who elaborated them, they can be seen as logical indeed. Southerners themselves admitted that their apologies were not directed primarily at the most obvious enemies of slavery; few expected to convince Northern abolitionists of the justice of the peculiar institution. Holmes intended to write essays "capable of doing good service within our borders"; Hammond and Tucker both hoped to have "fixed Slavery infinitely more firmly in the public opinion of the South." The significance of the proslavery argument, it seems, lay within ante-bellum Southern society itself.[1]

Accordingly, a number of twentieth-century historians have sought the meaning of the defense of slavery in the relationships between different social groups within the Old South. As early as 1936, William

Hesseltine suggested that the movement was part of an effort by the upper-class planter to win the nonslaveholder to his side. More recent scholars such as Charles Sellers and Ralph Morrow have seen the argument as an attempt by slaveholders to establish peace, not with other groups, but with their own consciences, to alleviate the feelings of guilt created by the nagging contradictions between slavery and the American democratic creed. While both these explanations may seem plausible, there is little historical evidence to support either. Studies of Southern social structure suggest that significant class cleavages, such as those upon which Hesseltine's thesis depends, did not exist in the ante-bellum period; planters' diaries and letters reveal few pangs of conscience about the Southern system.[2]

While Sellers, Morrow, and Hesseltine accurately characterized the defense of the peculiar institution as a manifestation of stress within Southern society, they did not inquire into the specific social origins of these tensions. In a presidential address before the Southern Historical Association in 1970, David Donald attempted to remedy this deficiency by examining individuals who wrote widely circulated proslavery tracts. All, he concluded, were "unhappy men," displaced persons "compensating" for "severe personal problems relating to their place in Southern society." Their proslavery utterances, he asserted, manifested a desire to escape this crisis of social identity by returning to a "by-gone pastoral Arcadia," to a past they had lost.[3]

Donald insightfully described a pervasive "sense of alienation" shared by slavery's defenders. But these feelings of distance from the contemporary world did not arise from a defensive and hopeless nostalgia. Even though many proslavery advocates did indeed deplore the demagogic tone of the new mass politics and the conscienceless exploitation of naked capitalism, they were not completely backward-looking in their views. Hammond and Simms directly opposed the control that South Carolina's tradition-bound aristocracy exerted in their state. All the members of the Sacred Circle advocated diversifying the Southern economy and reducing its dependence on agriculture; several worked actively to introduce industrial enterprise within the South.[4]

The unhappiness that Donald perceived as characteristic of slavery's defenders arose less from a desire to escape the present than from what he accurately identified as anxieties "relating to their place in Southern society." However, Donald's essay did not make the nature of this relationship entirely clear, for he found that proslavery advocates occupied a wide variety of social locations. Indeed, the members of the Sacred Circle themselves exemplify this puzzling diversity of origins. Hammond was a social parvenu; Simms the motherless child of an Irish immigrant; and Holmes a recent—and penniless—arrival from Britain. All three hoped through their own exertions to gain places in

Southern society to which heredity gave them little claim. Tucker, by contrast, was intimately connected with Virginia's aristocracy by virtue of his mother's Bland and Randolph connections. But because of her early death, Tucker grew up in the world of his father, a professor of moderate means and uncertain status. Ruffin unquestionably was descended from Virginia's finest blood and was experiencing a decline in status as a result of the increasing democratization of American life.[5]

The existence of similar attitudes among men in many ways so different might appear to subvert any attempt at social explanation of thought or action and to leave distressingly vague any common biographical basis for the social anxieties Donald attributed to all slavery's defenders. More constructively, however, the characteristics of this network might suggest some revised hypotheses concerning the interaction between society and belief. A single idea or form of behavior may prove meaningful to a number of individuals for quite different reasons, and, therefore, simultaneously may satisfy a variety of psychological, social, or cultural needs. Objectively different social experiences may likewise have equivalent emotional import and may influence men to respond positively to common configurations of belief. More specifically, although Ruffin's status may have been declining while Simms's and Hammond's were rising, all shared a similar anxiety about the social flux in which they found themselves.

Such an explanation provides a clue to the enormous influence "status-anxiety" interpretations have wielded among American historians of the past two decades. David Donald is but one of a number of scholars who have sought to explain ideologies and social movements as the result of tensions arising from a situation of rapidly changing—and most often diminishing—social status. Late nineteenth-century Populists, twentieth-century Progressives, early nineteenth-century temperance crusaders all have been portrayed as elites afraid of losing control of their society in the continuing democratization of American life. Donald himself described Northern abolitionists in this manner, and his essay on slavery's defenders expanded the scope of his interpretive framework, explaining stress as the result of movement upward as well as downward on the social ladder. Donald thus established a certain symmetry between the sections by finding proslavery ideology to be, like many Northern social movements, a search for "social stability in a rapidly changing world."[6]

Yet in a society as fluid as America has been, almost all social positions are in flux; everyone is plagued by feelings of "status anxiety"; everyone is searching for a secure social niche. Southern social structure was always extremely labile. Even in the earliest period of settlement—later remembered as the age of mythic "cavaliers"—no closed aristocracy ever maintained control for so long as a generation. As an explanatory device, therefore, the status-anxiety model suffers from the weakness of telling us too much and consequently telling us nothing. If everyone suffers from such insecurity, it is a factor in every social movement, but not a sufficient explanation for the particular characteristics of any group's ideology or behavior. The historian must go beyond the limitations of this interpretation to examine the relationship between particular sorts of social dislocations and the specific conceptual frameworks in which they are expressed. What is in the internal nature of a belief system that makes it meaningful to a particular group? Why was it in the specific terms of the proslavery argument—rather than, for example, in a crusade for temperance or in some sort of anti-social behavior—that these Southerners found meaningful and gratifying expression for their social dissatisfaction? The particular symbols a group chooses to resolve or explain social and psychological stress are not random or capricious; they must be carefully explored. The proslavery argument was not merely a symptom of social stress that possessed no significance in itself. It has bewildered historians because they have devoted too little attention to its internal structure and meaning, to its importance as a symbolic product.[7]

In defending slavery, the Southern intellectual made his most significant effort to establish for himself a cultural identity and a social place. His arguments for human bondage invoked his system of disinterested and transcendent values and identified his world view with Southern society's most distinctive, most peculiar institution. By uniting the cause of intellect with the proslavery movement, the man of mind hoped to elicit from fellow Southerners an affirmation of his fundamental beliefs. Justifying slavery became for the intellectual an evangelical act, a defense of morality and truth, a "sacred duty" for men who regarded themselves as a "sacred circle."[8]

The abolitionist attack that grew rapidly in strength after the founding of the *Liberator* in 1831 required some response from the South. The members of the network quickly recognized that the region's need for a plausible social philosophy potentially enhanced their importance as men of mind. Holmes warned that the South would regret her past failure to accord "material support and public favor" to learning, for the need to protect slavery had demonstrated the importance of an able and loyal intellectual class. Looking back over the decade of the forties, Holmes observed that Southern attempts to rebut the abolitionists had created a new appreciation in the region for the products of intellect: "We shall be indebted to the continuance and asperity of this controversy for the creation of a genuine Southern literature—in itself an inestimable gain to our people. For out of this slavery agitation has sprung not merely essays on slavery, valuable and suggestive as these

have been, but also the literary activity, and the literary movement
which have lately characterized the intellect of the South."⁹

Hammond, Simms, Tucker, Holmes, and Ruffin soon discovered that
their essays on slavery won recognition other intellectual endeavors
failed to secure. Hammond first publicly defended slavery during the
1836 congressional debates on the gag rule and subsequently printed
his speech and distributed it to his constituents. Overwhelmingly favor-
able responses greeted his communication, and Hammond was
delighted to find that, in the words of one of his admirers, "Your
friends are all more and more pleased with you." These proslavery
remarks first drew Beverley Tucker's attention to the young South
Carolinian. Tucker wrote Hammond enthusiastically, commending his
refusal to submit his principles to party rule. "If your people are prepared for your threatened crusade, now is the time and this the topic."
The battle over slavery appeared to Tucker even at this early date as
part of a much larger moral effort, a quasi-religious "crusade."¹⁰

Yet the reaction to Hammond's 1836 speech was mild in comparison
to the outburst of acclaim that greeted the publication in 1845 of his
two letters to the English abolitionist Thomas Clarkson. "You have
succeeded by these Letters, in placing yourself in such a position
before the eye of our public that, if you please, you will be able to take
the wind out of the sails . . . of any of the aspirants for the Senate."
Hammond received letters of praise from almost every important
South Carolinian, including John Calhoun. Tucker requested copies of
the pamphlet for use in his William and Mary law class; Ruffin for-
warded his compliments; and a friend wrote to Holmes declaring that
Hammond's views had achieved a circulation "seldom reached by any
intellectual effort of our times." The editor of the Charleston *Mercury*
observed to Hammond that "if your object had been to secure for
yourself a substantial and enduring popularity I do not believe you
could possibly have adopted any means so likely to accomplish the
end." Even Hammond was gratified by the response to his proslavery
work. "My letters to Clarkson," he wrote in his diary, "have produced
quite a sensation. . . . I think from all accounts they have considerably
advanced my reputation." But he remarked ruefully that his insights
on other subjects were greeted by "no gush of public sentiment as on
the publication of my Clarkson Letters."¹¹

Ruffin also found that his essays on slavery were given a reception
never accorded his purely agricultural writings. Shortly after the
appearance of *African Colonization Unveiled*, he confided to his diary,
"Already I have had more notice taken or reported to me, in letters,
both from members of my family & other friends, of my late pamphlet
than of anything I ever wrote before."¹²

By publicly defending slavery, a Southerner of the forties or fifties was certain to gain attention and earn the acclaim of his compatriots. Francis Lieber, an eminent German political scientist who taught at South Carolina College until the eve of the Civil War, remarked acidly that the publication of a proslavery tract was a prerequisite for the presidency of the institution and a requirement he chose not to meet. "Nothing," he remarked, "would give me greater renown than a pamphlet written for the South, especially in favor of slavery."[13]

Notwithstanding their delight at the recognition these efforts won them, Hammond, Holmes, Tucker, Ruffin, and Simms did not consciously undertake the defense of slavery as a calculated, self-serving effort to advance themselves and their reputations. Public acclaim unnerved them somewhat, for they feared it might be testimony that they had stooped to demagoguery. Thus Hammond manifested considerable ambivalence about his success. The letters, he wrote in his diary, "have exalted my reputation . . . tho' I do not regard them as altogether the best thing I have done. But what is fame for me. I despise the mass. I would not turn on my heel for temporary applause." He discovered that "Injudicious & absurd compliment makes one writhe as bad as calumny." Hammond's goal was "immortality. . . . And I mean by immortality to fill a niche in History to the end of time." He wrote to Simms for reassurance that the importance of his work did not lie simply in its "impression on the mob. I want the discriminating opinion of one capable of giving one that may be of real service to me."[14]

Even the public approval he desired could not entirely substitute for the transcendent values to which he had declared his commitment. The defense of slavery had to meet the criteria he, Simms, and the others had established for the products of mind; it must not be a simple offering to political expediency. The proslavery argument was not to be partisan and polemical. Hammond and Simms agreed that they regarded "nothing as more inauspicious & evil than that we should convert the slave question into political capital for any object." When Calhoun's lieutenants proposed that a proslavery newspaper be published in Washington, Hammond was opposed, for he believed it would be dedicated primarily to political agitation and the advancement of Calhoun's presidential ambitions. The men of mind intended to defend the South without abandoning their moral goals. As always, they made certain that their ambition and their convictions would coincide.[15]

Hammond and the other members of the network declared that they were dedicated above all to educating the South in the religious, social, and philosophical implications of slavery. Holmes hoped to remove the discussion of slavery "from the domain of sectional controversy and political warfare" to "the more temperate and authorita-

tive tribunal of sober and cautious reflection." He proposed to discover truth by exploring "those broad and general views and principles," which he sought in the "comprehensive study of the phenomena of societies, and the history of nations," and to avoid the "angry
arena of political controversy." Tucker, too, was committed to the
philosophical investigation of the issue and was eager to avoid the
"angry and contentious spirit" manifested by most discussions of the
issue. The man of mind would raise the consideration of slavery to a
"higher ground," a level free of the partisanship and factious discord
he condemned; from the "sphere of mere temporary expediency" to the
"immutable rock of right and justice." In this realm he might discover
the fundamental character of the institution and pronounce disinterested judgment upon it. Because of the peculiar attributes he had
defined as his own, the Southern intellectual did not doubt his ability
to penetrate the storm of controversy and faction to discern the essential nature of the peculiar institution.[16]

In their search for truth, Holmes advised, men should always turn
first to the Bible. On the particular subject of slavery, divine intentions seemed clear; God had sanctioned human bondage in the patriarchal age and had bestowed his special favor on a slaveholding
people. The New Testament contained no condemnation of slavery,
and so, the men of mind concluded, the peculiar institution could be
considered consistent with Christ's principles.

But if man was not completely satisfied by biblical guidance, he
could determine his moral duties more prescisely by examining the
past experience of the human race. "If, then," Holmes advised, "Revelation does not prohibit the Institution of Slavery, as seems apparent,
we are left to the examinations of history for the basis of our induc-
tions." Ruffin agreed that it was necessary to replace "false theory, and
sickly sentimentality, and mistaken philanthropy" with a study of the
"whole subject of slavery through the means of facts and sound reasoning." The examination of human bondage would be empirical and
would employ the "positive" and "scientific" methods the group had
advocated for the assessment of all social problems. An individual
searching for truth about the peculiar institution could not begin with
"ingenious reasoning from unascertained premises." Facts, not abolitionists' theories of natural right or human equality, would best reveal
God's intentions and nature's plan.[17]

"Philosophical" history thus became a central weapon in the defense
of slavery. In what they considered the scientific study of the past, the
group undertook to collect and criticize the "evidences which sustain
or condemn" the peculiar institution. Slavery, their researches soon
convinced them, had exerted a beneficent influence in every society in
which it had ever existed. Its opponents, Hammond concluded, were

simply "ignorant of the essential principles of human association revealed in history."[18]

"Greeley, Giddings and Fred. Douglass," Holmes agreed, had erred in attributing a pernicious social effect to ancient slavery. It had not, as these Northerners contended, "rendered labor disreputable . . . displaced the free labourers, and destroyed the population, the industry and the agriculture of the ancient world." Slavery, Holmes pointed out, had existed in Sparta during its period of ascendance. A slave society had produced Pindar, Thucydides, Plato, and Aristotle, and Roman slaveholders had "conquered the world, legislated for all succeeding ages, and laid the broad foundations of modern civilization and modern institutions." The decline of the ancient states and the coming of the Dark Ages resulted not from the influence of slavery but from a growth of public vice and corruption unrelated to the prevailing system of labor. Slavery, it seemed, had served as the underpinning of the world's greatest civilizations.[19]

These five apologists frequently invoked history simply to demonstrate that slavery was a venerable institution. Its existence throughout time, they believed, imbued it with a kind of transcendence and legitimacy. Ruffin began his best-known proslavery tract by declaring, "Slavery has existed from as early time as historical records furnish any information of the social and political condition of mankind." Invoking the widely revered theological argument from design, Edmund Ruffin cited the "continued duration of the institution . . . its almost universal extension" as evidence that it was manifestly established by God. The Southern men of mind transferred the discussion from the realm of natural theology to that of society and history. In their hands, history became teleological: whatever God had permitted to endure through the ages necessarily must accord with his purposes. Because they viewed society as organic, this extrapolation appeared to them unquestionably logical; rules or explanations that applied to biological creatures governed social organisms as well. By demonstrating that slavery had existed throughout time, they hoped to prove that it was of spontaneous social origin and therefore right. The first principle on which Holmes justified slavery was "it is natural; it is inevitable," because, as he had shown, "it has always existed."[20]

In the same way they seized upon the widely accepted argument from design to strengthen their case, the five Southerners identified their apologies with the concepts of natural law that had been established as fundamental American principles. But the "natural law" they invoked would have seemed foreign to the original proponents of this doctrine. The intellectuals carefully dissociated it from contractual theories of the state and redefined it to coincide with their organic social views. The study of the past, the group asserted, revealed that

men were in the reality of nature not born equal and free, as Rousseau
and Jefferson had maintained, but were manifestly unequal in attributes and circumstances. Simms found, "The artifices of a social condition were woven about him from the earliest periods, and the essential inequalities of such conditions, in differing societies, must always
have had the effect of establishing corresponding inequalities among
the individuals composing tribes and families, even if it had not been
the benevolent purpose of God that such inequalities should constitute
an essential feature of his plan of creation." This persistence of inequality among men implied to Simms that the freedom and "natural rights"
to which they were entitled differed considerably from those the abolitionists had identified. A natural right, according to Simms and his
network, took account of the reality of natural laws of inequality and
was "not intended to disturb the natural degrees of humanity, . . .—
not to make the butcher a judge, or the baker a president, but to protect them, according to their claims as butcher and baker." The natural
society, therefore, was inevitably hierarchical and provided for appropriate and orderly differentiations among men.[21]

Redefining natural rights necessitated a redefinition of freedom and,
in consequence, of slavery. "What is liberty, and how far it may be
enjoyed by all," Tucker observed, "are questions of acknowledged difficulty." Freedom was not just the absence of restraint. Rather, it had
a more positive aspect; a man was most free, Simms declared, when
permitted "to occupy his proper place. He, only, is the slave, who is
forced into a position in society which is below the claim of his intellect and moral." The exercise of man's natural rights and the realiza-
tion of his true liberty required compliance with natural laws that
recognized inherent human inequality. Men could be free only by
acknowledging and working within the context of their limitations.
"The truth is, that our natural rights depend entirely upon the degree
of obedience which we pay to the laws of our creation."[22]

Southern slavery, the men of mind asserted, was merely a benevolent institutionalization of these principles of inequality. The system of
human bondage structured the interdependence that characterized all
human interaction. Because the slave was guaranteed food, clothing,
and shelter, he seemed to the five Southerners far freer than the Northern operative who depended upon the mercies of an impersonal indus-
trialist with no investment in his workers' health or survival. Whatever
abstract theories the abolitionists might advance about liberty and
bondage, the actual "Hunger and cold," the daily suffering of impoverished laborers, always would be "the most exacting of all taskmas-
ters." The conflict between North and South was not that the former
was "free" and the latter "slave," for, as Ruffin proclaimed, "There
exists slavery, or the subjection of man to man, in every country under

the sun." The real issue was to evaluate the nature of human interdependence in each region, to determine which was more consonant with
principles of morality and Christianity, and which tended best to promote these principles in society as a whole.[23]

In comparing Northern and Southern labor systems, Hammond,
Simms, Tucker, Ruffin, and Holmes contrasted the selfish, avaricious
nature of the "miscalled" free society with the humanitarian Christian
arrangements of slavery. The exploitation of Northern laborers symbolized the soulless materialism and inherent depravity of the North.
While the Yankees cared only about the wealth their operatives might
produce, Southerners accepted responsibility for the entire lives of the
human beings God had "entrusted" to them. Slavery was in Tucker's
view not as much an economic arrangement as "an affair of the heart."
To prove the disinterested character of the South's commitment to the
peculiar institution, all five apologists repeatedly emphasized the cost-
liness of slave labor in comparison with free. "We must . . . content
ourselves," Hammond advised, "with the consoling reflection that what
is lost to us, is gained to humanity."[24]

The free labor system was testimony to the North's "insatiable avidity for gain," which promised to bring the region to "social and
national disaster." But slavery encouraged different values, creating a
"*community* of interests" between masters and slaves. The morality
that originated in the master-slave relationship permeated all of
society, Holmes asserted. Slavery "occasions harmony, good order, and
permanent prosperity in society. . . . It protects those that require pro-
tection, the young, the aged, and the infirm. It resists the tendency to
convert all life and all social action into a mechanism for the mere
augmentation of gain, and directs the minds and hearts of men to
other and more elevated objects."[25]

When these men of mind declared, as they frequently did, that
domestic slavery was "the basis of all our institutions," the foundation
to which they referred was essentially moral rather than economic. In
the idealized system of human bondage they portrayed, their particular
values seemed fully realized. Duty and responsibility, not despised
greed, tied master and slave together; the seemingly objective criteria
of racial differentiation structured and ordered society; men of superior
mind exercised leadership and authority. Yet they recognized that
this was not a realistic portrayal of the mid-nineteenth-century South,
for they frequently berated their compatriots' avarice and indifference
to intellect and morality. They realized that their call for a society
based upon the disinterested leadership of mind reflected their ideals
and anxieties more than their observations. They sought not to describe
the South, but to inspire it. The only way to legitimate slavery, their
arguments implicitly warned, was to transform the region into the

moral utopia of their essays. The proslavery argument was thus in
essence a charter for reform.[26]

The principles upon which this evangelical movement depended
were, not surprisingly, those the five Southerners had identified as
most advantageous to the advancement of mind. Slavery, they argued,
was the labor system most conducive to the elevation of intellect, for
it protected men from the allurements of greed and afforded leisure to
a master class for cultivation of "mental improvement and refinement
of manners." Slavery was "truly the 'cornerstone'" of Southern society,
Hammond explained, for it ensured that social control would rest
in the hands of those "both educated and independent in their circumstances."[27]

Most important, slavery established stewardship as the essential
social relationship of the South. The "true business of genius" was "to
lift and guide" humanity, and slavery provided an entire race over
which the man of mind might discharge this duty. Not only did the
peculiar institution encourage Christian values in whites, but it served
as a missionary institution for bondsmen. The master-slave relationship
was an "ameliorating influence . . . on the hearts and minds" of both,
and "its part" in God's overall design was "enlightening, evangelizing
and regenerating the human race." The dependence of the slave upon
his master, Tucker believed, was analogous to that of man upon God.
Like the slaveholder, God "has bought us with a price. We are his,
body and soul—for a time and for eternity." In a similar manner, the
master purchased the slave and assumed the obligation to educate and
civilize him and even to ensure his eternal salvation. The master was
indeed God's surrogate on earth; the structure of human society replicated the order of the divine cosmos. Not only did the concept of
stewardship embody the nineteenth century's evangelical propensities,
but it justified the essence of the Southern way of life. Thus it served
as a doubly effective legitimation of the intellectuals' claims to social
authority. In a lecture on the peculiar institution to his students at
William and Mary, Tucker addressed them at once as slaveholders and
as men of learning: "My countrymen let no man deceive you. You
have been chosen as the instrument, in the hand of God for accomplishing the great purpose of his benevolence."[28]

Slavery, Ruffin believed, was "an institution of divine origin, and
manifestly designed and used by the all-wise and all-good Creator to
forward his beneficent purposes." Negro slavery in the Southern states,
he pointed out, had made twice as many Christians as all other missionary efforts in the world. Because they believed slavery promoted
spiritual as opposed to material values in society, and because it
encouraged Christian behavior in both the master and the bondsman,
the five Southerners saw its defense as a "sacred duty," a "holy func-

tion"—clearly comprehended within their area of concern as men of special intellectual and moral insight. To defend slavery was to act as a moral philosopher, to outline for others their obligations and responsibilities, for the essence of slavery was the institutionalization of the Christian duties of charity in the master and humility in the slave.[29]

Innate human inequality legitimated the master-slave relationship in the same way it justified stewardship. As Simms explained, "Regarding our slaves as a dependent and inferior people, we are their natural and only guardians." The conviction that blacks were an inferior race was implicit in all Southern proslavery tracts and often was made quite explicit. Intellectually unequal to whites, blacks were especially suited—and therefore, the men of mind inferred, providentially designed—to serve as menial laborers, as the "mud-sill" class necessary to every society.[30]

Significantly, the men of knowledge identified the attribute that differentiated the Caucasian from the African as his intellect. Mind was the distinguishing characteristic of the white race, the testimony to its superiority, and the most logical criterion of all social differentiation. By implication, therefore, works of mind were the highest achievements of the race and men of mind its supreme manifestation and natural leaders. The same hereditarian theories that justified the black's enslavement legitimated the social aspirations of the genius. In his theories of race, as in his more general social philosophy, the man of mind portrayed himself as the most perfect representative of his race, the best example of "the intellectual Caucasian."[31]

Because their justifications of slavery rested ultimately upon racist assumptions, Hammond, Holmes, Ruffin, Tucker, and Simms displayed considerable interest in the developing science of ethnology. Objective verification of the hierarchy of races would demonstrate that divine truth was manifest in nature as well as in history; science would confirm that men were differentially endowed and thus providentially suited for social inequality. Like the philosophical study of history, empirical analysis of nature served as a kind of scientific formulation and legitimation of the traditional argument from design. Whatever harmonized with these seemingly objective truths clearly accorded with God's will. Thus ethnology promised to unite religious and scientific defenses of the peculiar institution. The five Southerners found such arguments especially appealing, for in all their intellectual endeavors they had sought to maintain the complementarity of divine and rational knowledge. By asserting the righteousness of the peculiar institution on both religious and scientific grounds, the men of mind defined themselves as both positivists and evangelicals; they simultaneously confirmed the sacredness and comprehensibility of their world.

Hammond's interest in ethnological discoveries encouraged him to maintain an active correspondence with his college friend Josiah Nott, a Southern physician deeply involved in research on what he called the "nigger business." Hammond introduced Ruffin to the science of ethnology, and Holmes, too, became so concerned with the study that he proclaimed racial difference as the "principal axiom" of his historical theories. Invoking J. A. Gobineau as justification for his racist views, Holmes collected data on "Negro Character," "Ethnology," and "Castes and Degraded Races" for his commonplace book.[32]

In the late 1840s and early 1850s, however, ethnology took a new direction, one somewhat inconsistent with the religious views for which it previously had supplied support. Prominent scholars such as Samuel Morton, George Gliddon, Louis Agassiz, and Nott increasingly concerned themselves with the origins of racial differences, seeking to determine whether blacks and whites had been created separately as two distinct and differentially endowed groups or whether variations had evolved in response to different environments. Although prior to Charles Darwin's publication in 1859, the weight of scientific evidence was clearly on the side of polygenist hypotheses, many Southerners were reluctant to accept these views, for they profoundly threatened biblical revelation.

Hammond sought to avoid publicly embroiling himself in the controversy these doctrines had incited. He found it made little difference to his argument whether Africans actually were a different species or simply inferior members of the same species as whites. In his Clarkson letters, Hammond dodged the issue agilely, declaring, "the African, if not a distinct, is an inferior, race, and never will effect, as it never has effected, as much in any other condition as in that of Slavery." Simms insisted that Christian faith "cannot be affected in any way by the decision of this controversy," and Ruffin complained that "the same facts & the same authorities" were used "to support the opposite doctrines." Holmes, too, found the debate on the origin of the races disturbing and the issues "enveloped in all the mist of obscurity." His solution to this uncertainty was much the same as Hammond's: "to steer a cautious middle course between the extreme views on this subject."[33]

But unpleasant as they found the intrusion of controversy into what they considered a realm of disinterested speculation, the group could not ignore the ethnological debate, for they were personally and intellectually committed to the proslavery movement and thus to the entire scope of issues it raised and forms it assumed. Essays by Hammond and Simms appeared in the most popular contemporary collections of proslavery classics, and all the members of the network were intimate with the other principals in the slavery debate. For example, Thomas Dew, author of the first famous defense of slavery as a "positive good," "The Review of the Debate in the Virginia Legislature," was Tucker's colleague and close friend at William and Mary; William Harper, who produced the widely circulated *Memoir on Slavery*, was a cousin to both Holmes and Tucker and a friend of Hammond and Simms; Albert Bledsoe was on the faculty with Holmes at both the University of Mississippi and the University of Virginia; J. H. Thornwell corresponded frequently with Holmes, as did George Fitzhugh and J. D. B. DeBow. These personal ties among proslavery writers arose in great part from the small size of the intellectual class in the South; most of its members were acquainted with one another either directly or through mutual friends, and their social interaction from the 1830s onward reinforced the similarities in their thought. Although one apologist might emphasize political questions and another ethnological ones, most sought ultimately to demonstrate the morality of the peculiar institution.[34]

Both ante-bellum observers and later historians have emphasized the uniformity of the South's arguments for slavery. But in *The Black Image in the White Mind*, George Fredrickson recently challenged this position by asserting that there existed two well-defined categories of apologists. Spokesmen for slavery in the seaboard South—men like Simms, Tucker, Ruffin, Hammond, and Holmes—evoked socially conservative, patriarchal principles in the institution's defense. Leaders of the newer states of the Southwest, however, tended to emphasize racial justifications for the peculiar institution and promised the Southern people a white "Herrenvolk" democracy built on the cornerstone of slavery, a society, Fredrickson asserts, totally at odds with the hierarchical social philosophy of the first group. While Fredrickson's characterization may accurately represent the divisions within the larger political movement for Southern nationalism, it overstates the differences among those who devoted their energies specifically to the systematic defense of slavery. In fact, the differences that did exist were more of tone and emphasis than of substance, for there were few challenges to the basic moral-philosophical assumptions of the mainstream of slavery's defenders.[35]

As we have seen, Simms and his circle were not the unwavering opponents of democracy they often have been portrayed; they did not object to a social system in which the common man would be elevated to what Simms called positions of "responsibility and trust." Indeed, all five men of mind employed the argument—which Fredrickson regards as the distinguishing position of the opposing "Herrenvolk" group—that slavery would serve as the cornerstone for white democracy. Simms, Ruffin, Tucker, Hammond, and Holmes also depended heavily upon racist assumptions to justify slavery, for they saw these as scientific proof of God's inegalitarian designs.[36]

Many of those individuals whom Fredrickson would classify in his "Herrenvolk" category because of their interest in ethnology shared with our Sacred Circle a commitment to the defense of slavery as a moral issue and to science as an instrument with which to illuminate moral truth. As W. S. Jenkins noted in 1935, the ethnological justification of slavery was an "appeal to nature as the proper moral foundation upon which the institution could be placed." Hammond's close friend Josiah Nott represented this fusion of interests in his approach to the slavery problem and even the title of his *Two Lectures on the Connection between the Biblical and Physical History of Man* accurately manifests the combination of religious and scientific commitments that characterized this position.[37]

Hammond, Simms, and the other members of network indeed took issue with statements made about slavery by Southwestern politicians such as William Yancey, whom Fredrickson identifies as a prime spokesman of the "Herrenvolk" position. But their opposition had little relationship to Yancey's geographical origins or political loyalties. The five Southerners objected less to the democratic implications of Yancey's arguments than to the self-interest and political calculation his proslavery utterances seemed to represent. The men of mind expressed similar aversion to political uses of the slavery argument by South Carolinians such as Robert B. Rhett and John Calhoun. "Mr. C., as some others," Hammond remarked to Simms in disgust, "thinks that you have but to say nigger to the South to set it on fire, as one whistles to a Turkey to make him gobble." The intellectuals insisted that the defense of the peculiar institution not become a mere instrument for political advancement.[38]

Because Hammond, Holmes, Simms, Ruffin, and Tucker regarded the argument as the vehicle for intellectual self-definition, they felt compelled to dissociate themselves explicitly from discussions of the peculiar institution that challenged the transcendent goals they had associated with slavery's defense. Simms and Hammond were unalterably opposed to the creation of a political newspaper that would "agitate" the issue in order to gain political advantage for the South. Hammond was also disturbed by Calhoun's praise for a slavery tract by Kentucky Methodist H. B. Bascom, for he found the defense squeamish at best and "*very unsound*. He says the Bible is neither for nor against slavery." The sacred nature of the peculiar institution as demonstrated by both Revelation and history was central to the network's position on slavery. Hammond could explain Calhoun's enthusiasm for Bascom only by attributing it to the base motivations of political self-interest. Calhoun's attitude "was chiefly dedicated by the hope of *securing* Kentucky Methodist influence. . . . He is dying to be President in spite of fate." Such politicization of the proslavery movement appeared to Hammond as a profanation.[39]

Significantly, George Fitzhugh, the proslavery writer who probably has attracted most attention from twentieth-century historians, was particularly criticized by many of his contemporaries, and the reasons for this dislike are revealing. Fitzhugh was in fact both personally and intellectually isolated from the society of most Southern defenders of the peculiar institution. Holmes found that Fitzhugh completely ignored the "philosophical" requirements for disinterested pursuit of truth, and, indeed, approached perilously near the realm of polemic. Holmes bemoaned the Virginian's "want of moderation" and found his theories "too broadly and incautiously asserted." He worried that Fitzhugh would lead Northerners to regard all Southerners as fanatics. Taken as a whole, Fitzhugh's "utter recklessness of both statement and expression" and his "idiosyncracy" made his work "incendiary and dangerous."[40]

Unlike Hammond, Simms, Holmes, Tucker, and Ruffin, Fitzhugh had little interest in the works of mind or the role of intellect in the South. In *Cannibals All!* he proudly proclaimed himself to be no scholar and denounced philosophy as a waste of time. To Holmes he confided that he never had read Aristotle, the equivalent in the mid-nineteenth century to admitting himself uneducated. As the two Southerners corresponded between 1854 and 1857, Holmes grew increasingly disenchanted with his new acquaintance. When Fitzhugh acknowledged him handsomely in the preface to *Cannibals All!* Holmes wrote disgruntledly in his diary, "I dislike notoriety."[41]

Fitzhugh, by contrast, delighted in the stir he caused with his writings and declared to Holmes that *Sociology for the South* sold well because it was "odd, eccentric, extravagant and disorderly." Holmes could not have been pleased by the Virginian's attempt to replace "sober and cautious" reflection on slavery with a literary side show. Holmes came to recognize that Fitzhugh was above all a "great egoist," intent on advancing his own reputation and unconcerned about either the cause of intellect or the disinterested pursuit of truth, ideals to which Holmes and the other members of the network repeatedly had pledged their devotion.[42]

Yet C. Vann Woodward, David Donald, Louis Hartz, Harvey Wish, George Fredrickson, and Eugene Genovese have paid Fitzhugh extravagant attention and thus implicitly, if not explicitly, stressed his centrality to the movement for Southern defense. Perhaps these scholars too eagerly have accepted Fitzhugh's egotistical self-evaluation. His vanity and his ignorance—as Genovese admits, he read too little and wrote too much—prompted him to declare in 1855 that he had within the last year "revolutionized public opinion at the South on the subject of Slavery. Then, not one paper vindicated Slavery in the abstract—now all endorse my book." Perhaps Dew's 1831 essay was a bit too squeamish to be considered more than a fledgling "positive good" argument, for Dew placed more emphasis on the implausibility of alternative labor systems than on the inherent virtues of slavery. But by the late 1830s, and certainly well before 1855, Tucker, Simms, Hammond, Ruffin, Holmes, and others, such as William Harper and A. T. Bledsoe, had defended slavery on theoretical grounds, declaring it, as we have noted, to be of divine appointment and a positive benefit to both master and slave.[43]

Fitzhugh himself emphasized the originality of a number of his ideas and the consequent significance of his contributions to slavery's defense. He was the first, he believed, to consider the slavery issue within the larger context of the organization of labor and of economic production and to re-evaluate the meaning of freedom and natural law. But in reality, many earlier apologists had made these arguments explicit. Dew had stated in 1831 that a so-called "Free" worker who had no assurance of subsistence was free to do little more than starve. Hammond, Simms, and Tucker extended this process of redefinition, broadening it to include a recasting of the concept of natural law long before Fitzhugh ever published.[44]

Fitzhugh's most enthusiastic modern champion has been Eugene Genovese, who declares that he has come to regard the Virginian as an "old friend." Genovese asserts that while neither "typical nor representative," Fitzhugh was nevertheless a "ruthless and critical theorist who spelled out the logical outcome of the slaveholders' philosophy and laid bare its essence." In Fitzhugh's defense of the peculiar institution Genovese discovers not just a particularly audacious rationale for slavery, but the meaning of the civilization of the Old South.[45]

Yet, as we have seen, Fitzhugh was in many ways atypical and even antithetical to the moral-philosophical mainstream of proslavery thought—not its "logical outcome." He had little intellectual or personal rapport with the Southerners who from 1830 onward had worked together in slavery's defense. Many of these authors explicitly disavowed the Virginian, for his tone and attitudes threatened to subvert the goals they had established for the endeavor.

Fitzhugh was a latecomer to the defense of slavery. By the time he published in 1849, the Southern intellectual class already had appropriated the argument, seizing upon the defense of the peculiar institution as an opportunity for the practical exercise of its Idealist views and as an occasion for justifying its would-be social role. Not himself a part of this class, Fitzhugh took up the argument for reasons very different from those that had motivated the men of mind who developed it. He did not understand that one goal of the *mariage de convenance* between intellectual values and the peculiar institution was to impress upon Southerners the importance of intellectuals and their peculiar skills. Oblivious to these concerns, which were an integral part of the proslavery movement, Fitzhugh was a mutant strain within it. His polemical tone and his anti-intellectualism profaned the ideals of the men of mind from Dew onward who sought a defender of slavery committed to "sober and cautious reflection."

A key impetus behind the most widely circulated proslavery arguments was the peculiar emotional and social dilemma associated with being an intellectual in the ante-bellum South. Because the man of mind hoped to gain a place for himself and his work by defending slavery, he could not in the course of this undertaking break the rules that defined the intellectual role he was trying to establish. Social and cultural factors directed the nature of the defense and contained inherent restraints that prevented the argument from reaching in other hands the form given it by George Fitzhugh.

But ultimately, Genovese is less interested in Fitzhugh's relationship to the proslavery movement than in the significance of his apologies to the broader Southern world view. In Fitzhugh's thought, indeed in the values he did share with other apologists, Genovese finds the essence of Southern distinctiveness, the antimaterialist—and what he calls anticapitalist and prebourgeois—outlook upon which Fitzhugh's defenses of slavery rested. Genovese regards these attitudes as dependent variables, the logical product of the particularly Southern relationship between the ownership and the means of production, between the master and the slave. Yet, these antimaterialist values were in large part the product of the peculiar needs of the alienated Southern intellectual class from which Fitzhugh borrowed the moral-philosophical bases for his arguments. And, as we have seen, they did not as much reflect the realities of Southern life as the ambivalence of a group of intellectuals about the changes taking place in their society and in societies throughout the Western world. Ironically, Genovese finds Southern antimaterialism best exemplified in George Fitzhugh, an individual accused by his contemporaries of consciously appropriating these "prebourgeois" ideas not for their intrinsic merit, but for his own fame and material advancement.

These unique precapitalist values, most explicitly formulated in the proslavery argument, seem to Genovese to constitute the essence of Southernness. Indeed, many Southerners overtly challenged the preoccupation with pecuniary gain, the "cash nexus" they believed characterized much of mid-nineteenth-century America. But slaveholders were not alone in feeling these anxieties. The most striking aspect of the proslavery argument was that the values upon which it depended and the confusions it reflected were not peculiar to the South. The men of mind who constructed slavery's defense sought a plausible belief system for their society, a formula that would at once direct, explain, and justify the Southern way of life. Thus they based their arguments upon moral and social values to which large numbers of Americans both North and South could assent. Stewardship, which Genovese defines as the essential principle of the master-slave relationship, was an important characteristic of the evangelicalism that pervaded all of nineteenth-century America and much of England as well. Historians have particularly emphasized its efficacy in the North, where it served as a motivating force behind the myriad of reform movements of the era. In explaining the acceptance of "direct social responsibility for others" as the product of a "prebourgeois" Southern world view, Genovese ignores the existence of these central aspects of Northern civilization.[46]

The social views of the conservative Boston divines Daniel Walker Howe describes in *The Unitarian Conscience* were surprisingly similar to the organicist social philosophy of the Southern defenders of slavery, as was the thought of British social philosophers such as Matthew Arnold and Thomas Carlyle. Indeed, self-conscious fears about growing materialism and declining morality were, as Marvin Meyers has shown, national rather than peculiarly Southern. The social ideas advanced by the apologists of slavery are more accurately characterized as sacred, communitarian, or traditional, than as pre- or anticapitalist, for they were shared by many Americans in no way influenced by their participation in the master-slave relationship. Many of these Northern "stewards" were among slavery's harshest opponents.[47]

Genovese's analysis of Fitzhugh is ultimately circular, for it defines the South as prebourgeois and then embraces the single Southerner who openly attacked capitalism as the most accurate exponent of the regional world view. Genovese portrays the tensions between the two cultures within the South brilliantly, but he errs in his explanation of these anxieties. These strains were not the product of slavery, for they existed widespread in the North as well, where the challenge to long-accepted values had produced the multitude of "isms"—from communitarianism to feminism—that the South found threatening. Perhaps these anxieties might best be defined as the product of conflicts between the sacred and the profane, tensions arising from the modernization and secularization of society. The cultural crisis of the Victorian era in both England and America arose from the growing difficulty of maintaining any system of belief that would offer emotional satisfaction to the individual and legitimacy for society at large. This dilemma was as real for the South as for the rest of the Western world.

The defense of slavery was thus in an important sense an effort by a self-conscious group of Southern thinkers to revitalize their society, to provide a system of beliefs that would impart meaning to the regional way of life and in so doing to establish an essential role for thought in the South. The proslavery argument was designed to provide the region as a whole with a conventionalized formula of self-affirmation, to allay the anxieties of Southerners about the nature of the world in which they lived. Traditional values and ideals would legitimate the Southern ethos, while constant repetition of loyalty to these same values would reduce the tension arising from their abandonment as absolute criteria for behavior. In regard to the slavery question, Hammond was certain that "the more it is discussed, the stronger we will become."[48]

At the same time that the intellectuals hoped to transform their society, they sought to demonstrate the essential relationship between the regional way of life and the particular values associated with their role. For the men of mind themselves, the defense of slavery provided the opportunity to act in terms of the system of beliefs they had embraced, to assert in what was to become almost ritualized form their social relevance as persons of both intellectual and moral insight, and to assume the role Raymond Williams describes as coveted by every alienated Romantic. Because every member of the group participated in defending slavery, the movement also enhanced their own solidarity. Tucker became personally acquainted with Hammond by congratulating him on his first proslavery speech; Simms arranged for his publisher to print Hammond's Clarkson letters; Hammond offered his franking privileges to help distribute Ruffin's essays on the peculiar institution.[49]

The Sacred Circle of men of mind thus discovered in the defense of slavery the most appropriate vehicle for self-expression. By transforming the argument into a comprehensive social and moral philosophy, they succeeded in translating the dilemmas they faced as intellectuals and those the Old South confronted as a civilization into transcendent religious and cultural terms. As men of mind, they were convinced that both their own problems and those of their culture had of necessity to be solved within this realm of belief and value.

SEVEN

Earth's Teachers Overborne

rom its inception, the intellectual friendship among Hammond, Holmes, Simms, Tucker, and Ruffin contained the elements that were to produce its eventual dissolution. The group s particular definition of the role of genius required a precarious balance between active and contemplative concerns. As the South moved toward war, the men of mind found it increasingly difficult to maintain their simultaneous commitment to the transcendent and the practical, to both ultimate conviction and mundane ambition. The beleagured region had neither time nor resources to spare on disinterested speculation; action, as Hammond long had warned, had become the watchword of the age. As they came fully to comprehend the obstacles that separated them from their shared goals, the intellectuals' sense of common purpose and thus the foundation for their intimacy began to erode.[1]

The Nashville Convention of 1850 represented an important turning point for the group. The five Southerners cherished extravagant expectations for this regionwide gathering, for it promised to realize the unity of moral purpose to which they long had been dedicated. Their disillusionment at the meager accomplishments of the meeting was correspondingly intense and compelled the men of mind to reappraise not just their immediate hopes for the South, but their earthly mission generally.

At Nashville, the region first directly confronted the issue of secession. Congress had been discussing a North-South agreement concerning slavery in the territories, enforcement of the fugitive slave law, and other questions under dispute between the sections. Fearful of concessions to Northern demands, a number of radical sectionalists had called for a convention to consolidate the South in her resistance. The prospect of regional unification excited the five intellectuals, and all eagerly supported the movement for a meeting in Tennessee. Hammond and Tucker were chosen as delegates by their home states; Simms and Ruffin were disappointed at their failure to be selected as representatives.[2]

The congressional proposals that eventually became the Compromise of 1850 appeared to the men of mind as a political bargain, the product of partisan machinations and self-seeking factionalism. Resisting such a compromise on constitutional grounds, the intellectuals believed, might unite the Southern people in the long-awaited crusade for disinterested truth. In keeping with the religious vocabulary and world view they had embraced, the men of mind portrayed the movement for Southern independence in sectarian terms, as a desire to withdraw and thereby to escape the pollution of a profane world. Indeed, to Tucker, those who shared his states' rights views appeared as the "small remnant of a persecuted though once triumphant church." Constitutional and religious issues merged inseparably; as saving remnant, the South would secede in order to preserve the reign of principle. In rejecting the Union, she would symbolically reject the materialism and corruption to which she had succumbed during the national period. Secession would be a ritual of purification.[3]

Simms explained the conflict of North and South within the same religious framework. The Northern states, he asserted in a discussion of the convention, "have become arrogant in strength and power. Affluence has corrupted their hearts; pride and vanity have sapped their virtues. . . . They are a doomed people," he warned. "Rottenness and corruption are seated in their marble palaces." The proposed Compromise of 1850 was yet further evidence of Northern baseness, for it represented the triumph of party over principle, the profane over the sacred. "It is the most melancholy history in the progress of the nations." Simms declared, "that their Clays and Websters, commissioned by heaven with endowments for a great work . . . will forever substitute man for God in the objects of their solicitude." In its call for regional unity in resistance to concession, however, the Nashville Convention transcended "the prejudice of faction . . . the scruples of party." A united South would dedicate herself not to mundane "success," but to issues "of the last importance," to moral principles.[4]

To men with such hopes, the Nashville Convention was a bitter disappointment. There was little evidence of the idealistic Southern solidarity the intellectuals had hoped the gathering would symbolize. Only nine states sent representatives, and even these were badly divided on the issue of withdrawal from the Union. Whig participants insisted publicly that the convention did not contemplate secession and indeed sought to prevent it. Sentiment in Nashville itself was hostile to the gathering, and such powerful Southerners as Robert Toombs and Alexander Stephens dissociated themselves from the movement by

announcing their support for the Clay compromise proposals under discussion in the Senate. The convention adjourned with little accomplished, but agreed to await the outcome of congressional debates on
the compromise and meet again in six weeks.

Hammond was disgusted with what he had witnessed in Nashville,
and he determined not to return when the group reconvened. He
informed the governor of his resignation as a delegate, officially attributing his reluctance to serve to his own and his children's ill health.
In private, however, he declared that the Nashville meeting had been
"from the first a mere abortion." Tucker largely agreed with Hammond's assessment and proclaimed himself greatly disheartened by the
prevailing spirit of compromise. The failure of Nashville, like the more
general moral failure of the South, was the fault of "men who have
formed for themselves ambitious plans the sweep of which depends on
the preservation of the Union at every sacrifice." The convention had
demonstrated that faction and ambition, not truth and principle, still
held sway in the South.[5]

Hammond was particularly depressed by the Nashville "abortion,"
and his low spirits were intensified by the widespread disapproval that
greeted his refusal to attend the second session of the convention.
When the state legislature rejected him as a replacement for Calhoun
in the United States Senate, Hammond became convinced that his
alienation from his society was irreversible. "A reign of terror is at
hand," he proclaimed to Tucker. Disinterested virtue and the products
of the mind could find no place "when men must cease to speak unless
they speak to stimulate the frenzy of the mob." Instead of improving
as a result of the group's myriad efforts at reform, the South seemed
to Hammond to be sinking deeper into iniquity. "It is lamentably true,"
he wrote Simms, "that independence, real spirit & intellectual endowment & acquirement are no longer appreciated here." Defeated once
again in the legislature's election for U.S. Senator, Hammond decided
that South Carolina had "assassinated" him, and in consequence he
contemplated leaving the state. As a symbolic gesture, he enrolled his
sons in the university at Athens, Georgia, instead of at South Carolina
College, the alma mater to which he long had been loyal. From public
affairs, Hammond turned to exclusively private concerns, farming and
the draining of marshlands. "Reclaiming swamps," he declared to
Simms, "has become my passion. It is creative. It is exercising the
highest functions without having to ask *votes*. I love their creep, gloom
& their solemn silence." They provided an appropriate setting, he
found, for his own state of mind.[6]

Embittered by his disappointments, Hammond retreated into melancholy and cynicism and declared to Ruffin that part of him was
"inclined to . . . turn my devotions more & more to the Almighty Dol-

lar, which as things go is the only 'guarantee' in which a man should
put any faith." The anxiety of further ambition seemed too much to
bear. "When men are ever crushed as completely as I have been," he
explained to Simms, "they can never be made up again *as they were.*
. . . they must draw themselves into themselves." He had no choice, he
felt, but to surrender to his fate. "I quit the Prophets," he proclaimed.
"I had no mission."[7]

But Hammond's private life seemed little more rewarding, for here
he encountered with renewed intensity the same isolation and rejection he had experienced within the public world. His children could
not understand him or his hopes for their future. "An abyss separates
us," he lamented. Even his private ambitions seemed destined to fail.
Because of what he described as his sons' "incompetency," he decided
that "all hope of establishing a rich, well-bred & predominant family
. . . of our name is over."[8]

Hammond's isolation encouraged introspection, and his private writings during the 1850s consist of what can only be described as a morbid attempt to understand his "inexorable destiny." He continually
sought to discover why he had been placed in a world for which he
was unfit, and he compared his efforts to awaken the Southern intellect
to the endeavors of Sisyphus. To his private "Thoughts and Recollections" he confided in 1853, "The ideal has expired—the intellectual has
been frozen, the moral has been crushed within me."[9]

Simms was determined to prevent Hammond from sinking into
complete depression, and he enlisted Tucker in the effort to provide
their mutual friend with encouragement and support. "Let me beg
that in writing to him," Simms entreated Tucker, "you take some pains
in urging him not to despond. . . . Show him that with his endowments he has much to live for." Simms was well aware, however, that
the convention had been a failure. The months following Nashville, he
recognized, would be crucial both for the South and for the Sacred
Circle, and he strove to shore up both his friends and his region in
their hour of common crisis. In the summer of 1851, he set off to visit
both Holmes and Tucker in Virginia and encouraged their active
assistance in his labors on behalf of the South. The mind of the region
had not been ready for Nashville, he concluded. But the convention
had represented, he hoped, the first step in a process of regional awak-
ening. In 1849 he had assumed the editorship of the *Southern Quarterly
Review* and intended with the aid of his intellectual friends to transform it into the instrument of Southern regeneration.[10]

But before long Simms, too, had begun to despair. Like every other
periodical with which he had been associated, the *Review* did not
attract the support required for its survival. Simms resigned in 1854,
and the magazine failed three years later. Bitter at yet another frustra-

tion of his aspirations, Simms retired to his plantation. As the decade
progressed, he found that increasingly "my ideas . . . revolve in a narrow, almost a domestic circle. . . . I am losing all ambition." His health
became a major occupation, and he nursed constant headaches, stomach, and eye trouble, diseases he readily acknowledged to be the
result of his worldly disappointments. "Fate," he wrote Hammond,
"would seem to have denied a field to all my more youthful aspirations."[11]

Simms was not alone in sharing Hammond's distress at the failure
of the Nashville Convention. Tucker, too, declared his disgust at
Southern moral cowardice. But the Virginian had derived some measure of satisfaction from the stir caused throughout the South by a radically disunionist address he had delivered to the delegates, a speech
which, as Hammond reported to Simms, "skins everybody." After the
first session of the convention, Tucker had returned with Hammond to
Silver Bluff, where over late-night games of billiards he assailed his
host with schemes for exploiting his new notoriety. At last he had
gained "possession of the public ear, and I do not mean to let go my
hold upon it"—or, apparently, upon that of his long-suffering friend.[12]

While Hammond had all but abandoned hope for any decisive
Southern action, Tucker proceeded with frenetic zeal on behalf of his
strategy of "prudent boldness." Southerners, he admonished, must
learn from Byron's words and from the example of his heroism in
Greece; " 'they must seize they cannot snare their prey.' " Even when
the failure of the second Nashville meeting made a united Southern
movement impossible, Tucker still urged Hammond to lead South Carolina in single-state resistance of federal encroachments, in treating
the Constitution as a "nullity," in forging independent alliances with
European states. In spite of his despondency, Hammond seemed to
his friend the obvious leader for their cause. "I cannot bear you should
droop and withdraw from the field," Tucker declared, and sent the
South Carolinian a case of brandy to uplift his failing spirits.[13]

Tucker seemed not to recognize that by the following spring the
passions of 1850 had for most Southerners subsided temporarily into a
reassuring routine of rising cotton prices and regional prosperity. He,
at least, was ready to go to war. "Is there any way which South Carolina can employ me?" he beseeched Hammond. "I have in my time
trained two regiments up to the *Regular* standard, am expert in the
duties of the general staff and understand the tactics of the infantry
battalion. . . . This question," he insisted soberly, "is not asked idly."[14]

Tucker perhaps recognized that if secession did not come soon, he
would be unable to play a role in the movement for which he had
waited so long. "When the tree falls," he wrote resignedly to Ham-

mond, "I wish it to be remembered that one of the first blows struck was mine. It will be for you to plant the acorn from which a healthier and noble growth shall spring, and hereafter when Virginia shall seek shelter under its shadow, she will do honour to my memory." In the summer of 1851, Tucker fell ill while visiting his brother in Winchester and died there on 26 August.[15]

While Tucker's death removed him from the Sacred Circle, other factors were at work to distance Ruffin and Holmes from their friends. While Hammond felt more alienated in the 1850s than he ever had, Ruffin encountered his first measure of public acceptance. His two favorite causes, agricultural reform and Southern independence, were gaining popularity. Virginians had begun by the fifties to recognize the importance of his prescriptions for renewal of their lands, and acclaim for Ruffin's methods was widespread. His new relationship to the public was symbolized by the reorganization of the Virginia Agricultural Society in accordance with many of his earlier suggestions and by his consequent selection as its president.[16]

This change of fortune created a distance between Ruffin and his friend Hammond, who increasingly regarded himself as a pariah. Ruffin urged the South Carolinian to abandon his self-pitying withdrawal: "I readily admit that you may have had enough of ingratitude & unmerited hostility & *wrong*. Also I can well sympathize with & enter into your wounded feeling—as for years *I* felt the like & acted in like manner. . . . My consequent entire seclusion *you* then opposed. . . . At that time, I felt much as you do now and acted comparably. And I was wrong & I think you are also." Hammond recognized that he and the Virginian no longer shared a common plight and spurned Ruffin's attempts to console and encourage him. "I do not believe that any evidences of appreciation, any testimonials of gratitude, any honors, however great from any quarter could resuscitate me." Overwhelmed with physical disorders much like those plaguing Simms, Hammond complained to Ruffin, "It is your peculiar happiness that having survived the neglect of the world, you have still life enough to appreciate & enjoy its tardy compensations." Hammond was certain that he would reap no such rewards.[17]

Hammond resented the Virginian's success, and this jealousy eroded their friendship. In 1853, Hammond wrote to Simms in disgust at Ruffin's "vanity and egotism." Public approval greeted Ruffin's growing commitment to action rather than thought and influenced the Virginian gradually to separate himself from the group and its intellectual and spiritual values. Ruffin no longer seemed concerned with the transcendent principles Southern political actions might symbolize; secession became for him an end in itself. While Simms and Hammond maintained a critical distance from their society throughout the fifties and even after the outbreak of war, Ruffin, by contrast, became an increasingly active participant in the conflicts around him. He appeared as an enthusiastic witness at John Brown's hanging; distributed Brown's pikes to all the governors of the South in order to urge forceful resistance upon them; fired the first shot at Sumter; then donned the uniform of the Palmetto Guards and at the age of sixty-five became a field soldier for the Confederacy. When he found himself unable to keep pace with his regiment's double-time march, Ruffin rode proudly into battle resting on a caisson.

Ruffin found the acclaim that greeted his activist endeavors during the course of the 1850s almost irresistible. The period of secession was for him "the happiest of my life"; the events of the sectional crisis "as gratifying to me as they are glorious and momentous. And there has been much to gratify my individual and selfish feelings." The outbreak of war provided him with even greater opportunities for distinction. "Since the beginning of my recent military service," he confided to his diary in 1861, "general popular favor & . . . applause have increased ten-fold."[18]

For most of his life, Edmund Ruffin had endeavored to communicate his opinions and values to the Southern people through the media of oratory and the press. But the South had seemed not to hear or comprehend his words. His agricultural principles, for example, had been acknowledged only when the increased productivity of soil under his management became undeniable. Frustrated at this neglect, Ruffin recognized that the mounting crisis provided him with the opportunity to adopt new and more effective means of self-expression. Instead of verbalizing his convictions, he would act them; he would not rely on words but make his life itself a symbol; he would communicate through bold—even extreme—gestures bearing meanings that would be unmistakable. Through heroism, through charismatic example, his life would educate the people in a way all his intellectual endeavors had not. The discontinuity between his actions and his age and appearance would render his behavior all the more striking; it would be hard to ignore or forget the image of a venerable gentleman with flowing white hair advancing into battle astride a wagonload of ammunition. It was the Old South herself riding to war.

Ruffin regarded himself as a kind of high priest, an exemplary figure enacting a public ritual with which he hoped the entire South would identify. As a genius, he long had believed himself the embodiment of the people; his actions in this crisis were designed simply to reaffirm this conviction—both for Ruffin and for his society. In firing the first shot at Sumter, he was only following the motivations for his pro-slavery tracts to their ultimate and logical conclusion. In both undertakings, he considered himself the incarnation of a regenerate South; he was transformed into a moral idea. Similarly, he greeted the defeat of the Confederacy with a final act of symbolic defiance.

On 18 June 1865, Ruffin waited for an unexpected succession of callers to depart the Virginia home where he had sought refuge from the war with his oldest son. It was almost noon when the family was left alone, and Ruffin proceeded at once with his long-considered intentions. In a most deliberate manner, Ruffin retired from the others and calmly shot himself, symbolizing, as he saw it, his refusal to compromise "my unmitigated hatred to Yankee rule." In the barren intellectual fields of the South, communication by gesture and by example seemed more successful than any effort by words. For Ruffin, the dilemma of thought and action had been resolved decisively in favor of action.[19]

In marked contrast, George Frederick Holmes retreated during the fifties into the realms of contemplation. Unable to find academic employment, Holmes, like Hammond and Simms, retired to his farm where he lamented his agricultural as well as his more general failures. "I am only too much afraid," he wrote, "that there is some propriety in applying to myself the following remark. . . . 'There, too, has a fine character been rendered almost useless by the force of circumstances: there was more in the heart of the tree than ever appeared in its foliage and blossoms.' "[20]

Holmes's withdrawal from the world was not simply geographical. The intellectual dilemma he had defined earlier now appeared to Holmes less a matter of reason and increasingly an issue of spirit and faith. While he previously had been preoccupied with discovering a new science of society, his writings in the 1850s reflected a growing sense of the limits of positivism. Any intellectual endeavor, he came to believe, of necessity must rest on a firm spiritual foundation. Personally, Holmes grew more and more devout in the course of the decade, began "diligent and beseeching" daily prayer, and considered converting to Roman Catholicism. His work during this period manifested a diminishing interest in social processes and a deepening concern with thought and belief. Although he published articles defending slavery throughout the 1850s, his primary intellectual preoccupation was the delineation of his "Philosophy of Faith."[21]

The changing focus of Holmes's interests was reflected in a changing pattern of correspondence and friendship. Simms, Holmes decided, lacked the depth required for true intellectual production, and scandals surrounding Hammond convinced Holmes that the South Carolinian had sacrificed his "powerful intellect" to "sensual outrages." Holmes began instead to cultivate James Henley Thornwell, the brilliant and rigidly pious president of the Presbyterian Theological Seminary at Columbia and later of South Carolina College. When Thornwell took over the editorship of the *Southern Quarterly* from Simms in 1856, Holmes's entry in his diary clearly manifested the nature of these shifting loyalties. Thornwell, Holmes wrote, was "one of the few real scholars in the South, one of the few competent to conduct a Review creditably." Both Holmes and Thornwell agreed that establishing religious certainty was the overriding duty of their age, and upon Thornwell's invitation, Holmes began to interact with the Presbyterian's "literary circle." In 1856, Holmes explained his priorities explicitly: "If poverty, and struggle, and debts and embarrassments would permit me, I would devote myself first to the settlement of my religious convictions, and then to the regular study of the Middle Ages, and the composition of my contemplated work on the Laws of Social Development." Holmes had not completely abandoned his interest in creating a new science of society, but this concern was far outranked in importance by the search for religious truth. Although he continued to write about slavery and the world around him, Holmes's real interests lay in the realms of contemplation and belief.[22]

In 1857, Holmes emerged from his isolation in the mountains to accept a professorship at the University of Virginia, where he was to remain until his death forty years later. From Charlottesville, he witnessed the approach and the outbreak of war. Holmes's reaction to the upheaval manifested his typological view of present occurrences and the otherworldly significance he had come to attribute to all events around him. The conflagration, he believed, was a divine judgment, God's chastening of man for his errors. "The days of the Martyrs have returned." Man's "speculative delusions" had not been "eradicated by more sober reflection" and thus God had decided they must be "burnt out by the fires of war." The failure of Holmes's efforts on behalf of intellectual and moral reform had undermined his faith in human agency. Man had demonstrated that he could not save himself. Thus God had intervened, dispatching the long-threatened "Hordes from the North" to purify him of his depravities, of the "misplaced ambition, desire of pay and plunder, love of notoriety, hope of popularity . . . greed, rapacity, drinking, gambling, dissipation" that "have gradually usurped the place of principle." What the men of mind had been unable to effect, Holmes now looked to God to accomplish. Holmes's understanding of the war symbolized his abandonment of the movement on behalf of intellect, for he denied the efficacy of human stewards in maintaining truth and principle on earth. Only God could determine the course of men's affairs. Therefore, Holmes concluded, only religious, otherworldly contemplation was of real value.[23]

Despite the death of Tucker and the gradual alienation of Holmes and Ruffin from the group, Hammond and Simms remained intimate. Their common despair during the middle years of the decade was interrupted in 1857 by Hammond's unsolicited election to the United States Senate. Despite earlier proclamations that nothing could rouse him from his despondency, Hammond was delighted and considered the event "a signal triumph over all my enemies." Simms rejoiced in his friend's good fortune and barraged him with political advice.[24]

In the remaining years before the outbreak of war, Simms and Hammond manifested a curious ambivalence toward the situation in the South. Alternately they exulted over increasing Southern unity and despaired over the unprincipled, self-interested quality of the regional consolidation that was taking place. To his constituents Hammond declared at Barnwell Courthouse in October 1858, "The abolitionists have, at length, forced upon us a knowledge of our true position, and compelled us into union." The national government, he declared, was "but a policy and not a principle. . . . But the union of the slaveholders of the South is a principle involving all our rights and all our interests." Yet less than a year later, Hammond was disgusted with the South's lack of principle and abandonment of ideals in the struggle for political advantage. "She seems to have surrendered," he declared to Simms, "*prostituted* herself all at once to every sort of adventurer— Cuban fillibusters, slave trade felons & political aspirants of the basest & *silliest* order. Who would have thought it? I am ashamed of her."[25]

In Washington, Hammond found himself continually torn between sectional loyalties and issues of principle. "I say little in the Senate," he wrote Simms in 1860. "I don't discourse North & South which is the topic because although I might interject here & there in the main I stand by all I have heretofore said & have nothing very important in addition. If anything rather more against the South than the North. . . . As things stand I don't wish to rebuke my side." Hammond himself advocated in the late fifties that the South reject independence and instead exert her power within the structure of the existing union. He warned Simms not to mistake the true motivations of those insisting on secession: "Do not suppose it is *Virtue* in the South, *Chivalry*, exalted *Patriotism* or inspired *Intellect*. . . . It is the insanity of one-idea *Enthusiasts*, the weak folly of besotted *Ignorance*, the rabid rage of disappointed *Aspirants* . . . whose unbridled ambition knows no check of knowledge or of conscience."[26]

But the actual process of secession nevertheless caught Hammond up in its excitement, and once again he began to believe that an independent South would embody the ideals for which he had worked so long. In March 1861, he exclaimed enthusiastically to Simms, "all honor & glory to that wise & noble Convention." Hammond was con-

vinced that regional autonomy would "at once redeem the Southern
character & Southern intellect from the slanders of the North & England & place our people in their true position." Yet Hammond's ambivalence persisted. Perhaps the frequent mention of his name for president tied him to the Union, for he was little involved with the activities of the Southern independence movement. When Lincoln was
elected, Hammond resigned his Senate seat, but thought himself "very
foolish." His action, he declared, was like responding to an insult by
committing hari-kari.[27]

When war broke out, Hammond and Simms were eager to assist in
the defense of their region. Simms was full of suggestions about the
best means of seizing Sumter and financing the Confederate war effort,
but found, as he had many times before, that no one cared to listen.
Despite what he considered the "scientific" reliability of his plan for
fortifying the Charleston harbor, no one would heed his advice. "One
feels a little sore," he wrote, "that there should be no record of a
patriotism & a devotion to his country which has left . . . little time or
thought for anything else." By November of 1861, Southern reverses
on the battlefield had begun to seem to Simms, as they had to Holmes,
a kind of divine judgment. In a letter to Hammond, Simms evoked the
themes of personal alienation and cultural declension that long had
formed the foundation of their shared vision of the world: "I was fated
like Cassandra to speak the truth with nobody to listen. My plans
would most effectually have kept the enemy from breaking in at Port
Royal. It is not the Yankee race alone that needs purging and scourg-
ing. We too need punishment to destroy the packed jury, & old family
systems, the logrolling & the corruption everywhere." Simms readily
acknowledged that his conviction of the need for reform in the South
was motivated by the region's failure to heed his inspired counsels.[28]

From the beginning of the conflict, even in the early days of Southern successes, Simms and Hammond bemoaned the unprincipled Confederate leadership. Political influences, Simms believed, had served
to "lay on the shelf the able men. . . . It is melancholy," he mused, "to
look about and see how resourceless we are in intellectual power."
Both Simms and Hammond were disgusted with Jefferson Davis and
especially with the suppressions of individual rights that he justified as
war measures. "The Yankees would not stand from Lincoln what we
do from Davis," Hammond declared to Simms. The principles of the
Constitution must be maintained even under the most pressing circumstances, Hammond insisted. When the Confederacy demanded the
produce of his plantation to feed the troops and the labor of his slaves
to fortify Charleston, Hammond refused to cooperate. "I can never,"
he declared, "cease to do battle against the tyrant's plea of 'Necessity'
& the Heathen proverb that 'in war Laws are Silent.'" Principles must

prevail even in times of crisis. "To surrender these," Hammond declared, "would be to surrender all that Christian civilization has been contending for these last Eighteen centuries."[29]

Despite these differences with the Confederate government, Hammond was in other respects an enthusiastic supporter of the Southern cause; he lent money to the government, sent his sons off to war, and prayed earnestly for Confederate victory. But the bodily ailments about which he had complained all his life seemed to intensify in proportion with Southern defeats on the battlefield. On 13 November 1864, Hammond died. Simms was desolated when he heard the news of his dear friend's death and composed an elegy in his memory. Simms's poem was not just a farewell to Hammond, but a tribute to their friendship. Its imagery of barrenness and exile depicted the common plight that had bound the two Carolinians together for more than twenty years:

> O Brave One! Thou has tilled a barren soil,
>> Thou reap'st no fruit, though thou did'st sow the seed.
> Thou has but exile for thy years of toil,
>> No voice in council, though thy children bleed.
> . . . .
> Faction and party stilled that mighty voice
>> Which yet would teach us wisdom could we hear.
> . . . .
> So all earth's teachers have been overborne
>> By the coarse crowd, and fainting, droop or die;
> They bear the cross, their bleeding brows the thorn,
>> And ever hear the clamor, "Crucify!"[30]

Epilogue

he Sacred Circle gradually came to recognize that what Hammond called the "frenzy of the mob" made the institutionalization of intellect all but impossible in the beleagured South. War required an effective unity of action and opinion and thus defeated their fledgling movement for cultural revitalization and reform. With the acknowledgment of the failure of their shared purpose, the five intellectuals lost the most pressing social motive for interaction. But the five Southerners' lack of ultimate success should not obscure their influence during their years as statesmen, editors, essayists, and teachers. Although they always felt themselves excluded from the Southern mainstream, these men of mind made an important contribution through their nonconformity. As the South grew increasingly modern and secular and as it—and indeed these intellectuals themselves—succumbed to the seductive allure of nineteenth-century progress and material wealth, the members of the Sacred Circle offered tribute to the values of the past. They insisted upon the continuing relevance of older beliefs and standards in spite of social-structural change. By embodying both tradition and transcendence, they incarnated the past and the future in the present and thus offered the South a means of easing the tension aroused by its changing way of life.[1]

The pervasive cultural anxiety to which these intellectuals were responding found one outlet for its expression and resolution within the framework of the nineteenth century's widespread evangelicalism. Many Americans who, like these Southerners, deplored the tone and style of enthusiastic revivalism nevertheless adopted much of the evangelical vocabulary and outlook. For a generation uncertain about their world and their place in it, this configuration of attitudes and beliefs provided both a social identity and location within a timeless cosmos. Intellectuals torn between the transcendent and the practical found in evangelicalism a means of reconciling their conflicting commitments to thought and to action; this religious outlook encompassed man's ultimate concerns at the same time it assigned him the more immediate practical—and rewarding—duty of saving others.[2]

The same aspects of evangelicalism that had produced the nineteenth-century ferment of reform therefore offered the Southern men of mind a plausible means of achieving the social legitimacy they eagerly sought. Because Simms, Hammond, Tucker, Ruffin, and Holmes never succeeded in finding or creating any satisfactory intellectual institution, they substituted this widely accepted configuration of religious attitudes. Social institutions often serve to embody and structure more abstract arrangements of common values and expectations and to function as the vehicle through which these beliefs are transformed into active and continuing influences within society. But for intellectuals in the Old South, no such formal organizations existed to intermediate between generalized norms and particular social actions. The men of mind therefore were rendered directly dependent on the shared system of belief itself to establish their mundane relevance. Thus they defined themselves not in terms of social location or affiliation, but in relationship to transcendent conceptions of duty and mission. Through the leverage of evangelical values, rather than through specific institutions, the men of mind came closest to establishing a personal, social, and cultural identity.

The meaning of evangelicalism to the five Southerners is in many ways representative of their more general relationship to all ideas. Their constant use of intellectual modes—religious, philosophical, scientific, or historical—to legitimate their own social aspirations may make their professed idealism seem transparently self-serving. Yet to a considerable extent, every belief system functions in this manner. An individual identifies with a particular configuration of thought because of its appeal to his emotional and social as well as his cognitive needs. But this in no way diminishes the influence or importance of an organizing framework of belief in human life. Ideas serve to restructure perceptions, as well as to legitimate them. In the same way in which human beings desire social recognition and personal happiness, so, too, they have an irreducible need for meaning. These varied requirements all interact and conjointly influence man's relationship to the world. Thought is thus neither a totally dependent nor a wholly independent factor in human life; sometimes it influences, always it reflects the more tangible realities of mundane existence. To describe the motivation for these Southerners' actions as a simple desire for social status is unjustifiably to restrict the scope of their genuine concerns.

But their social "exile," their distance from any more formal institutions through which to relate to the world, rendered the five intellectuals especially dependent upon the realm of ideas and values for the

personal, social, and cultural self-definition they sought. Their lack
of individual psychological and social security exacerbated their feelings of cultural anxiety and rendered them particularly sensitive to
the uncertainty of beliefs and values in their world. Contemporary
society seemed to them confronted by a series of apparent paradoxes
that replicated the most pressing problems of their own lives. The
need to resolve this persistent tension between idealism and realism,
conviction and ambition, appeared to arise from the more general
problem of reconciling thought and action. To the men of mind it was
imperative that they minimize the apparent conflict between these
principles by insisting upon the immediate relevance of speculation.
That which is truly useful, they maintained, always must encompass
more than just the concerns of the moment; the transcendent, they
argued, is genuinely practical.

But the base minds of the nineteenth century in their sordidness had
ignored ultimate values and transformed realism into crass materialism, pragmatism into greed. Thought had been rendered all but irrele-
vant. The dichotomies the men of mind had identified thus attained
their most extreme and distressing polarization in the conflict between
avarice and disinterested virtue that constituted the greatest moral
challenge of their age. The opposition seemed to represent the essence
of the cultural differences between North and South, as well as the
important cleavages within their own society and the conflicting loyalties of their own lives. Thus the five Southerners rationalized the
world in terms of a series of contrasts that appeared to them not only
inextricably intertwined, but simultaneously relevant to social and
cultural as well as individual levels of human experience. A species
of yin and yang, these dichotomies comprehended and condensed
life's paradoxes into a single image and thus imposed an integrated
structure on the world.

Like any belief system, their conception of the world was rendered
particularly meaningful by what anthropologist Victor Turner would
call its "multivocality," its capacity to encompass and explain the various levels of man's experience, to satisfy his desire for different sorts
of meaning within a single framework of ideas. Man's need for coher-
ence and consistency motivates him to identify personal with social
and cultural concerns. Thus he seeks a single set of ideas that will provide an interpretive key to the multiple facets of his life. Every belief
system is required to impart these several kinds of meaning, for indeed
there can be no satisfactory explanation of the cosmos that does not
explain to man his own significance and place within it. Human beings
formulate configurations of belief to satisfy their hunger for understanding, and in this sense it is tautological to describe a belief system as self-serving. But this in no way justifies belittling the role of

ideas in human life. What is most significant about beliefs is not that they are designed to be useful to men, but that the purposes they serve are so varied and their ramifications so widespread. The particular manner in which man fulfills his desire for meaning structures and to a considerable degree determines the way in which all his other human needs—economic, social, and so forth—are satisfied.[3]

The lives of these five Southerners forcefully demonstrate the pervasive effect an individual's system of beliefs about his identity may exert upon all aspects of his existence. The intellectuals' conception of their genius did not simply legitimate their more self-interested aspirations, but organized and in many instances prescribed the essential nature of their relationship to the world.

As part of this endeavor to determine their role and purpose, the intellectuals formed a group to function as the vehicle through which their search for meaning might be satisfied. Because groups are the means through which an individual relates to the world around him, they serve as the interface of social, personal, and cultural influences upon individual behavior. The social context of the group and the reactions and criticisms of others encouraged the formation of both personal and social identity; the five Southerners arrived at their understanding of genius by observing it in each other as well as in themselves. Their feelings of isolation and of rejection became communal; the shared nature of their plight imparted to it a universal and transcendent character; they were no longer exiles, but prophets. The group structure influenced the men of mind to develop both a cultural and a social explanation of their situation and expression of their dilemma and therefore to imbue it with a more general significance. Thus the group served as the social context and encouragement for atypicality, for behavior and beliefs that would satisfy the variety of human needs that must coexist in any society, particularly one changing as rapidly as mid-nineteenth-century America.

The existence of such conflicting human needs, of such diverse roles, and of deep-seated anxiety about change in the ante-bellum South is perhaps surprising. But in many ways, Simms, Hammond, Tucker, Ruffin, and Holmes expressed concerns not unlike those of James Fenimore Cooper and other Northern intellectuals preoccupied with the demise of traditional values and the decline of gentility. The prestige of empirical science and the importance of the evangelical world view in the South are evidence of the cultural similarity between the two sections.[4]

But the crisis developing in the South rendered the dilemma of the man of mind particularly acute. To remain within his society, he had to confront its "peculiar institutions." His transformation of soil exhaustion into moral corruption and of slavery into stewardship forcefully represent the attempt to deal with the intellectual's perpetual quandary: the necessity of both accepting and transcending the tradition and the social context from which he arises. In their simultaneous love and hate for the South, in their need both to justify and reform, Hammond, Holmes, Tucker, Ruffin, and Simms thus embody not just the dilemma of the thinking Southerner, but the universal plight of the intellectual. But in the Old South, the growing sense of crisis, the intensity of cultural identity, and the fear of regional inadequacy rendered both the love and hate particularly strong. The predicament of the intellectual was proportionately aggravated. For this group of Southerners, the pressures of such ambivalence proved too great to bear. Ultimately they concluded that being an intellectual in the South was as rewarding, as Simms phrased it, as "drawing water in a sieve."[5]

Manuscript Collections Cited

AL: Alderman Library, University of Virginia, Charlottesville
    Bryan Papers
    Cocke Papers
    George Frederick Holmes Papers
    Rawlings Papers
    Edmund Ruffin Papers
    University of Virginia Faculty Minutes

ASSC: Archives of the State of South Carolina, Columbia
    Legislative Papers, 1831–1859

EGSL: Earl Gregg Swem Library, College of William and Mary, Williamsburg, Va.
    Dew Family Papers
    Benjamin Ewell Papers
    Minutes of the Faculty, 1830–1836
    George Frederick Holmes Papers
    Tucker-Coleman Collection

LC: Manuscript Division, Library of Congress, Washington, D.C.
    Albert Taylor Bledsoe Papers
    James Henry Hammond Papers
    George Frederick Holmes Papers
    Edmund Ruffin Papers

SCL: South Caroliniana Library, University of South Carolina, Columbia
    Hammond-Bryan-Cummings Papers
    James Henry Hammond Papers
    Robert Henry Papers
    Henry Junius Nott Papers
    Giles Patterson Papers
    William Campbell Preston Papers
    Charles Carroll Simms Collection
    James Henley Thornwell Papers
    Andrew Wardlaw Papers
    University of South Carolina Collection

SHC: Southern Historical Collection, University of North Carolina, Chapel Hill
    James Henry Hammond Papers

VHS: Virginia Historical Society, Richmond
    Bagby Papers
    Preston Family Papers
    Edmund Ruffin Papers

149

WPL: William Perkins Library, Duke University, Durham, N.C.
        James Henry Hammond Papers
        George Frederick Holmes Papers
        D. F. Jamison Papers
        William Campbell Preston Papers

Notes

PREFACE

1. Although there has been controversy about the degree of difference between North and South, it is safe to assert that most scholars have agreed that they are two distinct regions. Even those who have stressed the "Americanness" of the South generally have not denied the importance of regional differences, but simply have insisted that similarities outweigh them. On the Americanness of the South, see Charles G. Sellers, ed., *The Southerner as American* (Chapel Hill: University of North Carolina Press, 1960), and Grady McWhiney, *Southerners and Other Americans* (New York: Basic Books, 1973). For two recent discussions of Jefferson's ambivalence about his Southernness, see Fawn M. Brodie, *Thomas Jefferson: An Intimate History* (New York: W. W. Norton, 1974), and Winthrop D. Jordan, *White over Black: American Attitudes toward the Negro, 1550–1812* (Chapel Hill: University of North Carolina Press, 1968). See also W. J. Cash, *The Mind of the South* (New York: Alfred A. Knopf, 1941); C. Vann Woodward, *Tom Watson, Agrarian Rebel* (New York: Macmillan, 1938), *The Strange Career of Jim Crow* (New York: Oxford University Press, 1955, 1957, 1966), and *The Burden of Southern History* (Baton Rouge: Louisiana State University Press, 1960); William Faulkner, *Absalom Absalom!* (New York: Random House, 1936). For Woodward reflecting on Cash's reflections, see "The Elusive Mind of the South," in C. Vann Woodward, *American Counterpoint* (Boston: Little, Brown, 1964). For reflections on Woodward's reflections, see Sheldon Hackney, "Origins of the New South in Retrospect," *Journal of Southern History* 38 (1972): 191–216.

2. William Gilmore Simms, "Southern Literature," *Magnolia* 3 (1841): 72–73.

3. Carl Degler has recently considered a number of Southerners critical of their society in *The Other South: Southern Dissenters in the Nineteenth Century* (New York: Harper & Row, 1974). The individuals with whom he is concerned, however, seem more isolated from the mainstream of Southern life and thought than were the five members of the Sacred Circle.

4. Edward Shils, *The Intellectuals and the Powers* (Chicago: University of Chicago Press, 1972), p. 3. See also: Shils, *Center and Periphery: Essays in Macrosociology* (Chicago: University of Chicago Press, 1975); Philip Rieff, ed., *On Intellectuals* (New York: Free Press, 1965); George B. de Huszar, *The Intellectuals: A Controversial Portrait* (Glencoe: Free Press, 1960); Florian Znaniecki, *The Social Role of the Man of Knowledge* (New York: Columbia University Press, 1940). Scholars frequently have remarked upon the high correlation between social marginality and the choice of an intellectual role. See Georg Simmel, "The Stranger," in *The Sociology of Georg Simmel,* ed. and trans. Kurt H. Wolff (Glencoe: Free Press, 1950); Alfred Schutz, "The Stranger," *American Journal of Sociology* 44 (1944): 500–507; Thorstein Veblen, "The Intellectual Pre-Eminence of Jews," *Political Science Quar-*

terly 24 (1919): 33–42. The anthropologist Victor Turner has broadened this conception from purely social to wider cultural lack of place, which he calls liminality. In this state, man is "liberated from normative demands," even if just for a brief period, and thus is able to reflect critically on his world. Out of liminality, Turner suggests, arise philosophy, science, art, and religion (*Dramas, Fields, and Metaphors: Symbolic Action in Human Society* [Ithaca: Cornell University Press, 1974]), pp. 18, 23–59.

INTRODUCTION

1. See description of Edmund Ruffin (1794–1865) in the Fredericksburg, Va., *Herald*, Editorial, clipping in "Incidents of My Life," 3:242, Edmund Ruffin Papers, VHS.

2. Ruffin, "Incidents," 1:1. The major secondary works on Ruffin are Avery Craven's biography, *Edmund Ruffin, Southerner: A Study in Secession* (1932; reprint ed., Baton Rouge: Louisiana State University Press, 1966), and William Scarborough's "Introduction" to Edmund Ruffin, *The Diary of Edmund Ruffin,* vol. 1, *October 1856 to April 1862,* ed. William Kauffman Scarborough (Baton Rouge: Louisiana State University Press, 1972). This is the first volume of Scarborough's edition of the manuscript Ruffin Diary in the Edmund Ruffin Papers, Manuscript Division, Library of Congress. The other major repository of Ruffin material is the Ruffin Papers, Virginia Historical Society, although there is a small collection of Edmund Ruffin Papers in the Manuscript Division, Alderman Library, University of Virginia, Charlottesville.

3. Ruffin, "Publication of the 'Southern Magazine and Monthly Review,' " *Farmers' Register* 8 (1840): 635; "The Farm and Farming of the Rev. J. H. Turner," ibid. 10 (1842): 155, n.

4. James Henry Hammond (1807–1864) to Edmund Ruffin, 14 Feb. 1844, Ruffin Papers, VHS. The major secondary sources on Hammond are a biography by Elizabeth Merrit, *James Henry Hammond, 1807–64* (Baltimore: Johns Hopkins University Press, 1923), and a more recent and more useful, but unpublished dissertation: Robert Cinnamond Tucker, "James Henry Hammond, South Carolinian" (Ph.D. diss., University of North Carolina, 1959). Hammond's voluminous personal papers are divided chiefly between the James Henry Hammond Papers, Manuscript Division, Library of Congress and the James Henry Hammond and Hammond-Bryan-Cummings Papers in the South Caroliniana Library at the University of South Carolina, Columbia, South Carolina, although there are small collections of Hammond material in the Manuscript Division, William Perkins Library, Duke University, and in the Southern Historical Collection at the University of North Carolina in Chapel Hill.

5. Ruffin, "Incidents," 1:221; Ruffin, *Diary,* ed. Scarborough, 20 April 1851, 1:75.

6. Hammond to Ruffin, 7 July 1844, 9 Nov. 1849, Ruffin Papers, VHS; Ruffin to Hammond, 6 July 1845, Hammond Papers, LC. See also Hammond to Ruffin, 12 May, 15 June 1846, Ruffin Papers, VHS.

7. See Robert Sutton, "Nostalgia, Pessimism, and Malaise: The Doomed Aristocrats in Late Jeffersonian Virginia," *Virginia Magazine of History and Biography* 76 (1968): 41–55.

8. William Gilmore Simms (1806–1870) to James Henry Hammond, 16 Feb. 1840, *The Letters of William Gilmore Simms,* coll. and ed. Mary C. Simms Oliphant, Alfred Taylor Odell, and T. C. Duncan Eaves, 5 vols. (Columbia: University of South Carolina Press, 1952–56), 1:168. In addition to these extremely valuable volumes, the major repository of Simms material is the Charles Carroll Simms Collection in the South Caroliniana Library, University of South Carolina. The secondary literature on Simms is extremely large and includes the classic though badly flawed biography by William Trent, *William Gilmore Simms* (Boston: Houghton Mifflin, 1892), and Jon Wakelyn, *The Politics of a Literary Man: William Gilmore*

Simms (Westport, Conn.: Greenwood Press, 1973), the most recent treatment of Simms's life. The literature by and about Simms is too enormous to summarize here. For more complete bibliographic information see Drew Gilpin Faust, "A Sacred Circle: The Social Role of the Intellectual in the Old South, 1840–1860" (Ph.D. diss., University of Pennsylvania, 1975), and the centennial edition of *The Writings of William Gilmore Simms* being published by the University of South Carolina Press.

9. James Henry Hammond, Diary, 30 March 1841, Hammond Papers, LC; Paul Hamilton Hayne, "Ante-Bellum Charleston," *Southern Bivouac* 1 (1885): 257–68; Hammond, Diary, 28 Feb. 1841, Hammond Papers, LC.

10. William Gilmore Simms to Edward Spann Hammond, 20 Nov. 1864, in *Letters of Simms,* 4:469–70.

11. Hammond, Diary, 5 Nov. 1841, Hammond to President James Polk, 4 Sept. 1847, both in Hammond Papers, LC; Simms to Thomas Burke, 7 Sept. 1856, *Letters of Simms,* 3:447.

12. Simms, "Southern Literature," *Magnolia* 3 (1841): 72–73.

13. George Frederick Holmes (1820–1897) to William Gilmore Simms, 3 Nov. 1843, Letterbook, Holmes Papers, WPL; Simms to Holmes, 5 Nov. 1844, *Letters of Simms,* 1:435; Simms to Holmes, 18 Nov. 1844, Letterbook, Holmes Papers, WPL; Holmes, "Present State of Letters," *Southern Literary Messenger* 10 (1844): 410. Holmes was not the only writer Simms arranged to meet this way. See Simms to Holmes 17 April 1844, *Letters of Simms,* 1:415. The major collections of Holmes materials are the George Frederick Holmes Papers at Duke and the George Frederick Holmes Papers in the Manuscript Division of the Library of Congress. There are also small collections of Holmes Papers in the Manuscript Division, Earl Gregg Swem Memorial Library, College of William and Mary, and the Manuscript Division, Alderman Library, University of Virginia. Neal C. Gillespie has written a very useful recent biography that devotes particular attention to Holmes's thought. See Gillespie, *The Collapse of Orthodoxy: The Intellectual Ordeal of George Frederick Holmes* (Charlottesville: University of Virginia Press, 1972).

14. The papers of Nathaniel Beverley Tucker (1784–1851) are part of the Tucker-Coleman Collection in the Manuscript Division of the Earl Gregg Swem Library of the College of William and Mary. The major secondary treatments of Tucker are Percy Winfield Turrentine, "The Life and Works of Nathaniel Beverly Tucker," 3 vols. (Ph.D. diss., Harvard University, 1952), and Robert J. Brugger, *Beverley Tucker: Heart over Head in the Old South* (forthcoming, Johns Hopkins University Press).

15. Hammond to Tucker, 12 Nov. 1847, Tucker-Coleman Collection, EGSL; Tucker to Hammond, 13 March 1847, Hammond Papers, LC. See Holmes to Tucker, 20 May 1850, Tucker-Coleman Collection, EGSL, for a summary of Tucker's influence on Holmes; Hammond to Tucker, 12 May 1847, Tucker-Coleman Collection, EGSL; Tucker to Hammond, 14 April 1848, Hammond Papers, LC.

16. Tucker to Hammond, 13 March 1847, Hammond Papers, LC; Simms to Tucker, 30 Jan. 1850, *Letters of Simms,* 3:8.

17. There are compelling justifications for moving away from more traditionally— and perhaps more easily—defined areas of historical inquiry to explore less formalized sorts of human interaction. In recent years, historians interested in the "history of the inarticulate" have paid extravagant attention to these sorts of problems, but they are just as relevant within the experience of the literate. For example, historians too long have ignored the importance of the small, largely unstructured group or network. As sociologists long have recognized, informal groups are the primary units of the social system.

On groups, see Theodore M. Mills, *The Sociology of Small Groups* (Englewood Cliffs: Prentice-Hall, 1967); Dorwin Cartwright and Alvin Zander, eds., *Group Dynamics: Research and Theory* (Evanston: Row Peterson, 1953); A. Paul Hare, *Handbook of Small Group Research* (New York: Free Press, 1962); Clovis Shepherd, *Small Groups: Some Sociological Perspectives* (San Francisco: Chandler, 1964); A. Paul Hare, E. F. Borgatta, and R. F. Bales, *Small Groups: Studies in Social Interaction* (New York: Alfred A. Knopf, 1955; rev. ed., 1965).

For examples of recent historical work on networks, see Carroll Smith-Rosenberg, "The Female World of Love and Ritual: Relations between Women in Nineteenth-Century America," *Signs* 1 (1975): 1–29, and Alice Rossi, "Social Roots of the Woman's Movement in America," in Alice Rossi, ed., *Feminist Papers From Adams to de Beauvoir* (New York: Columbia University Press, 1973). For a study of a circle of intellectual men, see Charles Rosenberg, "Science and Social Values in Nineteenth-Century America: A Case Study in the Growth of Scientific Institutions," in Arnold Thackray and Everett Mendelsohn, eds., *Science and Values* (New York: Humanities Press, 1974).

18. William Campbell Preston and William Harper, for example, were cousins to Tucker and Holmes and interacted with the other members of the network as well. Unfortunately, however, neither left personal papers extensive enough to permit close investigation of their personal and intellectual relationships. A similar situation exists with David F. Jamison of Orangeburg, South Carolina, neighbor to Simms, Hammond, and Holmes and a friend to Ruffin as well. See D. F. Jamison Papers, Manuscript Division, William Perkins Library, Duke University; Preston Family Papers, Virginia Historical Society, Richmond; William Campbell Preston Papers, Manuscript Division, William Perkins Library, Duke University, and William Campbell Preston Papers, South Carolniana Library, University of South Carolina, Columbia. The intellectual aristocracy of the South may have been nearly as closely integrated and related through ties of blood and marriage as was the English elite N. G. Annan describes in "The Intellectual Aristocracy," in J. H. Plumb, ed., *Studies in Social History: A Tribute to G. M. Trevelyan* (London: Longmans, Green, 1955).

CHAPTER ONE

1. Nathaniel Beverley Tucker, Lecture 5, Ms., n.d., Tucker-Coleman Collection, EGSL.

2. Robert W. B. Elliott, Jr., "Hindrances to the Progress of Literature at the South," Class Medal Essay, 3 Dec. 1860, South Carolina College, Ms., University of South Carolina Collection, SCL.

3. Ibid.

4. "Petition of Teachers' Association and Others," 1854, Union District Legislative Papers, 1831–59, Public Improvements, Education, Ms., ASSC. J. D. B. DeBow, *The Industrial Resources of the Southern and Western States*, 3 vols. (New Orleans: DeBow's, 1853), 1:71; B. B. Minor, "Education in the Southern and Western States," *Southern Literary Messenger* 13 (1847): 686–87. The secondary literature on education in the ante-bellum South is sparse. See, however, Edgar Knight, *Public Education in the South* (New York: Ginn, 1922); Knight, *Education in the United States* (New York: Ginn, 1951); Knight, ed., *A Documentary History of Education in the South Before 1860*, 5 vols. (Chapel Hill: University of North Carolina Press, 1949); William R. Taylor, "Toward a Definition of Orthodoxy: The Patrician South and the Common Schools," *Harvard Educational Review* 26 (1966): 412–26; M. C. S. Noble, *A History of the Public Schools of North Carolina* (Chapel Hill: University of North Carolina Press, 1930); Elbert W. G. Boogher, *Secondary Education in Georgia* (Philadelphia: I. F. Huntzinger, 1933); John F. Thomason, *Foundations of the Public Schools of South Carolina* (Columbia: State Company, 1925); James Isaac Copeland, "The Movement for Free Schools in South Carolina to 1868" (Ph.D. diss., University of North Carolina, 1957); Cornelius Heatwole, *A History of Education in Virginia* (New York: Macmillan, 1916); John S. Ezell, "A Southern Education for Southrons," *Journal of Southern History* 17 (1951): 303–27; Albea Godbold, *The Church College of the Old South* (Durham: Duke University Press, 1944); E. Merton Coulter, *College Life in the Old South* (New York: Macmillan, 1928), as well as histories of specific individual institutions of

higher learning. See, for example, Daniel Hollis, *University of South Carolina*, 2 vols. (Columbia: University of South Carolina Press, 1951, 1955); J. H. Easterby, *A History of the College of Charleston* (Charleston: Trustees of the College of Charleston, 1935). One is compelled to turn to primary sources to gain any sense of the educational situation. I used three major kinds of primary sources on education, chiefly in relationship to the states of Virginia and South Carolina, the two loci of most of the activities of the Sacred Circle. First, official documents and reports, as for example, Grand Jury Presentments to the South Carolina Legislature dealing with the Free School System, in Legislative Papers, 1831–59, Legal System, Presentments, ASSC, or R. F. W. Allston, *Report on the Free School System of South Carolina Printed by Order of the Legislature for the Use of the Commissioners of Free Schools* (Columbia: A. S. Johnston, 1846); second, the personal papers of students and professors at ante-bellum schools and colleges and manuscript records of these institutions as, for example, the Henry Junius Nott Papers, Giles Patterson Papers, Robert Henry Papers, Andrew Wardlaw Papers, James Henley Thornwell Papers, Faculty Minutes, South Carolina College, 1845–53, University of South Carolina Collection, all at South Caroliniana Library, University of South Carolina, Columbia; the Albert Taylor Bledsoe Papers, Manuscript Division, Library of Congress; the Faculty Minutes, University of Virginia, Manuscript Division, Alderman Library, University of Virginia; and the Dew Family Papers, Benjamin Ewell Papers, and Faculty Minute Books, William and Mary College Papers, all in the Manuscript Division of the Earl Gregg Swem Library, the College of William and Mary; third, printed addresses and articles in contemporary periodicals dealing with education. See, for example, B. B. Minor, "College Convention of Virginia," *Southern Literary Messenger* 10 (1844): 121–22; Richard Morris, "Southern Educational and Industrial Development," *DeBow's Review* 20 (1856): 622–26, or John Reuben Thompson, *Education and Literature in Virginia: An Address Delivered before the Literary Societies of Washington College, Lexington, Virginia, 18 June, 1850* (Richmond: H. K. Ellyson, 1850).

5. "Presentment of Barnwell District Grand Jury," 1853, Legislative Papers, 1831–59, Legal System, Presentments, Ms., ASSC.

6. Thompson, *Education and Literature*, p. 14.

7. "Address to the People of Virginia by the Education Convention in Richmond, August 28, 1845," *Southern Literary Messenger* 11 (1845): 605. Estimating literacy rates is extremely difficult, as is developing a useful working definition for the concept of literacy itself. The most recent effort to deal with the problem in historical terms is Kenneth Lockridge, *Literacy in Colonial New England: An Inquiry into the Social Context of Literacy in the Early Modern West* (New York: W. W. Norton, 1974). As its title indicates, however, Lockridge's work tells us little about the South. On the census of 1850, see J. D. B. DeBow, *Compendium of the Seventh Census* (Washington, D.C.: U. S. Government Printing Office, 1854), p. 153. Charles Sydnor estimated the Southern illiteracy rate at 33 percent (*The Development of Southern Sectionalism* [Baton Rouge: Louisiana State University Press, 1948], p. 59).

8. "Message of Governor John Manning," 29 Nov. 1853, Ms. in Legislative Papers, 1831–59, Public Improvements, Education, ASSC.

9. The classic treatment of this problem is Clement Eaton, *The Freedom of Thought Struggle in the Old South* (Durham: Duke University Press, 1940).

10. Henry Junius Nott to Governor George McDuffie, 25 Nov. 1835, Nott Papers, SCL.

11. *DeBow's Review* 31 (1861): 347–61.

12. "Fearful Riot at South Carolina College," New York *Weekly Tribune*, 15 March 1856, p. 6; Faculty Minute Books, 1830–36, pp. 15–19, EGSL; see also Maximilian LaBorde, *History of the South Carolina College, from Its Incorporation, December 19, 1801, to November 25, 1857, Including Sketches of Its Presidents and Professors, with an Appendix* (Columbia: P. B. Glass, 1859).

13. Robert Wardlaw to Andrew Wardlaw, 25 April 1850, Andrew Wardlaw Papers, SCL.

14. Scholarships were not numerous at most Southern colleges and universities, leading one Virginian to conclude that higher education was "resorted to principally by the sons of the wealthy" ("Education in Virginia," *Southern Literary Messenger* 7 [1841]: 633–34). See also "Appendix," LaBorde, *History of South Carolina College.*

15. George Frederick Holmes, Diary, 15 Dec. 1857, Holmes Papers, WPL.

16. Jay Hubbell, "Literary Nationalism in the Old South," in David Kelly Jackson, ed., *American Studies in Honor of William Kenneth Boyd* (Durham: Duke University Press, 1940); Elliott, "Hindrances," p. 3.

17. Henry Timrod, quoted in Willard Thorp, "The Writer as Pariah in the Old South," in R. C. Simonini, ed., *Southern Writers: Appraisals in our Time* (Charlottesville: University of Virginia Press, 1958), p. 4. See also Jay B. Hubbell, *The South in American Literature, 1607–1900* (Durham: Duke University Press, 1954); Richard Beale Davis, *Intellectual Life in Jefferson's Virginia, 1790–1830* (Chapel Hill: University of North Carolina Press, 1964).

18. "Free Schools and the University of Virginia," *Southern Literary Messenger* 20 (1854): 71.

19. Alfred Glaze Smith, Jr., *Economic Readjustment of an Old Cotton State: South Carolina, 1820–1860* (Columbia: University of South Carolina Press, 1958). The question of soil exhaustion and agricultural reform in the seaboard South has been debated by historians since Avery Craven published *Soil Exhaustion as a Factor in the Agricultural History of Virginia and Maryland, 1606–1860* (1926; reprint ed., Gloucester: Peter Smith, 1965) and Paul Gates undertook to challenge some of his conclusions in *The Farmer's Age: Agriculture 1815–1860* (1960; reprint ed., New York: Harper Torchbooks, 1968), pp. 109–10. In recent years, the condition of agriculture in the South has been subjected to increasing scrutiny by the tools of the new economic historians. As Harold Woodman recently summarized, we all used to know the South was poor, but now we are not so sure. Despite his reservations about Southern economic inferiority in the ante-bellum period, Woodman nevertheless challenges some of the data on the basis of which historians such as Stanley Engerman and Richard Easterlin have endeavored to overthrow the traditional picture of Southern economic backwardness. For our purposes—understanding the perceptions of Hammond, Holmes, Ruffin, Tucker, and Simms—it seems sufficient to note that whatever the *objective* reality of comparative regional per capita income and growth rates, these nineteenth-century Southerners clearly identified a crisis situation, at least in the eastern South. Plantations deserted by individuals moving west, decreasing productivity of uncared-for lands, and popular resistance to agricultural reforms seemed to them indications of severe economic distress. Woodman himself has pointed out that Easterlin and Engerman's optimistic assessments of Southern wealth do not for the most part take account of the striking differences between the seaboard and the southwestern states. It is also important to recognize that even in Engerman's terms, the South *had* experienced a relative decline since the time of the Revolution when its per capita income was 14.5 percent above that of the rest of the nation. The issue of Southern economic growth in this period thus poses difficulties on two levels: the objective level of what actually occurred—a question historians are vigorously debating; and a second, more subjective level of what the state of the Southern economy meant to the inhabitants of the region. See Richard Easterlin, "Interregional Differences in Per Capita Income, Population, and Total Income, 1840–1950," in William Parker, ed., *Trends in the American Economy in the Nineteenth Century,* National Bureau of Economic Research, Studies in Income and Wealth, vol. 24 (Princeton: Princeton University Press, 1960); Harold Woodman, "New Perspectives on Southern Economic Development; A Comment," *Agricultural History* 49 (1975): 374–80; Stanley Engerman, "A Reconsideration of Southern Economic Growth, 1770–1860," *Agricultural History* 49 (1975): 343–61; Morton Rothstein, "The Cotton Frontier of the Antebellum United States: A Meth-

odological Battleground," *Agricultural History* 44 (1970): 149–65. The evidence
for perception of decline among seaboard Southerners is extensive. For two examples
beyond the confines of the Sacred Circle, see the debates in the Virginia legislature
in "Appendix" to Joseph Robert, *The Road from Monticello: A Study of the Virginia Slavery Debate of 1832* (Durham: Duke University Press, 1941), and "Record
of the Proceedings of the Beech Island Agricultural Club 1856–62, Beech Island
South Carolina," typescript, SCL. I am grateful to Morton Rothstein for the helpful
comments he made to me regarding these issues.

20. Edmund Ruffin, "To Planters," undated clipping from the Charleston *Mercury* in Ruffin Diary, 1843, Ruffin Papers, VHS.

21. Craven, *Soil Exhaustion;* Robert Sutton, "Nostalgia, Pessimism, and Malaise:
The Doomed Aristocrats in Late Jeffersonian Virginia," *Virginia Magazine of History and Biography* 76 (1968): 41–55.

22. William Gilmore Simms to James Lawson, 23 Oct. 1846, *The Letters of William Gilmore Simms,* coll. and ed. Mary C. Simms Oliphant, Alfred Taylor Odell,
and T. C. Duncan Eaves, 5 vols. (Columbia: University of South Carolina Press,
1952–56), 3:195.

23. Holmes to W. G. Minor, 9 Jan. 1845, Holmes Letterbook, Holmes Diary,
9 Feb. 1853, Holmes to David Flavel Jamison, 14 April 1847, Holmes Letterbook,
all in Holmes Papers, WPL.

24. Simms to James Lawson, 12 Dec. 1846, *Letters of Simms,* 2: 238; Nathaniel
Beverley Tucker to St. George Tucker, 26 Feb. 1815, Tucker-Coleman Collection,
EGSL.

25. William Gilmore Simms, "Southern Agriculture," *Magnolia* 4 (1842): 131,
135; Edmund Ruffin, "Sketch of the Progress of Agriculture in Virginia and the
Causes of Its Decline and Present Depression: An Address to the Historical and
Philosophical Society of Virginia," *Farmers' Register* 12 (1836): 754; William Gilmore Simms, *The Social Principle: The True Source of National Permanence* (Tuscaloosa: Erosophic Society of the University of Alabama, 1843), p. 42; James Henry
Hammond, "Anniversary Oration," *Proceedings of the Agricultural Convention of
the State Agricultural Society of South Carolina, 1839–1845* (Columbia: Sumner
and Carroll, 1846), pp. 182–83. See also William Gilmore Simms, "Agriculture in
South Carolina," *Magnolia* n.s., 2 (1843): 200–203; Simms, "Ancient and Modern
Culture," *Magnolia* 4 (1842): 308–11; Simms, "Our Agricultural Condition," *Southern and Western Monthly Magazine* 1 (1845): 73–84; James Henry Hammond,
"Gov. Hammond's Report," *Southern Cultivator* 3 (1845): 114–15; "Marling in
South Carolina," *Farmers' Register* 10 (1842): 366–67; "Overseers," *Carolina
Planter* 7 (1844): 25–30; "Recent and Extensive Marling in South Carolina,"
Farmers' Register 10 (1842): 519–22; "Report of the Committee of the Barnwell
Agricultural Society on the Culture of Cotton," *Farmers' Register* 8 (1840): 341;
"Rules of the Plantation," *Carolina Planter* 1 (1840): 49–50.

26. Simms, "Southern Agriculture," p. 131.

27. Hammond to Simms, 27 Aug. 1841, Hammond Papers, LC; William Gilmore
Simms, *Views and Reviews in American Literature, History, and Fiction,* 1st ser.
ed. Hugh C. Holman (1845; reprint ed., Cambridge: Belknap Press of Harvard
University), p. 121.

28. Hammond, Diary, 6 Oct. 1839, Hammond Papers, SCL; William Gilmore
Simms, "Southern Literature," *Magnolia* 3 (1841): 71; Holmes to Auguste Comte,
21 Sept. 1853, Holmes Letterbook, Holmes Papers, WPL.

CHAPTER TWO

1. William Gilmore Simms to James Henry Hammond, 24 Nov. 1852, *The Letters
of William Gilmore Simms,* coll. and ed. Mary C. Simms Oliphant, Alfred Taylor
Odell, and T. C. Duncan Eaves, 5 vols. (Columbia: University of South Carolina

Press, 1952–56), 3:210; Simms, "Year of Consolation," *Southern Quarterly Review* 12 (1847): 195; Simms to John Esten Cooke, 26 July 1859, *Letters of Simms,* 4:164–65.

2. James Henry Hammond to M. C. M. Hammond, 12 May 1849, Hammond Papers, SCL; George Frederick Holmes to D. F. Jamison, 12 May 1846, Holmes Papers, WPL; Hammond to Simms, 19 June 1845, Hammond Papers, LC; Hammond to Edmund Ruffin, 6 Feb. 1846, Ruffin Papers, VHS.

3. Hammond to Simms, 8 Aug. 1848, Hammond Papers, LC; Simms to Holmes, 18 Nov., 1844, 30 Dec., 1844, *Letters of Simms,* 1:442, 449.

4. Holmes to Hammond, 21 Dec. 1846, Hammond Papers, LC. See, for example, Nathaniel Beverley Tucker's review of Hammond's Oration at South Carolina College in the *Southern Quarterly Review* 17 (1850): 37–48; William Gilmore Simms on Tucker in "Southern Convention," *Southern Quarterly Review* 18 (1850): 191–232; Simms, "Gen. Hammond's Letters on Slavery," *Southern and Western Monthly Magazine* 2 (1845): 71–72.

5. Simms to Holmes, 6 Nov. 1844, *Letters of Simms,* 1:434; Tucker to Hammond, 12 July 1849, Tucker-Coleman Collection, EGSL; Ruffin to A. P. Upshur, 24 Oct. 1840, Tucker-Coleman Collection, EGSL; Hammond to Simms, 1 April, 25 July, 1847, Hammond Papers, LC.

6. Tucker to Hammond, 26 March, 1850, Hammond Papers, LC.; Hammond to Tucker, 4 March, 1847, Tucker-Coleman Collection, EGSL.

7. Simms to John Esten Cooke, 26 July 1859, *Letters of Simms,* 4:164–65.

8. Simms to James Lawson, 7 April 1845, *Letters of Simms,* 2:48; Hammond, Diary, 5 Nov. 1841, Hammond Papers, LC.; Simms to Hammond, 20 May 1845, *Letters of Simms,* 2:64; Hammond to Simms, 10 Feb. 1849, Hammond, Diary, 21 June 1842, Hammond to Simms, 10 Feb. 1849, all in Hammond Papers, LC.; Edmund Ruffin, Diary, 4 Feb. 1861, Ruffin Papers, LC; Holmes, "Miscellaneous Notes," Holmes Papers, WPL; Tucker to John Randolph, 12 Sept. 1807, Tucker-Coleman Collection, EGSL.

9. Simms, "Year of Consolation," p. 200; Simms, "A New Spirit of the Age," *Southern Quarterly Review* 4 (1845): 314.

10. See Tucker's comparison of himself and the adored Randolph to Byron in Manuscript Fragments, Tucker-Coleman Collection, EGSL, and Holmes's discussion of Tennyson as a model of Romantic genius, "Tennyson's Poems," *Southern Literary Messenger* 19 (1853): 649–58. On the Byronic model of genius, see Peter Thorslev, *The Byronic Hero: Types and Prototypes* (Minneapolis: University of Minnesota Press, 1962), and Howard Mumford Jones, *Revolution and Romanticism* (Cambridge: Belknap Press of Harvard University, 1974). See also William Longton's discussion of the importance of the idea of suffering and Romantic agony to the Southern intellectual in "Some Aspects of Intellectual Activity in Ante-Bellum South Carolina, 1830–1860" (Ph.D. diss., University of North Carolina, 1969). The debate about differences among Romanticisms was inaugurated by Arthur O. Lovejoy in "On the Discrimination of Romanticisms" in his *Essays in the History of Ideas* (New York: George Braziller, 1955). On this issue, see also: Meyer H. Abrams, *The Mirror and the Lamp: Romantic Theory and the Critical Tradition* (New York: Oxford University Press, 1953); Jacques Barzun, *Classic, Romantic, and Modern* (Boston: Little, Brown, 1961), Raymond Benoit, *Single Nature's Double Name: The Collectedness of the Conflicting in British and American Romanticism* (The Hague: Mouton, 1973), Northrop Frye, ed., *Romanticism Reconsidered: Selected Papers from the English Institute* (New York: Columbia University Press, 1963); Lilian Furst, *Romanticism in Perspective: A Comparative Study of Aspects of the Romantic Movements in England, France, and Germany* (New York: St. Martins, 1969); Irving Babbitt, *Rousseau and Romanticism* (Boston: Houghton Mifflin, 1919). On more general problems of intellectual periodization and categorization in this era see Michael Timko, "The Victorianism of Victorian Literature," in *New Literary History* 6 (1975): 607–28; Robert Langbaum, *The Modern Spirit: Essays on the Continuity of Nineteenth and Twentieth Century Literature* (New York:

Oxford University Press, 1970); Morse Peckham, *Victorian Revolutionaries: Speculations on Some Heroes of a Culture Crisis* (New York: George Braziller, 1970); Gertrude Himmelfarb, *Victorian Minds* (New York: Alfred A. Knopf, 1968), Walter Houghton, *The Victorian Frame of Mind, 1830–1870* (New Haven: Yale University Press, 1970).

11. See Hammond's Commonplace Book, Hammond Papers, SCL, and Holmes's "Miscellaneous Notes," "Notes on Various Books," and Commonplace Book, Holmes Papers, WPL. On the characterization of a world view as both a "model of" and a "model for" human life, see Clifford Geertz, *The Interpretation of Cultures* (New York: Basic Books, 1973).

12. Hammond to My Dear Friend, 17 July 1826, Hammond to Elisha Hammond, 23 Feb. 1827, both in Hammond Papers, SCL; Hammond, Diary, 19, 30 April 1837, Hammond Papers, LC.

13. Tucker, "Midnight. March 23, 1830," Manuscript Fragments, Tucker-Coleman Collection, EGSL.

14. See Babbitt, *Rousseau and Romanticism*, p. 250; Carlyle was acknowledged by the members of the Sacred Circle to be a particularly important influence. Tucker informed Hammond in a letter of 29 May 1849 that he had just sent his collected works to Carlyle (Hammond Papers, LC). For a discussion of the influence of Carlyle on Simms, see Hugh Holman, "Introduction" to Simms, *Views and Reviews in American Literature, History, and Fiction*, 1st ser. ed. Hugh C. Holman (1845; reprint ed., Cambridge: Belknap Press of Harvard University, 1962), p. xi. See also Gerald Straka, "The Influence of Thomas Carlyle in the Old South, 1848–1865" (M.A. thesis, University of Virginia, 1953).

15. Raymond Williams, *Culture and Society, 1780–1950* (1958; reprint ed., New York: Harper Torchbooks, 1966).

16. Holmes, "The Present Condition of Letters," *Southern Literary Messenger* 11 (1845): 172; Holmes, "Miscellaneous Notes," p. 85, Holmes Papers, WPL.

17. Hammond to Simms, 12 Nov. 1849, Hammond Papers, LC.

18. Williams, *Culture and Society*, p. xvi.

19. On this conception of the artist, see Chapter 3, as well as Wordsworth's "Advertisement" (1798) and "Prefaces" to succeeding editions of *Lyrical Ballads* in *Selected Poems and Prefaces*, ed. Jack Stittinger (Boston: Houghton Mifflin, 1965), pp. 443–92; and Percy B. Shelley's description of geniuses as "legislators" who are "unacknowledged" in "A Defense of Poetry," 1821, reprinted in *Shelley's Prose: Or the Trumpet of a Prophecy*, ed. David Lee Clark (Albuquerque: University of New Mexico Press, 1954), p. 279; Victor Hugo, "Ce Siècle avait deux ans," in *Les Feuilles d'automne, oeuvres complètes, poésie*, 46 vols. (Paris: L'lmprimerie Nationale, 1904–52), 2: 249–52.

20. On Romanticism in the Old South specifically, see Rollin G. Osterweis, *Romanticism and Nationalism in the Old South* (New Haven: Yale University Press, 1949). For student addresses, see commencement programs for 7 Dec. 1846, 9 May 1851, 5 May 1848, University of South Carolina Papers, SCL.

21. "Fate of Genius," Hammond, Commonplace Book, Hammond Papers, SCL.

22. Simms, "Year of Consolation," p. 201; Tucker to John Randolph, 19 Feb. 1807, Tucker-Coleman Collection, EGSL.

23. Simms, "Year of Consolation," p. 195.

24. Tucker to Elizabeth Coalter Bryan, 24 Aug. 1839, Bryan Papers, AL.

25. Tucker, Autobiographical Fragment, n.d., Tucker-Coleman Collection, EGSL.

26. Ibid.; Tucker to John Randolph, July 1808, 19 Feb. 1806, Tucker-Coleman, EGSL.

27. On the issue of St. George Tucker's alleged mistreatment of his sons, see Anna B. Dudley to Nathaniel Beverley Tucker, 7 Jan. 1840, Tucker-Coleman Collection, EGSL. On Beverley's feelings of rejection, see his letter to St. George Tucker, 11 March 1808, Tucker-Coleman Collection, EGSL.

28. Tucker to John Randolph, 19 Feb. 1807, Tucker-Coleman Collection, EGSL.

29. Tucker to John Randoph, 19 Feb. 1807, Tucker-Coleman Collection, EGSL; Tucker to Elizabeth Coalter, 15 May 1829, Bryan Papers, AL.

30. Tucker to John Randoph, 19 Feb. 1806, Tucker-Coleman Collection, EGSL. He also described Randolph as a surrogate father in a letter to Lucy Tucker, 30 March 1833, Tucker-Coleman Collection, EGSL.
31. Tucker to Elizabeth Coalter, 13 July 1839, Bryan Papers, AL.
32. Tucker to John Randolph, 26 March 1808, 15 March 1832, 26 May 1825, Tucker-Coleman Collection, EGSL.
33. Simms, "Year of Consolation," pp. 194–95.
34. In an address before the Euphradian Society at South Carolina College, 26 May 1848, J. Richardson exemplified this common conception when he characterized Byron as a genius with "no fond mother to smile upon her boy but with an unnatural woman who neither loved nor cared for him" (Euphradian Society Papers, University of South Carolina Collection, SCL).
35. Simms to John Esten Cooke, 14 April 1860, *Letters of Simms*, 4:216.
36. Simms to James Lawson, 29 Dec. 1839, ibid., 1:159–60; Simms, "A New Spirit of the Age," pp. 317–18.
37. Hammond to Simms, 13 Feb. 1850, Hammond Papers, LC.
38. Simms to Hammond, 30 April 1842, *Letters of Simms*, 1:304.
39. Simms to James Lawson, 29 Dec. 1839, ibid., 1:165.
40. Simms to Hammond, 18 Aug. 1852, ibid., 3:196; Simms to James Lawson, 7 April 1845, ibid., 2:48; Simms to Lawson, 17 March 1846, ibid., 2:154; Simms to Lawson, 26 Jan. 1847, ibid., 2:262; Simms to Lawson, 19 July 1834, ibid., 1:59.
41. D. F. Jamison to Holmes, 26 May 1852, Holmes Papers, LC; Mary Anne Holmes to G. F. Holmes, 7 Feb. 1828, Holmes Papers, WPL.
42. Peter Miller to Mary Anne Holmes, 28 June 1832, typescript from original in the possession of Charles Holmes of Marion, Virginia, in Holmes Papers, WPL; Neal C. Gillespie, *The Collapse of Orthodoxy: The Intellectual Ordeal of George Frederick Holmes* (Charlottesville: University of Virginia Press, 1972), p. 7.
43. Holmes to Professor Fraser, 29 July 1854, Holmes Papers, WPL.
44. Holmes to Lavalette Floyd Holmes, 22 Oct. 1846, Holmes Papers, WPL.
45. Cited by Holmes in "Miscellaneous Notes," pp. 106, 70, Holmes Papers, WPL.
46. Mary Anne Holmes to Edward Holmes, 18 Oct. 1859, typescript in Holmes Papers, WPL.
47. Holmes to Lavalette Floyd Holmes, 21 Nov. 1846, Holmes to Robert McCandlish, 22 Jan. 1848, both in Holmes Papers, WPL.
48. Holmes to Robert McCandlish, 14 Aug. 1848, Holmes Papers, WPL.
49. Holmes, Diary, Jan. 1856, Holmes Papers, WPL; Holmes, "Sir William Hamilton's Discussions," *Southern Quarterly Review* n.s., 8 (1853): 297.
50. On Ruffin's childhood, see "Gallery of Industry and Enterprise: Edwin Ruffin: Agriculturalist," *DeBow's Review* 11 (1851): 431–36. DeBow's erroneous spelling of his name must only have confirmed Ruffin's feelings of neglect.
51. "Address to the Agricultural Society of Rappahannock," n.d., Ruffin to Mildred Ruffin Sayre, 13 Feb. 1860, both in Ruffin Papers, VHS.
52. Edmund Ruffin, Jr., to Edmund Ruffin, 18 Feb. 1862, Ruffin, "Incidents of My Life," 1:160, 162, both in Ruffin Papers, VHS; Ruffin, Diary, 14 Sept., 20 Jan. 1863, Ruffin Papers, LC.
53. Elisha Hammond to James Henry Hammond, 25 April 1829, 26 Jan., 11 Aug. 1826, 7 April 1827, Hammond Papers, SCL.
54. Hammond, Diary, 12 April 1836, Hammond Papers, LC. On the various manifestations of the ambivalence of the nineteenth-century American about success see William R. Taylor, *Cavalier and Yankee: The Old South and American National Character* (New York: George Braziller, 1957); Marvin Meyers, *The Jacksonian Persuasion: Politics and Belief* (Stanford: Stanford University Press, 1957); Charles E. Rosenberg, "Sexuality, Class, and Role," *American Quarterly* 25 (1973): 131–53.
55. Hammond, Diary, 21 Feb. 1847, Hammond Papers, SCL.
56. Elisha Hammond to James Henry Hammond, 7 April 1827, J. H. Hammond to Elisha Hammond, 23 Feb. 1827, both in Hammond Papers, SCL.
57. Elisha Hammond to James Henry Hammond, 1827, Hammond, Diary, 22

Feb. 1853, both in Hammond Papers, SCL; Hammond to H. I. Caughman, 29 Dec. 1833, Hammond Papers, LC.

58. Hammond, Diary, 3 July 1841, Simms to Hammond, 30 Jan. 1851, both in Hammond Papers, LC.; Hammond to M. C. M. Hammond, 26 March 1835, Hammond Papers, SCL; Hammond to Isaac Hayne, 7 Dec. 1833, Hammond Papers, LC. On his own estimates of his increasing wealth, see Hammond, Diary, 5 Nov. 1841, Hammond Papers, LC.

59. See Hammond, Diary, 29 Nov. 1839, 4 April 1840, Hammond Papers, SCL; Hammond, Diary, 7 Feb. 1841, Hammond Papers, LC.

60. Hammond, Diary, 18 April, 16 May 1836, Hammond Papers, LC; Hammond to M. C. M. Hammond, 4 March 1838, Granville Pattison to J. H. Hammond, 19 April 1836, both in Hammond Papers, SCL. See Hammond's Medical Diary, 1836–37, Hammond Papers, SCL.

61. Hammond, Diary, 12 April 1836, Hammond Papers, LC.

62. Hammond, Diary, 12 Dec. 1844, 1 March 1841, Hammond to Simms, 27 Sept. 1852, Hammond, Diary, 17 April 1836, all in Hammond Papers, LC; Hammond, Diary, 6 Oct. 1839, Hammond Papers, SCL. See also Hammond to Simms, 19 Feb. 1846, Hammond Papers, LC. On Hammond's weight gain, see Hammond to Ruffin, 1 May 1854, Ruffin Papers, VHS.

63. J. L. Clark to Hammond, 8 Jan. 1850, Hammond, Diary, 12 Dec. 1844, Hammond Papers, LC. Through illness, Hammond—and perhaps the hypochondriacal Simms as well—could gain what Carroll Smith-Rosenberg has described as legitimation to "stay in bed and thus be relieved of day to day responsibilities, to enjoy the special prerogatives and indulgences and sympathy the sick role entailed" ("The Hysterical Woman: Sex Roles and Role Conflict in 19th Century America," *Social Research* 39 [1972]: 652). Indeed, the South Carolinian once confessed, "I pass most of my time stretched out on a sofa dreaming or at best reading" (Hammond to Ruffin, 16 June 1846, Ruffin Papers, VHS). On the "true woman," see Barbara Welter, "The Cult of True Womanhood: 1820–1860," *American Quarterly* 18 (1966): 151–74.

64. Hammond to W. G. Hodgson, 1 Jan. 1846, Hammond Papers, WPL.

65. Hammond to Simms, 8 July 1848, Hammond, Diary, 3 July 1845, Hammond Papers, LC; Hammond, Diary, 9 Dec. 1846, Hammond Papers, SCL; Hammond to Simms, 8 July 1848, Hammond Papers, LC; Hammond to John F. Hammond, 6 March 1842, Hammond Papers, SCL.

66. Hammond, Diary, 31 Jan., 20 Nov., 10 Dec. 1844, Hammond Papers, LC.

67. Simms to Tucker, 12 March 1851, *Letters of Simms*, 3:91; Hammond to Simms, 21 Aug. 1852, clipping 6 Oct. 1858, Hammond Scrapbook, both in Hammond Papers, LC.

68. Max Weber, *The Theory of Social and Economic Organization* (New York: Oxford University Press, 1947), p. 88.

69. Tucker to St. George Tucker, 11 July 1807, Tucker-Coleman Collection, EGSL; Hammond, Diary, 6 Feb. 1841, Hammond Papers, LC.

70. Simms to Tucker, 12 March 1851, *Letters of Simms*, 3:98, 100–101; Simms to Holmes, 3 Feb. 1846, ibid., 2:138; Tucker to Hammond, 8 Feb. 1850, Hammond Papers, LC; Hammond to Tucker, 29 April 1850, Tucker-Coleman Collection, EGSL; Tucker to Hammond, 7 May 1850, Hammond Papers, LC. Beverley Hammond Simms was born 24 July 1854.

71. Intense friendships were regarded as peculiarly characteristic of intellectuals and geniuses: Tennyson had his Apostles, Hugo his Cenacle, Byron and Shelley their Pisan entourage. See Linda Kelly, *The Young Romantics* (New York: Random House, 1976); John Buxton, *Byron and Shelley: The History of a Friendship* (New York: Harcourt Brace, 1968); R. C. Bald, ed., *Literary Friendships in the Age of Wordsworth* (Cambridge: Cambridge University Press, 1932).

72. Simms, "Headley's Life of Cromwell," *Southern Quarterly Review* 14 (1848): 507–8.

CHAPTER THREE

1. James Henry Hammond, *An Oration on the Life, Character, and Services of John Caldwell Calhoun,* quoted in Nathaniel Beverley Tucker, "South Carolina: Her Present Attitude and Future Action," *Southern Quarterly Review* n.s., 4 (1851): 273; Nathaniel Beverley Tucker, *Prescience. Speech Delivered by Hon. Beverley Tucker of Virginia in the Southern Convention Held at Nashville, Tenn., April 13th, 1850* (Richmond: West and Johnston, 1862), pp. 14–15; William Gilmore Simms, "Modern Prose Fiction," *Southern Quarterly Review* 15 (1849): 61. "In ancient days," Simms observed, "the man of mind had been part of that 'ministering priest-hood, which . . . made of the poet a prophet who was alone permitted to ascend the sacred eminences, receiving for his people, the laws and judgments of the . . . Eternal father."

2. Tucker to Hammond, 7 May 1850, Hammond Papers, LC.

3. George Frederick Holmes to R. R. Howison, 28 Dec. 1846, Letterbook, Holmes Papers, WPL. As Donald Mathews recently has re-emphasized, "The South and evangelical Protestantism have had a peculiarly intimate relationship for perhaps two hundred years" ("Religion in the Old South: Speculation on Methodology," *South Atlantic Quarterly* 73 [1974]: 34). On the religious nature of the American self-conception, see Sydney Ahlstrom, *A Religious History of the American People* (New Haven: Yale University Press, 1973); Fred Somkin, *Unquiet Eagle: Memory and Desire in the Idea of American Freedom* (Ithaca: Cornell University Press, 1967); Conrad Cherry, *God's New Israel: Religious Interpretations of American Destiny* (Englewood Cliffs, N.J.: Prentice-Hall, 1971); Paul Nagel, *This Sacred Trust: American Nationality, 1798–1898* (New York: Oxford University Press, 1971); Ernest Lee Tuveson, *Redeemer Nation: The Idea of America's Millenial Role* (Chicago: University of Chicago Press, 1968); Sacvan Bercovitch, "Horolog-icals to Chronometricals: The Rhetoric of the Jeremiad," *Literary Monographs* 3 (1970): 1–24, 187–215; Perry Miller, *The New England Mind: From Colony to Province* (Cambridge: Harvard University Press, 1953), pp. 46–52.

4. William Gilmore Simms, "Southern Agriculture," *Magnolia* 4 (1842): 131; Nathaniel Beverley Tucker, "Religious Reflections," Bryan Papers, AL; Jer. 1:13; Holmes, Commonplace Book, Holmes Papers, WPL; Nathaniel Beverley Tucker, "South Carolina: Her Present Attitude and Future Action," *Southern Quarterly Review* 20 (1851): 275; Tucker to Hammond, 27 Dec. 1849, Hammond Papers, LC; William Gilmore Simms, "The Southern Convention," *Southern Quarterly Review* 18 (1850): 192–93. On the psychological bases of human perception and symbolic communication and the significance of choices of metaphor, see Walker Percy, "The Symbolic Structure of Interpersonal Process," *Psychiatry* 24 (1961): 39–52; and Percy, "Metaphor as Mistake," *Sewanee Review* 64 (1958): 79–99.

5. Miller, *New England Mind,* p. 50; David Bertelson, *The Lazy South* (New York: Oxford University Press, 1967); see also William R. Taylor, *Cavalier and Yankee: The Old South and American National Character* (New York: George Braziller, 1957). Edward Shils has described the great dilemma of the intellectual as a need to accept tradition and at the same time to change it. Perhaps this is part of the reason why the jeremiad has proved such an appealing form. Bercovitch makes a similar point about Norman Mailer and other modern American intellectuals in his recent discussion of the jeremiad. By uniting man's time and God's time, "horologicals" and "chronometricals," the intellectual achieves both relevance and transcendence. See Edward Shils, *The Intellectuals and the Powers* (Chicago: University of Chicago Press, 1972), and Bercovitch, "Horologicals to Chronometricals."

6. William Gilmore Simms, "A New Spirit of the Age," *Southern Quarterly Review* 7 (1845): 314. On Ruffin as a prophet, see Edmund Ruffin, Jr., to Edmund Ruffin, 16 Nov. 1860, Ruffin Papers, VHS.

7. William Gilmore Simms, *Views and Reviews in American Literature, History, and Fiction,* 1st ser., Hugh C. Holman, ed. (1845; reprint ed., Cambridge: Belknap Press of Harvard University, 1962), p. 44; Simms, "Modern Prose Fiction," pp. 57, 82.

8. Hammond to M. C. M. Hammond, 13 Feb. 1849, Hammond Papers, SCL; Hammond to Simms, 2 Sept. 1849, Hammond Papers, LC; Hammond, Diary, 9 Dec. 1857, Hammond Papers, SCL.

9. Holmes, "Original Observations in Excerpts from Various Books," Holmes Papers, WPL.

10. Hammond to Simms, 8 Jan. 1853, Hammond Papers, LC.

11. Hammond to Simms, 13 Feb. 1850, Hammond Papers, LC.

12. Hammond to Edmund Ruffin, 22 July 1846, Ruffin Papers, VHS.

13. Nathaniel Beverley Tucker, *A Lecture Delivered to the Law Class of William and Mary, June 17, 1839* (n.p., n.d.), p. 2. Tucker described his own ambition as to be remembered by posterity "as one of the founders of that glorious Southern Confederacy which I begin to see in prophetic vision" (Tucker to Hammond, 2 Feb. 1850, Hammond Papers, LC).

14. William Gilmore Simms, "The Epochs and Events of American History, as Suited to the Purposes of Art in Fiction," *Southern and Western Monthly Magazine and Review* 1 (1845): 182; Simms, "Topics in the History of South Carolina," *Southern Quarterly Review* 18 (1850): 71; Simms, "Letter to the Editor," *Magnolia* 3 (1841): 378. Hammond found that there were many levels at which man might contribute to his world. "He who dispenses harmony and kindly feeling thro' the domestic circle" was worthy of admiration. On a still "nobler scale" was "he whose efforts are directed to the preservation of his country." But "above all . . . to be admired" was the "lofty genius, wh. elevating itself from the grovelling mass of the world's creatures, confines its vision to no place or time." This was a man of unmeasurable worth who was concerned not with family or country, but with the "Human Race" in "his own age & ages yet to come" (see Hammond, "Fugitive Peices" [sic], Hammond Papers, SCL).

15. The centrality within Romanticism of the contrast of real and ideal is stressed by Jacques Barzun in *Classic, Romantic, and Modern* (Boston: Little, Brown, 1961), p. 16, as well as by Irving Babbitt, *Rousseau and Romanticism* (Boston: Houghton Mifflin, 1919), p. 58.

16. Ruffin to J. H. Cocke, 2 April 1822, Cocke Papers, AL. Simms thought that falsehood derived from "selfishness" and "cowardice" and declared that the man of knowledge must be dedicated to that "great antagonist quality opposed to Self" (Simms, "Southern Convention," p. 232); Simms, "Poetry and the Practical," Charles Carroll Simms Collection, SCL, quoted in Edd Winfield Parks, *Ante-Bellum Southern Literary Critics* (Athens: University of Georgia Press, 1962), p. 111; Tucker, "Miscellaneous Notes," Tucker-Coleman Collection, EGSL. Tucker, quoted by James Rawlings in "Notes on a Course of Lectures Delivered before the Law Class of William and Mary College on the Philosophy of Government by Judge Beverley Tucker, 1838–9," Rawlings Papers, AL; Holmes, Diary, 19 April 1862, Holmes Papers, WPL.

17. Ruffin spoke of the need to promote the "regeneration and disenthrallment" of the Southern people. Ruffin to G. W. Bagby, 14 Feb. 1861, Bagby Papers, VHS; William Gilmore Simms, "A Year of Consolation," *Southern Quarterly Review*, 12 (1847): 216.

18. Simms, "Modern Prose Fiction," p. 61. On the hero, see Thomas Carlyle, *On Heroes, Hero-Worship, and the Heroic in History* (1841; reprint ed., London: Chapman and Hall, 1897).

19. Simms, "Modern Prose Fiction," p. 61.

20. Hammond, Diary 22 Feb. 1853, Hammond Papers, SCL; Simms to Tucker, 17 May 1851, *The Letters of William Gilmore Simms*, coll. and ed. Mary C. Simms Oliphant, Alfred Taylor Odell, and T. C. Duncan Eaves, 5 vols. (Columbia: University of South Carolina Press, 1952–56), 3:20.

21. Simms, "Year of Consolation," pp. 202–3. The real intellectual was always a man of wide-ranging knowledge and interests. Hammond explained to Tucker, "A great Teacher should never be confined to a topic. There are common minds enough now to elaborate on special subjects & back by details. From you I should prefer a

disputation de omnibus rebus giving in the essences of a thousand of these—the ultimate of observation, experience & thought" (Hammond to Tucker, 31 Aug. 1849, Tucker-Coleman Collection, EGSL).

22. Nathaniel Beverley Tucker, *A Running Commentary on Vattel's Law of Nations, Consisting of Short Notes and Parallel Remarks Intended for Use of the Class of National Law at William and Mary College* (n.p., n.d.), pp. 1–3; Tucker, "Miscellaneous Writings," 4 March 1840, Miscellaneous Lectures, Tucker-Coleman Collection, EGSL; Nathaniel Beverley Tucker, *A Series of Lectures on the Science of Government, Intended to Prepare the Student for the Study of the Constitution of the United States* (Philadelphia: Carey and Hart, 1845), p. 31. The other group members shared this pansophism. It was impossible, Holmes noted in his commonplace book, to separate politics, economics, law, or religion from morality (Holmes, quoting Laveleye, in Commonplace Book on Law, 1845–80, Holmes Papers, WPL). Simms declared the concerns of the intellectual unbounded: "His humanity, like his genius is catholic" (William Gilmore Simms, "Southern Literature," *Magnolia* 3 [1841]: 72).

23. Charles C. Cole, *The Social Ideas of the Northern Evangelists, 1826–1860* (New York: Columbia University Press, 1954), p. 189. Simms, the only member of the group who did not attend an institution of higher learning, was considered for the presidency of South Carolina College; Holmes taught at Richmond College, William and Mary, and the University of Virginia, and served briefly as president of the University of Mississippi; Hammond was in constant communication with South Carolina College, where he delivered his important 1849 address on the conflict of intellect and utility; Ruffin was one of William and Mary's Board of Visitors; and Tucker was a professor at the same institution. See Hammond, College Notebook on Lectures of Robert Henry, 1824, Hammond Papers, SCL.

24. D. H. Meyer, *The Instructed Conscience: The Shaping of the American National Ethic* (Philadelphia: University of Pennsylvania Press, 1972). In addition to Meyer, see Wilson Smith, *Professors and Public Ethics: Studies of Northern Philosophers before the Civil War* (Ithaca: Cornell University Press, 1956); Hammond, "South Carolina College Oration, December 4, 1849," p. 2, Ms., Hammond Papers, LC.

25. Meyer, *The Instructed Conscience*, p. 125; see also Francis Wayland, *The Elements of Moral Science*, ed. Joseph Blau (1837; reprint ed., Cambridge: Belknap Press of Harvard University, 1963).

26. Fiering, "President Samuel Johnson and the Circle of Knowledge," *William and Mary Quarterly* 28 (1971): 233, quoted in Meyer, *The Instructed Conscience*, p. 10.

27. Holmes to Francis Lieber, 12 Nov. 1846, Letterbook, Holmes Papers, WPL; Simms, "Southern Literature," p. 72.

28. Tucker, *A Discourse on the Dangers That Threaten the Free Institutions of the United States, Being an Address to the Literary Societies of Hampden Sydney College, Virginia, Read on the 22nd of September, 1841 at the Request of the Philanthropic Society of That College* (Richmond: J. B. Martin, 1847), p. 75; Hammond to Ruffin, 19 Dec. 1853, Ruffin Papers, VHS; Simms to Hammond, 29 July, 1848, *Letters of Simms*, 2:425.

29. Tucker, William and Mary Lecture fragments, Tucker-Coleman Collection, EGSL; Tucker, "Religious Reflections," Bryan Papers, AL; William Gilmore Simms, "Ellet's Women of the Revolution," *Southern Quarterly Review* 17 (1850): 316–17; William Gilmore Simms, "Headley's Life of Cromwell," *Southern Quarterly Review* 14 (1848): 507–8. The concept of stewardship had wide legitimacy in early nineteenth-century America. A number of historians have described this phenomenon in the North. See Clifford S. Griffin, *Their Brothers' Keepers: Moral Stewardship in the United States, 1800–65* (New Brunswick: Rutgers University Press, 1960); Charles Foster, *An Errand of Mercy: The Evangelical United Front, 1790–1837* (Chapel Hill: University of North Carolina Press, 1960); John R. Bodo, *The Protes-*

tant Clergy and Public Issues, 1812-1848 (Princeton: Princeton University Press, 1954). For a consideration of the idea of stewardship in the South, see Drew Gilpin Faust, "Evangelicalism and the Meaning of the Pro-Slavery Argument: Reverend Thornton Stringfellow of Virginia," *Virginia Magazine of History and Biography,* 85 (1977): 3-17.

30. Hammond, "South Carolina College Oration," draft ms. 4 Dec. 1849, Ms., Hammond Papers, LC; Hammond, Diary, 6 Oct. 1839, 22 Feb. 1853, Hammond Papers, SCL; Hammond, "South Carolina College Oration," draft ms., 5 June 1849, Hammond Papers, LC; Simms, "Year of Consolation," p. 216; "Gen. Hammond's Letters on Slavery," *Southern and Western Monthly Magazine and Review* 2 (1845): 72; Holmes to W. C. Preston, 6 March 1849, Preston Papers, VHS; Tucker, *A Series of Lectures,* p. 26.

31. Tucker to Hammond, 20 Nov. 1848, Hammond Papers, LC; Simms, "Southern Literature," p. 72.

32. Hammond to M. C. M. Hammond, 10 Dec. 1834, Hammond Papers, SCL; Tucker, *A Series of Lectures,* p. 13.

33. Simms, "Bulwer's Genius and Writings," *Magnolia* n.s., 1 (1842): 332.

34. Hammond to M. C. M. Hammond, 8 March 1853, Hammond Papers, SCL.

35. Hammond, "South Carolina College Oration," 4 Dec. 1849, draft ms., pp. 1, 19.

36. Ibid., pp. 35, 23.

37. Ibid., pp. 39-40.

38. Ibid., pp. 43-44.

39. Tucker, "An Oration Delivered before the Two Societies of the South Carolina College on the 4th of December 1849," *Southern Quarterly Review* 17 (1850): 37-48; Simms, "Modern Prose Fiction," p. 55; Simms, "Poetry and the Practical," cited in Parks, *Ante-Bellum Southern Literary Critics,* p. 111; Simms, "Southern Literature," p. 72.

40. George Frederick Holmes, "The Present Condition of Letters," *Southern Literary Messenger* 11 (1845): 172.

41. Holmes, "Present Condition of Letters," *Southern Literary Messenger* 10 (1844): 542; George Frederick Holmes, *Address Delivered before the Beaufort District Society* (Columbia: A. S. Johnson, 1845), pp. 23-24; Holmes, "Sir William Hamilton's Discussions," *Southern Quarterly Review* n.s., 8 (1853): 309; George Frederick Holmes, *Inaugural Address Delivered on Occasion of the Opening of the University of the State of Mississippi, November 6, 1848* (Memphis: Franklin, 1849), p. 15; Holmes to Nicholas Nemo, 19 Sept. 1843, Holmes Papers, LC.

42. Hammond, "South Carolina College Oration," 4 Dec. 1849, draft ms., pp. 37-38; Simms to E. A. Duyckinck, 8 June 1845, *Letters of Simms,* 2:73.

CHAPTER FOUR

1. On changing American religion and on the growing importance of reason and science in American belief systems, see Joseph Haroutunian, *Piety Versus Moralism: The Passing of the New England Theology* (New York: Henry Holt, 1932); Perry Miller, *The Life of the Mind in America from the Revolution to the Civil War* (New York: Harcourt Brace, 1965); Joseph L. Blau, *Men and Movements in American Philosophy* (Englewood Cliffs, N.J.: Prentice-Hall, 1952); William A Clebsch, *From Sacred to Profane America: The Role of Religion in American History* (New York: Harper and Row, 1968); George H. Daniels, *American Science in the Age of Jackson* (New York: Columbia University Press, 1968); Edward A. White, *Science and Religion in American Thought: The Impact of Naturalism* (Stanford: Stanford University Press, 1952); Ian Barbour, *Issues in Science and Religion* (Englewood Cliffs, N.J.: Prentice-Hall, 1966), A number of studies of this problem in England provide useful comparative material. In particular, see Frank Miller Turner, *Between Science and Religion: The Reaction to Scientific Naturalism in Late Victorian Eng-*

land (New Haven: Yale University Press, 1974); Walter Cannon, "Darwin's Vision in *On the Origin of Species*," in George Levine and William Madden, eds., *The Art of Victorian Prose* (New York: Oxford University Press, 1968); Cannon, "Scientists and Broad Churchmen: An Early Victorian Intellectual Network," *Journal of British Studies* 4 (1964): 65–88; Cannon, "William Whewell, FRS 1864–1866: Contributions to Science and Learning," *Notes and Records of the Royal Society of London* 19 (1964): 168–91; Cannon, "The Impact of Uninformitarianism," *Proceedings of the American Philosophical Society* 105 (1961): 301–14; Cannon, "The Normative Role of Science in Early Victorian Thought," *Journal of the History of Ideas* 25 (1964): 487–502.

2. See Daniel Walker Howe, *The Unitarian Conscience: Harvard Moral Philosophy, 1805–1861* (Cambridge: Harvard University Press, 1970), and Gladys Bryson, *Man and Society: The Scotish Inquiry of the Eighteenth Century* (1945; reprint ed., New York: A. M. Kelley, 1968). I am grateful to Murray G. Murphey for permitting me to see parts of the manuscript for Elizabeth Flower and Murray G. Murphey, *A History of American Philosophy*, forthcoming.

3. Howe, *Unitarian Conscience*, p. 31.

4. George Frederick Holmes to Samuel Tyler, 25 Aug. 1854, Holmes to August Comte, 20 June 1853, Holmes to Comte, 8 July 1852, all in Letterbook, Holmes Papers, WPL; George Frederick Holmes, "The Nineteenth Century," *Southern Literary Messenger* 17 (1851): 462; Holmes to John R. Thompson, 20 Nov. 1850, Holmes Papers, WPL. Modern society's three greatest problems, Holmes concluded, which most warranted the attention of serious reformers, were the "want of an earnest religious faith," the need for a "healthy restoration of the predominance of moral sentiment over all calculations of worldly profit," and the recognition of "the duties of life as duties . . . not as demonstrated expediency" (George Frederick Holmes, "Greeley on Reforms," *Southern Literary Messenger* 17 [1851]: 267).

5. George Frederick Holmes, "Whewell on the Inductive Sciences," *Southern Quarterly Review* 2 (1842): 194; Holmes, "Latter Day Pamphlets," *Southern Quarterly Review* n.s., 2 (1850): 341.

6. In other words, Holmes explained, "the object must be to re-establish the authority of religion, by conciliating speculative and scientific knowledge, by prescribing the limits of each, and discovering the mutual analogies, which can only be done by a revisal of our logic and metaphysics" (Holmes, "The Spirit of Positivism," p. 9, Ms., 1853, Holmes Papers, LC).

7. See Walter Houghton, *The Victorian Frame of Mind, 1830–1870* (New Haven: Yale University Press, 1957), for a general consideration of this dilemma.

8. George Frederick Holmes, "Old Notes on the Scriptures," 20 March 1854, "Excerpts from Various Books," 2:49, both in Holmes Papers, WPL; Holmes, "Whewell," pp. 216–17.

9. Holmes, "Whewell," p. 194; see also in general Holmes, "The Present State of Letters," *Southern Literary Messenger* 10 (1844): 410–14.

10. Holmes, "Spirit of Positivism," p. 3.

11. Holmes, "Philosophy and Faith," *Methodist Quarterly Review* 3 (1851): 187, 205.

12. Letty Preston Lewis to Holmes, 16 March 1846, Letterbook, Holmes Papers, WPL; Neal C. Gillespie asserts that reading Hume provoked an "existential terror" in young Holmes. See his *The Collapse of Orthodoxy: The Intellectual Ordeal of George Frederick Holmes* (Charlottesville: University of Virginia Press, 1972), p. 105.

13. Simms to Hammond, 24 Dec. 1847, *The Letters of William Gilmore Simms*, coll. and ed. Mary C. Simms Oliphant, Alfred Taylor Odell, and T. C. Duncan Eaves, 5 vols. (Columbia: University of South Carolina Press, 1952–56), 2:385; Simms to Justin Starr Redfield, 4 May 1856, ibid., 3:431; Simms to Hammond, 8 Dec. 1856, ibid., 3:469; Simms to Hammond, 23 Jan. 1857, ibid., 3:491–92; Simms to Hammond, 30 Dec. 1856, ibid., 3:475–82; Hammond to Simms, 2 Oct. 1856, Hammond Papers, LC.

14. Hammond, Diary, 13 Dec. 1853, Hammond Papers, SCL; On spiritualism, see Burton Gates Brown, Jr., "Spiritualism in Nineteenth Century America" (Ph.D. diss., Boston University, 1973).

15. Hammond, Diary, 29 Jan. 1848, Hammond Papers, SCL; Hammond to William Hodgson, 2 April 1852, Hammond Papers, WPL; Hammond, "Untitled Thoughts," Hammond-Bryan-Cummings Papers, SCL; Hammond to F. W. Byrdsall, 8 July 1861, Hammond Papers, LC.

16. Hammond, "An Oration Delivered before the Two Societies of the South Carolina College on the Fourth of December, 1849," in *Selections from the Letters and Speeches of the Hon. James H. Hammond* (New York: J. F. Trow, 1866), also cited in Nathaniel Beverley Tucker, "An Oration Delivered before the Two Societies of the South Carolina College, on the 4th of December, 1849," *Southern Quarterly Review* 17 (1850): 48. Anthropologist Mary Douglas has suggested that philosophical discussion about the problem of mind versus matter is always a symbolic expression of the concrete social problem of the relationship of the individual to his society. This network of Southerners would corroborate this point, for they explicitly recognized their individual social difficulties as mere manifestations of the conflict between thought and action and of mind and matter in their age. See Mary Douglas, "Social Preconditions of Enthusiasm and Heterodoxy," *Forms of Symbolic Action, Proceedings of the 1969 Spring Meetings of the American Ethnological Society*, ed. Robert F. Spencer (Seattle: University of Washington Press, 1969), p. 52.

17. Tucker, "An Oration, Delivered before the Two Societies," p. 48.

18. Ibid., p. 41.

19. Nathaniel Beverley Tucker to St. George Tucker, 26 Sept. 1819, Tucker-Coleman Collection, EGSL; Nathaniel Beverley Tucker, "Sermons and Religious Reflections," Bryan Papers, AL; Tucker to St. George Tucker, 17 May 1825, Tucker-Coleman Collection, EGSL.

20. Tucker, "Sermons and Religious Reflections"; Tucker to Elizabeth Coalter, 28 April 1826, Tucker-Coleman Collection, EGSL.

21. Edmund Ruffin, "African Colonization Unveiled," Ms., Ruffin Papers, VHS, also in "Liberia and the Colonization Society," *DeBow's Review* 26 (1859): 416; see Ruffin to J. H. Cocke, 25 May 1855, Cocke Papers, AL. To combat this divisiveness and confusion, Ruffin wrote a number of religious parables and planned to publish them as a guide to the discovery of religious verities.

22. See the general interpretation by Daniels, *American Science in the Age of Jackson,* who has argued that strict Baconianism ultimately retarded the growth of scientific understanding; Holmes, "Notes on Theology," 1845–65, Holmes Papers, WPL.

23. George Frederick Holmes, "The Bacon of the Nineteenth Century," *Methodist Quarterly Review* 5 (1853): 330.

24. George Frederick Holmes, "Notebook on Francis Bacon," 1858, Ms., Holmes Papers, AL; George Frederick Holmes, "The Present Condition of Letters," *Southern Literary Messenger* 10 (1844): 673. Hammond explained to Simms that he was writing a book on metaphysics and theology (Hammond to Simms, 2 March 1848, Hammond Papers, LC). For Hammond on Bacon, see "Index Rerum," 1840, and "Untitled Thoughts," Hammond-Bryan-Cummings Papers, SCL, as well as his "Oration Delivered before the South Carolina College," in *Letters and Speeches.*

25. Holmes, "The Bacon of the Nineteenth Century," p. 509.

26. Tucker, "An Oration Delivered before the Two Societies," p. 44. The moral philosophers of the nineteenth century agreed upon the necessity of rejecting the utilitarian philosophy that had been made popular in the United States in Paley's textbook on ethics, standard fare in American colleges in the first quarter of the century. D. H. Meyer finds that the rejection of Paleyanism and its Benthamite ancestry was central to moral philosophy and arose from the conviction that the United States "needed no philosophical justification for practicality." See D. H. Meyer, *The Instructed Conscience: The Shaping of the American National Ethic* (Philadelphia: University of Pennsylvania Press, 1972), p. 136. Hammond found the

utilitarians "cankered with worldly cares & scarcely looking beyond the morrow. . . . unmindful that Christianity has revealed a soul to man." "South Carolina College Oration," p. 35, draft ms., 4 Dec. 1849, Hammond Papers, LC.

27. Hammond, "An Oration Delivered before the South Carolina College," *Letters and Speeches*, p. 199; Holmes, "Whewell," p. 210.

28. Holmes, "Philosophy and Faith," p. 198.

29. Holmes, "The Bacon of the Nineteenth Century," p. 490.

30. Holmes, "History of Literature," *Southern Quarterly Review* 2 (1842): 476.

31. Holmes, "Whewell," p. 196; William Gilmore Simms, "The Southern Convention," *Southern Quarterly Review* 18 (1850): 195; Nathaniel Beverley Tucker, *A Lecture, Delivered to the Law Class of William and Mary, June 17, 1839* (n.p. n.d.), p. 5; Hammond, "South Carolina College Oration," 4 Dec. 1849, p. 6, draft ms., Hammond Papers, LC. For Holmes on the deficiencies of moral science, see George Frederick Holmes, "Sir William Hamilton's Discussions," *Southern Quarterly Review* n.s., 8 (1853): 321–23 and his *Inaugural Address Delivered on Occasion of the Opening of the University of the State of Mississippi, November 6, 1848* (Memphis: Franklin, 1849).

32. Holmes to David Flavel Jamison, 14 April 1847, Holmes Papers, WPL.

33. Nathaniel Beverley Tucker, "Macauley's History of England," *Southern Quarterly Review* 15 (1849): 374; William Gilmore Simms, "Prescott's Conquest of Peru," *Southern Quarterly Review* 13 (1848): 137; William Gilmore Simms, *Views and Reviews in American Literature, History, and Fiction*, 1st ser. ed. Hugh C. Holman (1845; reprint ed., Cambridge: Belknap Press of Harvard University, 1962), p. 37.

34. Hammond, "South Carolina College Oration," p. 19, 4 Dec. 1849, draft ms., Simms, "Preface" to *The Partisan: A Tale of the Revolution* (New York: Harper Bros., 1835), p. viii; Gillespie, *Collapse of Orthodoxy*, p. 67.

35. William Gilmore Simms, "The Epochs and Events of American History as Suited to the Purposes of Art in Fiction," *Southern and Western Monthly Magazine and Review* 2 (1845): 94; Simms, *Views and Reviews*, pp. 214–15, 34; Tucker, "Macauley's History," p. 377–78; see George H. Callcott, *History in the United States: Its Practice and Purpose* (Baltimore: Johns Hopkins University Press, 1970); David Levin, *History as Romantic Art* (Palo Alto: Stanford University Press, 1959); David D. Van Tassel, *Recording America's Past: An Interpretation of the Development of Historical Studies in America, 1607–1884* (Chicago: University of Chicago Press, 1960); Duncan Forbes, *The Liberal Anglican Idea of History* (Cambridge, Eng.: Cambridge University Press, 1944); George Peabody Gooch, *History and Historians in the Nineteenth Century* (Boston: Beacon, 1959); Jurgen Herbst, *The German Historical School in American Scholarship* (Ithaca: Cornell University Press, 1965); Frederick Merk, *Manifest Destiny and Mission in American History* (New York: Alfred A. Knopf, 1965).

36. William Gilmore Simms, *The History of South Carolina, from Its First European Discovery to Its Erection into a Republic: With a Supplementary Chronicle of Events to the Present Time* (Charleston: S. Babcock, 1840); William Gilmore Simms, *The History of South Carolina from Its Erection into a Republic; With a Supplementary Book, Bringing the Narrative Down to the Present Time* (New York: Redfield, 1860).

37. William Gilmore Simms to James Henry Hammond, 15 Dec. 1848, *Letters of Simms*, 2:465; Simms to John Reuben Thompson, 7 Feb. 1856, ibid., 3:421. See also George Frederick Holmes, "Schlegel's Philosophy of History," *Southern Quarterly Review* 3 (1843): 263–317.

38. Simms, "South Carolina in the Revolution" in *Letters of Simms*, 3:523.

39. William Gilmore Simms, "Ellet's Women of the Revolution," *Southern Quarterly Review* 17 (1850): 328–29.

40. Ruffin, "The Blackwater Guerilla: A Tradition of Revolutionary Times, 1851," Ms., Ruffin Papers, VHS; William Gilmore Simms, *The Life of Francis Marion* (Boston: Cooledge, 1856).

41. Holmes, "Schlegel's Philosophy of History," pp. 276, 278; Holmes, "Antonina," *Southern Literary Messenger* 17 (1851): 104–10, Holmes, "Roman History," *Southern Literary Messenger* 12 (1846): 508. Hammond shared Holmes's interest in Rome and its decline as a prototype for the American experience, and Simms, too, turned to the Classical Age to gain perspective on his own time. The ancient agriculturalists, Simms believed, could serve as a model to the tillers of the South's "bald and sterile fields," for the Greeks and Romans had diligently studied farming methods. The members of the network also portrayed slavery in these ancient societies as a model for modern instruction. This institution, Holmes and the others insisted, had been the basis for democracy and republicanism in the classical world, as indeed it was in the South. Only when such an underclass existed, they contended, could there be true equality among men. Thus through both positive and negative example, the ancient experience might prevent a reversion to the Dark Ages. See William Gilmore Simms, "Ancient and Modern Culture," *Magnolia* 4 (1842): 308–11.

42. In his desire to increase Southern self-awareness, Tucker modeled his characters on existing Southerners, illustrating both their virtues and vices. His own brother, Henry St. George Tucker, was enraged by his appearance in the novel as Hugh Trevor, an ineffectual gentleman of lukewarm—and thus in the context of the work misguided—sentiments about Southern independence (Nathaniel Beverley Tucker, *The Partisan Leader: A Tale of the Future* [1836; reprint ed., New York: Alfred A. Knopf, 1933]).

43. Wistfully, Holmes observed that the professors of earlier ages had not been required to stand in loco parentis to their students and had been able to devote all their time to scholarship. Holmes found this a particularly important issue, for he had tried to institute an honor system during his presidency of the University of Mississippi, but it had produced such chaos that eventually he had been dismissed. Undoubtedly this experience and the generally notorious rowdiness of Southern college students prompted him to long for an age when intellectuals had not been required to occupy themselves with problems of student discipline. See Holmes, "Universities and Colleges," *Southern Literary Messenger* 20 (1854): 449–60; 577–90; 641–52; Holmes, "History of Literature," pp. 472–517; Holmes, "History of the Christian Church," *Southern Quarterly Review* 9 (1846): 541–43; Tucker, "Macauley's History," p. 378; Simms, "Ellet's Women," p. 314; see also Simms, *The Social Principle: The True Source of National Permanence* (Tuscaloosa: Erosophic Society of the University of Alabama, 1843), p. 54; Simms, *The Sources of American Independence* (Aiken, S. C.: The Council, 1844), pp. 9–10.

44. George Frederick Holmes, "Athens and Athenians," *Southern Quarterly Review* 11 (1847): 314; George Frederick Holmes, *Address Delivered before the Beaufort District Society* (Columbia: A. S. Johnson, 1845), p. 19; William Gilmore Simms, "Kennedy's Life of Wirt," *Southern Quarterly Review* 17 (1850): 193; Nathaniel Beverley Tucker, "*The Writings of George Washington* by Jared Sparks," *Southern Literary Messenger* 1 (1835): 592; William Gilmore Simms, *The Life of Captain John Smith, the Founder of Virginia* (Philadelphia: Cooledge, 1846), pp. 349, 373.

45. William Gilmore Simms, *The Life of the Chevalier Bayard* (New York: Harper, 1847), pp. 1, 393, 396–97, 3; Simms viewed Francis Marion in a similar manner. He, too, was distinguished by "noble and disinterested characteristics," and his life could serve as the "best model" for the sons of South Carolina. Like other great men, he was insufficiently honored by his own time, for he received "no reward for his sacrifices and services" (Simms, *Life of Francis Marion*, p. 334).

46. Simms, "Kennedy's Life of Wirt," p. 193; Holmes, "Schlegel's Philosophy of History," p. 316.

47. George Frederick Holmes, "Observations on a Passage in the Politics of Aristotle Relative to Slavery," *Southern Literary Messenger* 16 (1850): 200. Thomas F. Gossett, *Race: The History of an Idea in America* (Dallas: Southern Methodist

University Press, 1963); George W. Stocking, *Race, Culture, and Evolution: Essays in the History of Anthropology* (New York: Free Press, 1968); Simms, *Social Principle*, pp. 12, 28.

48. Holmes, "Observations on a Passage," p. 200.

49. George Frederick Holmes, "The History of the Working Classes," *Southern Literary Messenger* 21 (1855): 199.

50. Hammond to Simms, n.d., Hammond to John Fox Hammond, 22 March 1842, both in Hammond Papers, SCL. Holmes related this insight to the criticisms made by northerners about the peculiar institution. He admitted that the abuses Harriet Beecher Stowe described in *Uncle Tom's Cabin* might have occurred on rare occasions. But, he insisted, the blame should be placed not on the system of slavery but on the depravity of individual masters. "It is only the malignant hate of a splenetic and frenzied fanaticism which would venture to charge upon a particular institution as its peculiar and characteristic vice the common incidents of humanity in all times and under all its phases" (Holmes, "Uncle Tom's Cabin," *Southern Literary Messenger* 18 [1852]: 727–28).

51. Holmes, "History of the Working Classes," p. 201; William Gilmore Simms, "The Fine Arts," *Magnolia* n.s., 1 (1842): 323–24.

52. Hammond to Tucker, 26 Jan. 1847, Tucker-Coleman Collection, EGSL; Hammond, Ms., Notes, n.d., Hammond Papers, LC; Ruffin, "African Colonization."

53. George Frederick Holmes, "Speculation and Trade," *Southern Quarterly Review* n.s., 2 (1856): 31.

54. Tucker, *George Balcombe* (New York: Harper Bros., 1836), p. 24.

55. Tucker, "Miscellaneous Notes," Tucker-Coleman Collection, EGSL.

56. Theodore D. Bozeman, "Joseph LeConte: Organic Science and a 'Sociology for the South,'" *Journal of Southern History* 39 (1973): 565–82; on Southern organicism generally, see Harvey Wish, *George Fitzhugh, Propagandist of the Old South* (Baton Rouge: Louisiana State University Press, 1943); William Sumner Jenkins, *Pro-Slavery Thought in the Old South* (Chapel Hill: University of North Carolina Press, 1935); Louis Hartz, *The Liberal Tradition in America* (New York: Harcourt Brace, 1955). Bozeman specifically mentions the organicism of William Harper and William C. Preston, who were friends of long standing to Tucker and Hammond and cousins to Holmes. As part of the larger circle of Southern men of mind within which our network was located, Harper, Preston, and the others no doubt had shared their ideas with the members of our group long before LeConte began to publish on the subject. See also William Martin Smallwood with Mabel Smallwood, *Natural History and the American Mind* (New York: Columbia University Press, 1941).

57. Hammond, "Manuscript on Natural Right," 26 Jan. 1847, Tucker-Coleman Collection, EGSL; Holmes, "Notes on Theology," 1845–65, Holmes Papers, WPL; Simms, *Social Principle*, p. 28; Tucker, "A Lecture, March 4, 1840," Miscellaneous Writings," Ms., Tucker-Coleman Collection, EGSL.

58. Holmes, "Illustrations of Historical Law and Development," Notes in the Social Sciences, Commonplace Book, Holmes Papers, WPL.

59. Hammond to Simms, 18 Nov. 1863, Hammond Papers, LC.

60. Simms, "Kennedy's Life of Wirt," p. 193.

CHAPTER FIVE

1. William Gilmore Simms, "Southern Agriculture," *Magnolia* 4 (1842): 142; George Frederick Holmes, "Education," Commonplace Book on Law, p. 356, Holmes Papers, WPL; Simms, "Southern Literature," *Magnolia* 3 (1841): 2.

2. Simms, "Editorial," *Southern and Western Monthly Magazine* 2 (1845): 189.

3. Simms, "The Fine Arts," *Magnolia* n.s., 1 (1842): 324.

4. See Daniel Walker Howe, *The Unitarian Conscience: Harvard Moral Philosophy, 1805–61* (Cambridge: Harvard University Press, 1970); Raymond Williams,

Culture and Society, 1780–1950 (1958; reprint ed., New York: Harper Torchbooks, 1966); Francis Wayland, *The Elements of Moral Science,* ed. Joseph Blau (1837; reprint ed., Cambridge: Belknap Press of Harvard University, 1963); Morse Peckham, *Victorian Revolutionaries: Speculations on Some Heroes of a Culture Crisis* (New York: George Braziller, 1970); John L. Thomas, "Romantic Reform in America, 1815–1860," *American Quarterly* 17 (1965): 656–81.

5. William Gilmore Simms to Nathaniel Beverley Tucker, 6 Sept. 1849, *The Letters of William Gilmore Simms,* coll. and ed. Mary C. Simms Oliphant, Alfred Taylor Odell, and T. C. Duncan Eaves, 5 vols. (Columbia: University of South Carolina Press, 1952–56): 2:554; Simms to Tucker, 15 March 1849, ibid., 2:496; Simms to James Henry Hammond, 22 Nov. 1847, ibid., 2:372; Simms to Tucker, 8 May 1850, ibid., 3:40.

6. James Henry Hammond, "Agricultural Address, before the Matlock, South Carolina, Agricultural Club," 3 July 1847, Ms., Hammond Papers, LC.

7. Holmes to Auguste Comte, 8 July 1852, Letterbook, Holmes Papers, WPL.

8. See David Brion Davis, "Introduction," *Ante Bellum Reform,* ed. David Brion Davis (New York: Harper and Row, 1967); Stanley Elkins, *Slavery: A Problem in American Institutional and Intellectual Life* (Chicago: University of Chicago Press, 1959); John Bodo, *The Protestant Clergy and Public Issues, 1812–48* (Princeton: Princeton University Press, 1954); Clifford Griffin, *Their Brothers' Keepers: Moral Stewardship in the United States, 1800–65* (New Brunswick: Rutgers University Press, 1960); Howe, *Unitarian Conscience.* James Henry Hammond, "Anniversary Oration before the State Agricultural Society," 1841, p. 50, Ms., Hammond Papers, LC.

9. Hammond, "Anniversary Oration," p. 50; William Gilmore Simms to Charles Wheler, 9 May 1849, *Letters of Simms,* 2:515–23. See John J. Gross, *The Rise and Fall of the Man of Letters* (New York: Macmillan, 1969); and Frank Luther Mott, *A History of American Magazines,* 5 vols. (Cambridge: Harvard University Press, 1930–68).

10. Simms's first venture was the *Album,* a literary periodical he founded in Charleston when he was only nineteen. This was succeeded by the *Tablet* in June 1828, then the *Pleiades* shortly later. In 1829, Simms purchased the *City Gazette,* a traditionally Unionist newspaper that vigorously opposed nullification throughout the crisis of the next few years. After these bitter battles, Simms retreated somewhat from political writing and abandoned the *City Gazette* for the *Cosmopolitan,* another short-lived literary journal. During the 1830s, Simms wrote constantly for the *Southern Literary Journal,* as well as for a host of other periodicals North and South. See John C. Guilds, "Simms as a Magazine Editor, 1825–1845" (Ph.D. diss., Duke University, 1954).

11. "Editorial," *Southern Times,* inaugural issue, 29 Jan. 1830, p. 1; James Henry Hammond to M. C. M. Hammond, 10 Dec. 1834, Hammond Papers, SCL; Edmund Ruffin to Hammond, 24 Oct. 1845, Hammond Papers, LC; Hammond, "Oration at South Carolina College," *Selections from the Letters and Speeches of the Hon. James H. Hammond of South Carolina* (New York: J. F. Trow, 1866), p. 229.

12. The *Farmers' Register* was recognized as the most scholarly, the most scientific, and by many critics, the best agricultural paper. See Albert Lowther Demaree, *The American Agricultural Press, 1819–1860* (New York: Columbia University Press, 1941); Edmund Ruffin to Tucker, 24 Jan. 1841, Tucker-Coleman Collection, EGSL.

13. Simms to E. A. Duyckinck, 28 Oct. 1845, *Letters of Simms,* 2:110; Introductory Editorial, *Southern Magazine,* 1841; Daniel Whitaker, "Prospectus of the Southern Quarterly Review," 1 Oct. 1843, *Letters of Simms,* 1:373–74; Simms, "Southern Literature," p. 1. For almost identical statements, see George Frederick Holmes to Simms, 19 Nov. 1844, Letterbook, Holmes Papers, WPL; William Gilmore Simms, "Modern Prose Fiction," *Southern Quarterly Review* 15 (1849); 64;

George Frederick Holmes, "Leverett's Latin Lexicon," *Southern Quarterly Review*
3 (1843): 248; Hammond to Tucker, 4 July 1851, Tucker-Coleman Collection,
EGSL.

14. Holmes, "The Wandering Jew," *Southern Quarterly Review* 9 (1846): 74;
Introductory Editorial, *Southern Magazine*, 1841; Hammond to Simms, 22 Dec. 1848,
Hammond Papers, LC; Hammond to M. C. M. Hammond, 5 March 1849, Hammond
Papers, SCL; Edmund Ruffin, "Incidents of My Life," 1837, 1:149, Ruffin Papers,
VHS; Ruffin to Tucker, 24 Jan. 1841, Tucker-Coleman Collection, EGSL.

15. Simms to William Elliott, 7 Feb. 1849, *Letters of Simms*, 3:477. They were
discussing the editorship of the *Southern Quarterly Review;* Nathaniel Beverley
Tucker, "The Present State of Europe," *Southern Quarterly Review* 16 (1850):
279; Simms to Holmes, 15 Aug. 1842, *Letters of Simms*, 1:319.

16. Editorial, *Southern Quarterly Review* 12 (1847): i–xii.

17. George Frederick Holmes, "Uncle Tom's Cabin," *Southern Literary Messenger* 18 (1852): 721–31; 19 (1853): 321–30; William Gilmore Simms, "Miss Martineau on Slavery," *Southern Literary Messenger* 3 (1837): 641–57; B. B. Minor,
"To Our Patrons," *Southern Literary Messenger* 11 (1845): 760–61 (at the time of
the merger with *Simms' Magazine*).

18. Simms to P. Pendleton, 1 Dec. 1840, *Letters of Simms*, 1:197; Simms to
Charles Wheler, 9 May 1849, ibid., 2:516; Simms to Hammond, 20 June 1853, ibid.,
3:239. For examples of "puffing," see Simms on Hammond: "Southern Agriculture";
"Gen. Hammond's Letters on Slavery," *Southern and Western Monthly Magazine*
2 (1845): 71–72; on Ruffin: "Agriculture in South Carolina," *Magnolia n.s.*, 2
(1843): 200–203; on Tucker and Hammond at Nashville: "The Southern Conven-
tion," *Southern Quarterly Review* 18 (1850): 66–84; Tucker on Hammond: "An
Oration Delivered before the Two Societies of the South Carolina College, on the
4th of December, 1849," *Southern Quarterly Review* 17 (1850): 48; Holmes to
Tucker, "Origin and History of the High Court of Chancery," *Southern Literary
Messenger* 16 (1850): 303–15; to Simms: "The Present State of Letters," *Southern
Literary Messenger* 10 (1844): 410–14, 538–42, 673–78.

19. Simms, "Southern Literature," p. 2; Holmes hoped to transform reviews into
a source of economic as well as intellectual and emotional support for professional
men of knowledge in the South. The lack of firm social place that plagued the men
of mind was paralleled by a financial insecurity that made it nearly impossible for
an individual to devote his life wholly to the pursuit of wisdom. A university professor was paid according to the number of students he attracted to his classes, and
thus he, too, had no assurance of adequate income. In 1844, Holmes wrote to Daniel
Whitaker, publisher of the *Southern Quarterly Review*, proposing that he enter into
a contract to produce two articles for each number of the periodical. "My means
are limited and uncertain—and some sort of certainty I wish to arrive at," he
explained. Holmes sought a professional niche where both his status and his income
would be firmly fixed. Unfortunately for the young writer, however, Whitaker did
not agree to his suggestion, and Holmes was compelled to scrounge for money and
struggle with debt for the rest of his life. His request indicates, however, that the
Southern man of mind perceived the review as a potential organ for a learned profession. See Holmes to Daniel Whitaker, 26 Oct. 1844, Letterbook, Holmes Papers,
WPL.

20. Simms, "Southern Agriculture," p. 129.

21. Hammond, "Agricultural Address before the Matlock, South Carolina Agri-
cultural Club," 3 July 1847, Ms., Hammond Papers, LC; Simms, "Southern Agri-
culture," p. 130; Holmes, *Address Delivered before the Beaufort District Society*
(Columbia: A. S. Johnson, 1845), p. 17; Edmund Ruffin, "Apology for Book
Farmers," *Essays and Notes on Agriculture* (Richmond: J. W. Randolph, 1855), and
Diary, 1 March 1843, Ruffin Papers, VHS.

22. Hammond to Ruffin, 14 Feb. 1844, Ruffin Papers, VHS; Arthur R. Hall,
Early Erosion Control Practices in Virginia (Washington, D.C.: USDA Misc. Pub.
256, 1937); and Hall, *The Story of Soil Conservation in the South Carolina Piedmont,*

1800–60 (Washington, D.C.: USDA Misc. Pub. 407, 1940); Avery Craven, *Soil Exhaustion as a Factor in the Agricultural History of Virginia and Maryland, 1606–1860* (1926; reprint ed., Gloucester: Peter Smith, 1965).

23. See Chapter 2.

24. Ruffin, "Incidents," 1:161, Hammond to Ruffin, 6 Feb. 1846, both in Ruffin Papers, VHS.

25. *Proceedings of the Agricultural Convention and State Agricultural Society of South Carolina, 1839–45* (Columbia: Sumner and Carroll, 1846). See also, Hammond, Diary, 22 Nov. 1839, Hammond Papers, SCL. See "Record of the Proceedings of the Beech Island Agricultural Club, 1856–62 and Journal of the Proceedings of the Beech Island Agricultural and Police Society," WPA typescript, SCL. Hammond, "Anniversary Oration," 1841, pp. 29, 1, Ms., Hammond Papers, LC.

26. The State Agricultural Society also encouraged the establishment of district organizations to disseminate information more widely and to create a community of educated planters. Hammond was a leader in his local group, which met monthly and discussed such issues as "Best cheapest & most economical mode of fencing . . . Deep Plowing" and "Can not each community make its negro shoes cloth &c cheaper than buying them?" ("Beech Island Farmers Club," Ms., 1860, Hammond Papers, SCL).

27. Avery Craven, *Edmund Ruffin, Southerner: A Study in Secession* (1932; reprint ed., Baton Rouge: Louisiana State University Press, 1966); Ruffin, "Incidents," 1:155.

28. Ruffin, "Incidents," 2:224, 230.

29. Hammond, "Anniversary Oration," in *Proceedings of the Agricultural Convention,* pp. 182–83; Simms, "Ancient and Modern Culture," *Magnolia* 4 (1842): 309. Hammond to Ruffin, 15 Aug. 1849, Ruffin Papers, VHS; Hammond, "South Carolina Institute Address," 30 June 1849, Ms., Hammond Papers, LC; Simms, "Ancient and Modern Culture," p. 311. A number of recent studies by economic historians have challenged the belief of these nineteenth-century Southerners that their region was not self-sufficient in the production of foodstuffs. See Robert E. Gallman, "Self-Sufficiency in the Cotton Economy of the Ante-Bellum South," *Agricultural History* 44 (1970): 5–24; Diane Lindstrom, "Southern Dependence upon Interregional Grain Supplies: A Review of the Trade Flows, 1840–1860," *Agricultural History* 44 (1970): 101–13; Raymond C. Battalio and John Kagel, "The Structure of Ante-Bellum Southern Agriculture: A Case Study," *Agricultural History* 44 (1970): 25–38; Marjorie Stratford Mendenhall, "A History of Agriculture in South Carolina, 1790 to 1860: An Economic and Social Survey" (Ph.D. diss., University of North Carolina, 1940). See also a contemporary estimate of growing dependence on food imports: R. W. Roper, "Report before the Agricultural Society of South Carolina," *Southern Agriculturist* 2 (1844): 347–48.

30. *Proceedings of the Agricultural Convention,* p. 65; Hammond, "South Carolina Institute Address," p. 14.

31. Simms, "Summer Travel in the South," *Southern Quarterly Review* 18 (1850): 24–65, 32.

32. Hammond to M. C. M. Hammond, 2, 27 Nov. Hammond to M. C. M. Hammond, 7 May 1849, all in Hammond Papers, SCL. See Thomas P. Martin, "The Advent of William Gregg and the Graniteville Company," *Journal of Southern History* 11 (1945): 389–422.

33. A. H. Brisbane to Hammond, 22 Sept. 1849, Hammond Papers, LC; Hammond, Diary, 25 Dec. 1850, Hammond Papers, SCL. See J. Mauldin Lesesne, *The Bank of the State of South Carolina: A General and Political History* (Columbia: University of South Carolina Press, 1970); Hammond, "Message to the Senate and the House of South Carolina, November 28, 1843," in *Letters and Speeches,* p. 63.

34. Simms to Hammond, 15 Dec. 1848, *Letters of Simms,* 2:466; "Critical Notices," *Southern Quarterly Review* 18 (1850): 251; see Edmund Ruffin, *An Address on the Opposite Results of Exhausting and Fertilizing Systems of Agricul-*

ture, Read before the South Carolina Institute at Its Fourth Annual Fair, November 18, 1852 (Charleston: Walker and James, 1853), for general information on the fair.

35. Edmund Ruffin, "True Policy of the Southern States," Ms., Ruffin Papers, VHS; George Frederick Holmes, "The Failure of Free Societies," *Southern Literary Messenger* 21 (1855): 132.

36. Nathaniel Beverley Tucker to Hammond, 13 March 1850, Tucker to Hammond, 16 March 1848, both in Hammond Papers, LC; Tucker, *A Series of Lectures on the Science of Government Intended to Prepare the Student for the Study of the Constitution of the United States* (Philadelphia: Carey and Hart, 1845), pp. 39, 396, 398; Tucker to Hammond, 16 March 1848, Hammond Papers, LC.

37. See Eugene Genovese, *The Political Economy of Slavery* (New York: Pantheon, 1966); Neal C. Gillespie, *The Collapse of Orthodoxy: The Intellectual Ordeal of George Frederick Holmes* (Charlottesville: University of Virginia Press, 1972), pp. 162–63; Fred Batemen, James Foust, and Thomas Weiss, "The Participation of Planters in Manufacturing in the Ante Bellum South," *Agricultural History* 48 (1974): 277–97; Hammond to Tucker, 3 July 1849, Tucker-Coleman Collection, EGSL; George Frederick Holmes, "Failure of Free Societies," *Southern Literary Messenger* 21 (1855): 133; Tucker to Hammond, 13 March 1847, Hammond Papers, LC.

38. Hammond, "South Carolina Institute Address," p. 4.

39. Simms remarked upon "an unwonted activity in the popular mind shown in the general eagerness to procure good schools—in the increased diffusion of books and studies" ("Agriculture in South Carolina," *Magnolia* n.s., 2 [1843]: 201). See also John F. Thomason, *Foundations of the Public Schools of South Carolina* (Columbia: State Company, 1925); "Education in Virginia," *Southern Literary Messenger* 7 (1841): 633–34.

40. Hammond, "Education," Ms., 1848, Hammond to Simms, 10 Nov. 1846, both in Hammond Papers, LC.

41. Hammond, "Message to the Senate and House of South Carolina, 28 Nov. 1843," *Letters and Speeches*, pp. 71, 88; "Message to the Senate and House of South Carolina, November 26, 1844," ibid., p. 90.

42. See, for example, the *Southern Quarterly Review*, Oct. 1849; William Gilmore Simms, "Southern Education—Books," *Magnolia* n.s., 1 (1842): 59.

43. George Frederick Holmes, *Inaugural Address Delivered on Occasion of the Opening of the University of the State of Mississippi, November 6, 1848* (Memphis: Franklin, 1849), p. 12; Holmes, *Address before the Beaufort District Society*, p. 1.

44. Hammond, Diary, 15 May 1842, Hammond Papers, LC; Ruffin, Diary, 20 Jan. 1863, Ruffin Papers, LC.

45. Tucker, "Sermons and Religious Writings," Ms., Bryan Papers, AL; Tucker, *A Series of Lectures*, pp. 12–13.

46. Nathaniel Beverley Tucker, *A Discourse on the Dangers that Threaten the Free Institutions of the United States* (Richmond: Martin, 1841), p. 13; *Southern Magazine* 1 (1841), Masthead.

47. See Charles S. Sydnor, *Gentleman Freeholders* (Chapel Hill: University of North Carolina Press, 1952); and Robert Weir, " 'The Harmony We Were Famous For': An Interpretation of Pre-Revolutionary South Carolina Politics," *William and Mary Quarterly* 26 (1969): 473–501.

48. Tucker to R. K. Cralle, 18 Feb. 1838, Tucker-Coleman Collection, EGSL; William Gilmore Simms, "The Morals of Slavery," in *The Pro-Slavery Argument as Maintained by the Most Distinguished Writers of the Southern States* (Philadelphia: Walker and Richards, 1852), p. 64; the best example of their nonpartisanship is probably their support for Zachary Taylor in 1848, despite the supposed hostility of the Whig party to the South and despite Calhoun's support for Lewis Cass. On Simms's evolution away from the Democratic party, see John Higham, "The Changing Loyalties of William Gilmore Simms," *Journal of Southern History* 9 (1943): 210–23.

49. Simms to Hammond, 1 May 1847, *Letters of Simms*, 2:310; George Frederick

Holmes, "John C. Calhoun," *Southern Literary Messenger* 16 (1850): 301. Tucker was also a harsh critic of Calhoun. See his letter of 13 March 1847 to Hammond, Hammond Papers, LC.

50. James Henry Hammond, *An Oration on the Life, Character, and Services of John Caldwell Calhoun* (Charleston: Walker and James, 1850), p. 63; Hammond, "Thoughts and Recollections," 28 March 1852, Hammond Papers, SCL. Hammond declined to serve as a pallbearer for Calhoun (Hammond to Simms, 26 April 1850, Hammond Papers, LC).

51. Tucker, *A Series of Lectures,* p. 96.

52. Ibid., pp. 192, 108–9, 14.

53. Tucker, "The Seat of Government," n.d., Ms., Tucker-Coleman Collection, EGSL.

54. Tucker, *A Series of Lectures,* p. 450.

55. Ibid., p. 278.

56. Hammond to M. C. M. Hammond, 6 Aug. 1839, Hammond Papers, LC; Hammond, "Address at Barnwell Courthouse, October 1858," *Letters and Speeches,* p. 358; Savannah *Republican,* 26 Feb., 4 March 1859, clippings in Hammond Papers, SCL. The paper was nominating Hammond for president.

57. Hammond to M. C. M. Hammond, 30 April 1840, Hammond to Simms, 23 Nov. 1846, 4 Feb. 1851, all in Hammond Papers, LC. "Nostalgics said that Hammond's election was a return to the good old days when the office sought the man, a rebuke to electioneering" (Harold S. Schultz, *Nationalism and Sectionalism in South Carolina* [Durham: Duke University Press, 1950], p. 148).

58. Hammond to Simms, 19 April 1847, Hammond Papers, LC. The others in the network did not always agree with Hammond's political positions, but all perceived these disagreements as tactical rather than substantive. Tucker and Ruffin, for example, were far more adamant than the South Carolinian about the necessity of immediate secession, but they did not feel threatened by Hammond's stance, for they perceived that his ultimate goals were the same. Hammond was not, Ruffin insisted, a conciliator, but urged delaying secession as a strategic move to gain additional support for the revolutionary movement. Although they sometimes disagreed about means, they were in complete harmony on the ultimate purposes of political action: the elevation of the mind and spirit of the South.

59. Simms to Tucker, 8 May 1850, *Letters of Simms,* 3:40. "The *stump,* during the political canvass," Simms explained, was one of the few "sources of popular tuition" in the South. Simms to Charles Wheler, 9 May 1849, *Letters of Simms,* 2:515–23; Simms to Hammond, 25 Dec. 1846, *Letters of Simms,* 2:242.

60. Simms to Hammond, 25 Dec. 1846, *Letters of Simms,* 2:243. Simms's defeat resulted in large part from the position he had taken in the legislature against Calhoun and the other "Hunkers" of South Carolina politics. The "Young Carolina" movement he promoted was a political equivalent of the literary Young America movement in which Simms had played a prominent part. Designed to encourage intellectual independence, the effort centered on uniting the state and the South behind tariff reduction and the annexation of Texas.

Simms and Hammond worked closely together in this endeavor, for they shared a desire to liberate the mind of the state from its domination by the older politicians. The power of Calhoun and his lieutenants far exceeded that of the two men of knowledge, and they defeated Simms's movement for a Southern or a state convention to consider encroachments on regional autonomy. Almost simultaneously, Simms and Hammond were retired from public office; see Hammond to Tucker, 20 Jan. 1850, Tucker-Coleman Collection, EGSL.

61. Ruffin, Diary, 20 Jan. 1863, Ruffin Papers, LC; Ruffin, "Incidents," 1:214.

62. Tucker, *A Series of Lectures,* p. 463; Tucker to Hammond, 29 Dec. 1846, Hammond Papers, LC.

63. Tucker, *A Series of Lectures,* pp. 288, 14; it is important to recognize that the relationship between moral reform and social control was the natural product of the nineteenth-century world view, not, as some historians have implied, a cynical and

conspiratorial design by a small group to exert political and social power. Order, these Southerners assumed, was God's intention for his creation and had to be maintained through either external or internal restraint. For a summary of literature on social control, see Lois Banner, "Religious Benevolence as Social Control: A Critique of an Interpretation," *Journal of American History* 40 (1973): 23–41.

64. George Frederick Holmes explained, "The reformer who would hope for success in his lofty aspirations must literally become 'all things to all men,' " "Latter-Day Pamphlets," *Southern Quarterly Review* n.s., 2 (1850): 319; Tucker discovered that his duty in regard to the "bodies and souls of others" made him a doctor as well as a politician, a teacher, and a judge. "In one department my exertions, however unskillful have been blessed, and who knows but I may find the like blessing in the others" (Tucker to Elizabeth Coalter, 31 Oct. 1826, Tucker-Coleman Collection, EGSL).

CHAPTER SIX

1. David Donald, "The Proslavery Argument Reconsidered," *Journal of Southern History* 37 (1971): 4; George Frederick Holmes, "On Slavery and Christianity," *Southern Quarterly Review* 3 (1843): 252; James Henry Hammond to Nathaniel Beverley Tucker, 23 Feb. 1849, Tucker-Coleman Collection, EGSL. Simms pronounced his arguments explicitly directed at "our people of the South" (Simms to Hammond, 10 April 1845, *The Letters of William Gilmore Simms*, coll. and ed. Mary C. Simms Oliphant, Alfred Taylor Odell, and T. C. Duncan Eaves, 5 vols. [Columbia: University of South Carolina Press, 1952–56], 2:50–51).

2. William Hesseltine, "Some New Aspects of the Pro-Slavery Argument," *Journal of Negro History* 21 (1936): 1–15; Ralph E. Morrow, "The Proslavery Argument Revisited," *Mississippi Valley Historical Review* 47 (1961): 79–94; Charles G. Sellers, "The Travail of Slavery," in Sellers, ed., *The Southerner as American* (Chapel Hill: University of North Carolina Press, 1960), pp. 40–71. For other supporters of this position, see William W. Freehling, *Prelude to Civil War: The Nullification Controversy in South Carolina, 1816–1836* (New York: Harper Torchbooks, 1965), and James M. McPherson, "Slavery and Race," *Perspectives in American History* 3 (1969): 460–73. For a recent, statistical discussion of the proslavery argument, see Larry Tise, "Proslavery Ideology: A Social and Intellectual History of the Defense of Slavery in America, 1790–1840," (Ph.D. diss., University of North Carolina, 1975).

3. Donald, "Proslavery Argument," pp. 12–18.

4. Ibid., p. 17.

5. Hammond was cited as an example of social mobility by J. D. B. DeBow in his most famous defense of slavery, *The Interest in Slavery of the Southern Non-Slaveholder. The Rights of Peaceful Secession. Slavery in the Bible* (Charleston: Evans and Cogswell, 1860), p. 6. Simms's social origins are a bit more complex. His nineteenth-century biographer, William Trent, stressed Simms's lowly origins, but later scholars have found Trent's descriptions somewhat exaggerated, for they point to one of Simms's ancestors who fought in the Revolution and another who was a sizable landholder. Simms's father was an Irish immigrant who made and then lost a fortune in the South; his mother was of what Jon Wakelyn describes as "a respected if not affluent Charleston family." This controversy indicates how difficult it is to assign individuals to objective social categories or classes in a society as mobile as nineteenth-century America. A marriage between an Irish immigrant and a respected Charlestonian produced an offspring of anomalous social status, and Simms's objective position therefore was unclear to Simms himself, as well as to his numerous biographers. Unquestionably, however, he perceived himself to be very distant from the traditional South Carolina elite. In terms of Simms's view of his own status—which was, of course, the perception operative in his life—the Trent version is far more accurate than that of later writers. See William P. Trent, *William*

Gilmore Simms (Boston: Houghton Mifflin, 1895); John Rushing Welsh, "The Mind of William Gilmore Simms: His Social and Political Thought" (Ph.D. diss., Vanderbilt University, 1951); Jon L. Wakelyn, *The Politics of a Literary Man: William Gilmore Simms* (Westport, Conn.: Greenwood Press, 1973), p. 3. See also William R. Taylor, *Cavalier and Yankee: The Old South and American National Character* (New York: George Braziller, 1957).

6. On "status-anxiety," see Richard Hofstadter, *The Age of Reform* (New York: Vintage Books, 1955); Joseph Gusfield, *Symbolic Crusade* (Urbana: University of Illinois Press, 1963); David Donald, "Toward a Reconsideration of Abolitionists," in *Lincoln Reconsidered: Essays on the Civil War Era* (1947, reprint ed., New York: Vintage Books, 1961), pp. 19–36. Explanations that fit this "status-anxiety" model often do not make clear whether the anxious individual himself is experiencing mobility or whether he is simply aware of predecessors who seemed to have had different, usually higher, status. This would seem a distinction worth exploring. Donald suggests that slavery's defenders remembered "an earlier day . . . when men like themselves—their own ancestors—had been leaders in the South," but at the same time he recognizes that at least some of the proslavery advocates were experiencing stress resulting from their own movement upward in society.

7. On social structure and mobility in the colonial South, see Bernard Bailyn, "Politics and Social Structure in Virginia," in James Morton Smith, ed., *Seventeenth-Century America: Essays in Colonial History,* (1959; reprint ed., New York: W. W. Norton, 1972), pp. 90–118. On the relationship of ideas and society, see Clifford Geertz, "Ideology as a Cultural System," in Geertz, *The Interpretation of Cultures* (New York: Basic Books, 1973), pp. 193–233.

8. William Gilmore Simms, 'The Morals of Slavery," *The Pro-Slavery Argument as Maintained by the Most Distinguished Writers of the Southern States* (Philadelphia: Walker and Richards, 1852), p. 275.

9. George Frederick Holmes, "Uncle Tom's Cabin," *Southern Literary Messenger* 18 (1852): 725; George Frederick Holmes, "Bledsoe on Liberty and Slavery," *DeBow's Review* 21 (1856): 133.

10. James Clark to James Henry Hammond, 18 Jan. 1836, Tucker to Hammond, 18 Feb. 1836, both in Hammond Papers, LC.

11. Simms to Hammond, 10 July 1845, *Letters of Simms,* 2:87; D. F. Jamison to Holmes, 28 Aug. 1845, Holmes Papers, WPL; J. E. Carew to Hammond, 18 Nov. 1847, Hammond Papers, LC. A less sympathetic correspondent, New York abolitionist Lewis Tappan, ventured to suggest that public acclaim had been Hammond's primary goal. "You must forgive me," he wrote, "but I cannot get rid of the idea that you have written these letters partly for effect" (Lewis Tappan to Hammond, 23 July 1845, Hammond Papers, LC); Hammond, Diary, 20 June, 14 July, 3 July 1845, Hammond Papers, LC; Hammond, Diary, 29 Jan. 1848, Hammond Papers, SCL.

12. Edmund Ruffin, *The Diary of Edmund Ruffin,* ed. William Kauffman Scarborough (Baton Rouge: Louisiana State University Press, 1972), 29 Jan. 1859, 1:276.

13. Francis Lieber, quoted in Daniel Hollis, *University of South Carolina: South Carolina College* (Columbia: University of South Carolina Press, 1951), p. 183.

14. Hammond, Diary, 3 July 1845, Hammond to Simms, 3, 19 June 1845, all in Hammond Papers, LC.

15. Simms to Hammond, 20 Oct. 1847, *Letters of Simms,* 2:354; Hammond to Nott, 3 Aug. 1845, Hammond Papers, LC.

16. George Frederick Holmes, "The Failure of Free Societies," *Southern Literary Messenger* 21 (1855): 129; Holmes, "Aristotle on Slavery," Ms., Holmes Papers, LC; Nathaniel Beverley Tucker, "An Essay on the Moral and Political Effect of the Relation between the Caucasion Master and the African Slave," *Southern Literary Messenger* 10 (1844): 329; Holmes, "Bledsoe," p. 137.

17. George Frederick Holmes, "Observations on a Passage in the Politics of Aris-

totle Relative to Slavery," *Southern Literary Messenger* 16 (1850): 197. "Every investigation of social questions" must encompass the "history of the institutions discussed," Holmes advised ("Ancient Slavery," *DeBow's Review* 19 [1855]: 560); Ruffin, "African Colonization," pp. 2–3, Ms., VHS; Holmes, "Observations on a Passage," p. 197.

18. Holmes, "Ancient Slavery," p. 561; Hammond, "Hammond's Letters on Slavery," in *The Pro-Slavery Argument*, p. 154.

19. Holmes, "Ancient Slavery," pp. 572–73, 617.

20. Edmund Ruffin, *The Political Economy of Slavery; or, The Institution Considered in Regard to Its Influence on Public Wealth and the General Welfare* (Washington, D.C.: L. Towers, 1857), p. 3; Edmund Ruffin, *Address to the Virginia State Agricultural Society, on the Effects of Domestic Slavery on the Manners, Habits, and Welfare of the Agricultural Population of the Southern States; and the Slavery of Class to Class in the Northern States* (Richmond: P. D. Bernard, 1853), p. 19; George Frederick Holmes, "Slavery and Freedom," *Southern Quarterly Review* n.s., 1 (1856): 86; Holmes, "Ancient Slavery," p. 564.

21. Simms, "Morals," pp. 251–52. They also explicitly opposed natural rights doctrines. See, for example, Hammond's repudiation of Jefferson in "Hammond's Letters on Slavery," p. 110; Simms, "Morals," p. 256. For a discussion of persistence and change in ideology from the Revolution to the proslavery argument, see Kenneth S. Greenberg, "Revolutionary Ideology and the Proslavery Argument: The Abolition of Slavery in Ante Bellum South Carolina," *Journal of Southern History* 42 (1976): 365–84.

22. Nathaniel Beverley Tucker, "An Essay on the Moral and Political Effect," p. 330; Simms, "Morals," pp. 258, 259.

23. Ruffin, *Address to the Virginia State Agricultural Society*, p. 12.

24. Hammond, "Hammond's Letters on Slavery," pp. 125, 134; Tucker, "An Essay on the Moral and Political Effect," p. 337; Hammond, "Hammond's Letters on Slavery," p. 122. See also Holmes, "Slavery and Freedom," p. 84.

25. Holmes, "Slavery and Freedom," pp. 81, 87.

26. Nathaniel Beverley Tucker, "Slavery," *Southern Literary Messenger* 2 (1836): 337.

27. Ruffin, *Political Economy*, p. 5. See also, Simms, "Morals," p. 185; Hammond, "Hammond's Letters on Slavery," p. 111.

28. Tucker, "An Essay on the Moral and Political Effect," p. 339; Nathaniel Beverley Tucker, *A Series of Lectures on the Science of Government Intended to Prepare the Student for the Study of the Constitution of the United States* (Philadelphia: Carey and Hart, 1845), p. 349.

29. Ruffin, *Address to the Virginia State Agricultural Society*, p. 18; Ruffin, *Political Economy*, p. 10; Simms, "Morals," p. 275.

30. Simms, "Morals," p. 229. Hammond, Speech before the Senate, 4 March 1858, *Appendix to the Congressional Globe*, 35 Cong., 1 sess. (Washington, D.C.: John C. Rives, 1858), p. 68.

31. Tucker, "An Essay on the Moral and Political Effect," p. 332.

32. Josiah C. Nott to Hammond, 4 Sept. 1845, Hammond Papers, LC; Holmes, Notes on Social Science, Commonplace Book, Holmes Papers, WPL. Hammond declared to abolitionist Lewis Tappan, "You make no allowance for difference of races and colors and these constitute the main features of the case" (4 Sept. 1850, Hammond Papers, LC).

33. William Stanton, *The Leopard's Spots: Scientific Attitudes toward Race in America, 1815–59* (Chicago: University of Chicago Press, 1960); Hammond, "Hammond's Letters on Slavery," p. 145; Holmes to Daniel Whitaker, 25 Sept. 1844, Letterbook, Holmes Papers, WPL. Ruffin's position on polygenesis is not entirely clear. In his diary, he stated that he found John Bachman's monogenist arguments "unanswerable," but William K. Scarborough states in the Introduction to the diary that Ruffin disagreed with his friend Bachman. See Ruffin, *Diary*, ed. Scarborough, 3

March 1859, p. 290, and Scarborough's "Introduction," p. xxxii. Simms, "Critical
Notices," *Southern Quarterly Review* 13 (1849): 265; Ruffin, Diary, 10 Jan. 1861,
Ruffin Papers, LC.
    34. E. N. Elliott, ed., *Cotton Is King and Proslavery Arguments,* (Augusta:
Pritchard, Abbott, and Loomis, 1860); *The Pro-Slavery Argument;* see Thomas
R. Dew, "Review of the Debate in the Virginia Legislature of 1831 and 1832," in
The Pro-Slavery Argument; DeBow, *The Interest in Slavery of the Southern Non-
Slaveholder;* A. T. Bledsoe, *An Essay on Liberty and Slavery* (Philadelphia: Lippin-
cott, 1856); Thornton Stringfellow, *Slavery: Its Origin, Nature, and History, Con-
sidered in the Light of Bible Teachings, Moral Justice, and Political Wisdom* (New
York: J. F. Trow, 1861); Stringfellow, *A Brief Examination of Scripture Testimony
on the Institution of Slavery* (Richmond: Religious Herald, 1841); William Harper,
*Memoir on Slavery, Read before the Society for the Advancement of Learning, of
South Carolina, at Its Annual Meeting at Columbia, 1837* (Charleston: J. S. Burges,
1838); James H. Thornwell, *Report of the Subject of Slavery; Presented to the
Synod of South Carolina, November 6, 1851* (Columbia: A. S. Johnston, 1852);
Henry Hughes, *A Treatise on Sociology, Theoretical and Practical* (Philadelphia:
Lippincott, Grambo, 1854). For heuristic purposes, I have overlooked minor changes
in the positions taken by the five members of the network and have not detailed
differences among them which they themselves found insignificant enough to ignore.
As one would expect, their arguments became more forceful toward the end of the
ante-bellum period. While Simms's "Miss Martineau on Slavery," *Southern Literary
Messenger* 3 (1837): 641–57, anticipated the eventual end of the peculiar institution, his "Morals of Slavery," essentially a rewrite of the earlier article, reversed
this position. The five disagreed somewhat on the slave-trade question. Ruffin
evolved from opposition to support, while Hammond remained opposed because of
the political upheaval any change would engender. See Ruffin to J. Mitchel, 14 June
1859, Ruffin Papers, VHS; Ruffin, *Diary,* ed. Scarborough, 17 Jan. 1859, p. 270.
Ruffin also objected to use of "natural law" concepts in slavery's defense, for he felt
that even his friends' total redefinition of the theory to serve essentially as an argument from design gave unwarranted reinforcement to unsound doctrines.
    35. William Sumner Jenkins has noted how "viewing the history of American
slavery in perspective, one is . . . impressed with the similarity in the character of
the basic types of arguments . . . presented . . . in defense of slavery" (*Pro-Slavery
Thought in the Old South* [Chapel Hill: University of North Carolina Press, 1935],
p. 2). E. N. Elliott introduced his 1860 collection of proslavery classics from the entire ante-bellum period by remarking that "earlier and later writers both stood on substantially the same ground" (*Cotton Is King,* p. xii); George Fredrickson, *The Black
Image in the White Mind: The Debate on Afro-American Character and Destiny,
1817–1914* (New York: Harper and Row, 1971). David Donald has noted differences between eastern and southwestern spokesmen for slavery, although he finds
them far less significant than does Fredrickson. In his view, the differences were
not as much a matter of substance as of rhetoric. The "theme of nostalgia," he notes,
"was more characteristic of proslavery advocates from the eastern seaboard states
than of such southwestern polemicists as DeBow and Henry Hughes, whose rhetoric
resembles that of the New South spokesmen of a later period. These southwesterners
shared the sense of alienation which, as I have tried to show, was a basic motivation
of the proslavery defenders. Being, however, from newly settled states, which had
no colonial history to be glorified, they necessarily had to look to the future, rather
than to the past, for the paradigm of the perfect society" (Donald, "Proslavery
Argument," p. 17). The emphasis of the arguments did differ, for the southwesterners
tended to tilt the balance between religious and scientific justifications slightly in
favor of science. What Simms and his circle described with the religious terms
"stewardship," Hughes referred to in his protosociological word, "warranteeism."
Nevertheless, both science and religion were dedicated to illuminating God's design,
and the moral purpose of both arguments was the same. The easterners were sym-

pathetic to the southwesterners' ideals of progress, while, by the same token, DeBow and Hughes wholeheartedly accepted the Southern heritage so important to their eastern compatriots. As Paul Gaston demonstrated in *The New South Creed: A Study in Southern Mythmaking* (New York: Random House, 1970), it is almost impossible to label Southern social movements as either forward- or backward-looking, for even the most radical of Southern reformers have disguised their prescriptions for reform programs as a return to traditional Southern and especially Christian values. The most recent example of this is perhaps the rhetoric of Martin Luther King, Jr.

36. Simms to Tucker, 6 Sept. 1849, *Letters of Simms*, 2:554; see Hammond, "Hammond's Letters on Slavery," p. 111; Simms, "Morals," p. 185; Ruffin, *Political Economy*, pp. 5, 23; Holmes, "Slavery and Freedom," p. 92; Tucker, "Slavery," p. 336.

37. Jenkins, *Pro-Slavery Thought*, p. 242. The use of science to prove moral truth was characteristic of ethnology. Note, for example, the title of J. A. Gobineau's seminal work in the field, *The Moral and Intellectual Diversity of Races, with Particular Reference to Their Respective Influence on the Civil and Political History of Mankind, from the French by Count A. deGobineau*, trans. Josiah C. Nott (Philadelphia: Lippincott, 1856); Josiah Clark Nott, *Two Lectures on the Connection between the Biblical and Physical History of Man, Delivered by Invitation from the Chair of Political Economy of the Louisiana University in December 1848* (1849; reprint ed., New York: Negroes Universities Press, 1969). Fredrickson cites Nott as an example of the Southwestern group of apologists, ignoring the moral-philosophical emphasis of the doctor's ideas, as well as his close friendship with Hammond and his frequent expressions of support for the Carolinian's views.

38. Hammond to Simms, 20 June 1848, Hammond Papers, LC.

39. Hammond, Diary, 9 Aug., 6 Sept. 1845, Hammond Papers, LC.

40. Holmes, "Failure of Free Societies," p. 192; A. C. Cole has asserted that Abraham Lincoln's ultimate position on the slavery issue was determined by his reaction to the extremes of the proslavery argument, especially Fitzhugh's attack upon the principle of free labor. Cole provides evidence that Lincoln read *Sociology for the South, or the Failure of Free Society* (Richmond: A. Morris, 1854), and the Richmond *Enquirer*, for which Fitzhugh wrote. Thus Holmes's fear that Northerners would look upon Southerners as fanatics was not unfounded. See Arthur Charles Cole, *Lincoln's House Divided Speech* (Chicago: University of Chicago Press, 1923). See also, Holmes, "Failure of Free Societies," pp. 130–31; Holmes Diary, 21 Feb. 1857, Holmes Papers, WPL. Ruffin also found Fitzhugh objectionable, even "foolish." See Ruffin, *Diary*, ed. Scarborough, 26 Oct. 1858, p. 228. Fredrickson, however, regards Fitzhugh as the foremost representative of the patriarchal defense characteristic of the seaboard states of the Old South (*The Black Image*, pp. 59–60).

41. Fitzhugh to Holmes, 11 April 1855, Holmes, Diary, 9 Aug. 1856, both in Holmes Papers, WPL.

42. Fitzhugh to Holmes, 11 April 1855, Letterbook, Holmes, Diary, 16 April 1857, both in Holmes Papers, WPL.

43. C. Vann Woodward, "George Fitzhugh, Sui Generis," in *Cannibals All! or Slaves without Masters* (1857; reprint ed., Cambridge: Belknap Press of Harvard University, 1960); Harvey Wish, *George Fitzhugh: Propagandist of the Old South* (Baton Rouge: Louisiana State University Press, 1943); Louis Hartz, *The Liberal Tradition in America* (New York: Harcourt Brace, 1955); Eugene Genovese, *The World the Slaveholders Made* (New York: Pantheon, 1969), p. 128; Fitzhugh to Holmes, 27 March 1855, Letterbook, Holmes Papers, WPL.

44. Dew, "Review of the Debate," p. 322.

45. Genovese, *World the Slaveholders Made*, pp. 119, 129. Genovese has accorded undue prominence to the observations Fitzhugh made on the economic bases of Southern society. While he explicitly admits that Fitzhugh was concerned primarily with questions of morality and social values, in the course of his essay, Genovese reduces these issues to a position of much lesser importance than he gives to Fitz-

hugh's attacks on capitalism. While the bulk of Fitzhugh's argument was devoted to moral questions, the great part of Genovese's argument is devoted to material ones. See Genovese, *World the Slaveholders Made*, p. 154. Genovese's analysis of planter ideology in *Roll Jordan Roll: The World the Slaves Made* (New York: Pantheon, 1975) more nearly accords with the explanation presented here.

46. See Clifford S. Griffin, *Their Brothers' Keepers: Moral Stewardship in the United States, 1800-65* (New Brunswick: Rutgers University Press, 1960); Charles Foster, *An Errand of Mercy: The Evangelical United Front, 1790-1837* (Chapel Hill: University of North Carolina Press, 1960); John R. Bodo, *The Protestant Clergy and Public Issues, 1812-1848* (Princeton: Princeton University Press, 1954); Genovese, *World the Slaveholders Made*, p. 148.

47. See Daniel Walker Howe, *The Unitarian Conscience: Harvard Moral Philosophy, 1805-1861* (Cambridge: Harvard University Press, 1970), and Marvin Meyers, *The Jacksonian Persuasion: Politics and Belief* (Stanford: Stanford University Press, 1957).

48. Hammond, Diary, 24 May, 1845, Hammond Papers, LC. These intellectuals might be described as attempting to introduce what anthropologist Anthony F. C. Wallace has described as a "revitalization movement, . . . a deliberate, organized, conscious effort by members of a society to construct a more satisfying culture." See Wallace, "Revitalization Movements," *American Anthropologist* 58 (1956): 264.

49. Tucker to Hammond, Feb. 1836, Simms to Hammond, June 1845, both in Hammond Papers, LC; Hammond to Tucker, 11 Aug. 1850, Tucker-Coleman Collection, EGSL; Ruffin, *Diary*, ed. Scarborough, 26 April 1858, p. 181; Ruffin to Hammond, 23 July 1858, Hammond Papers, LC.

CHAPTER SEVEN

1. The men of mind indicated that they felt increasing pressure to conform as war approached. Holmes wrote, "In other countries, even in the midst of civil wars, scholars have continued to pursue their vocations successfully. . . . Is there room or hope for such employment here? I fear not—there is a fury of war abroad in the land which maddens or consumes every thing" (George Frederick Holmes, Diary, 12 April 1862, Holmes Papers, WPL). Hammond also found growing difficulty in serving as the voice of disinterested truth after the Nashville Convention. See James Henry Hammond to William Gilmore Simms, 11 Oct. 1851, Hammond Papers, LC; Hammond to Nathaniel Beverley Tucker, 25 Feb. 1851, Tucker-Coleman Collection, EGSL. On the growing power of demagoguery, see Hammond to Simms, 13 March 1859, Hammond Papers, LC; William Gilmore Simms to William Porcher Miles, 22 Dec. 1861, *The Letters of William Gilmore Simms*, coll. and ed. Mary C. Simms Oliphant, Alfred Taylor Odell, and T. C. Duncan Eaves, 5 vols. (Columbia: University of South Carolina Press, 1952-56), 4:391; Simms to Hammond, 2 Dec. 1861, ibid., 4:389. For evidence of the same demand for intellectual solidarity on an institutional level, see William R. Taylor, "Toward a Definition of Orthodoxy: The Patrician South and the Common Schools," *Harvard Educational Review* 26 (1966): 412-26; and John S. Ezell, "A Southern Education for Southrons," *Journal of Southern History* 17 (1951): 303-27. In one sense, the five intellectuals exploited the demand for solidarity at the same time they deplored it. Simms and Holmes were active in the movement for distinctively Southern education and for Southern textbooks. This is yet further evidence of the unworkability of the balance they sought to maintain between practical and ultimate commitments. See Hammond, "South Carolina College Oration," 4 Dec. 1849, draft ms., Hammond Papers, LC.

2. On the Nashville Convention, see Holman Hamilton, *Prologue to Conflict: The Crisis and Compromise of 1850* (Lexington: University of Kentucky Press, 1964); Melvin Johnson White, *The Secession Movement in the United States, 1847-1852* (New Orleans: Tulane University Press, 1910); Major L. Wilson, "Of Time and the Union: Webster and His Critics in the Crisis of 1850," *Civil War History*

14 (1968): 293–306; Allen Nevins, *The Ordeal of the Union*, 1 (New York: Charles Scribner and Sons, 1947); Avery Craven, *The Coming of the Civil War* (Chicago: University of Chicago Press, 1942); Henry T. Shanks, *The Secession Movement in Virginia, 1847–1861* (Richmond: Garrett and Massie, 1934); Chauncy Boucher, *The Secession and Co-operation Movements in South Carolina, 1848 to 1852* (St. Louis: Washington University Press, 1918); Robert R. Russel, "What Was the Compromise of 1850?" *Journal of Southern History* 22 (1956): 292–309.

3. Nathaniel Beverley Tucker, Letter XII to Henry Clay from "A Friend of States Rights," clipping from the Richmond *Whig*, July 1838, in N. Beverley Tucker Scrapbook, Tucker-Coleman Collection, EGSL. In 1864, Holmes characterized the war as a whole as such a ritual. "Every age and country has its own form of trial, through which the people must pass to purification. . . . The greater the trial, the brighter the reward" (Holmes, Diary, Dec. 1864, Holmes Papers, WPL). On the nature of sectarianism, see Ernst Troeltsch, *The Social Teaching of the Christian Churches*, trans. Olive Wyon (New York: Macmillan, 1931); H. Richard Niebuhr, Wilhelm Pauch, and Francis Miller, *The Church against the World* (Chicago: Willett, Clark, 1935); Peter Berger, "The Sociological Study of Sectarianism," *Social Research* 21 (1954): 967–85.

4. William Gilmore Simms, "The Southern Convention," *Southern Quarterly Review* 18 (1850): 197–98, 232, 209.

5. Hammond to Governor Gist, 2 Dec. 1850, Tucker to Hammond, 26 March 1850, both in Hammond Papers, LC.

6. Hammond to Tucker, 25 Feb. 1851, Tucker-Coleman Collection, EGSL; Hammond to Simms, 11 Oct. 1851, 14 May 1854, Hammond Papers, LC.

7. Hammond to Edmund Ruffin, 27 March 1850, Ruffin Papers, VHS; Hammond to Simms, 22 Aug. 1852, 4 Feb. 1851, Hammond Papers, LC.

8. Hammond to M. C. M. Hammond, 24 June, 1859, 10 Aug. 1858, Hammond Papers, SCL.

9. Hammond, Diary, 18 April 1855, 3 Jan. 1854, Hammond, "Thoughts and Recollections," 22 Feb. 1852, both in Hammond Papers, SCL.

10. Simms to Tucker, 4 April 1851, *Letters of Simms*, 3:109.

11. Simms to Hammond, 8 May 1858, ibid., 4:54; Simms to Hammond, 2 June 1858, ibid., 4:60. Simms and Hammond accused themselves and one another of hypochondria. Simms declared himself "a frequent invalid . . . rather . . . from mental than physical causes" (Simms to James Lawson, 20 June 1867, ibid., 5:61). Hammond declared that "Dyspepsia and hypochondria have been preying on me from my birth" (Hammond, "Thoughts and Recollections"). Simms was certain that Hammond's "mind . . . has generated all your physical infirmities" (Simms to Hammond, 10 Jan. 1859, *Letters of Simms*, 4:102–3). Perhaps this might be seen as yet another species of idealism, of the primacy of mind over matter.

12. Hammond to Simms, 27 June 1850, Hammond Papers, LC; Tucker *Prescience. Speech Delivered by Hon. Beverley Tucker of Virginia in the Southern Convention* (Richmond: West and Johnston, 1862); Tucker to Hammond, 26 March 1850, Hammond Papers, LC.

13. Tucker to Hammond, 18 Dec., 17 July, 18 Dec. 1850, 4 Feb. 1851, Hammond Papers, LC.

14. Tucker to Hammond, 21 Sept. 1850, Hammond Papers, LC.

15. Tucker to Hammond, 30 July 1850, Hammond Papers, LC.

16. See Avery Craven, *Soil Exhaustion as a Factor in the Agricultural History of Virginia and Maryland, 1606–1860* (1926; reprint ed., Gloucester: Peter Smith, 1965), and Ruffin to Hammond, 3 Dec. 1853, Hammond Papers, LC.

17. Ruffin to Hammond, 3 Dec. 1853, Hammond Papers, LC; Hammond to Ruffin, 1 May 1854, Ruffin Papers, VHS.

18. Hammond to Simms, 8 July 1853, Hammond Papers, LC; Ruffin, *Diary*, ed. Scarborough, 15 April 1861, p. 602. Ruffin to Julian Ruffin and Edmund Ruffin, Jr., 11 Nov. 1860, Ruffin Papers, VHS.

19. Ruffin, Diary, 18 June 1865, Ruffin Papers, LC. On symbolic action, see Clif-

ford Geertz, *The Interpretation of Cultures* (New York: Basic Books, 1973), and Geertz, "Centers, Kings, and Charisma: Reflections on the Symbolics of Power," in J. Ben David and T. Clark, eds., *Culture and Its Creators,* forthcoming.

20. Holmes, "Excerpts from Various Books," 1850, Holmes Papers, WPL.

21. Holmes, Diary, 18 April 1862, Holmes Papers, WPL; see Holmes's critical articles on Comte of this period: "Faith and Science—Comte's Positive Philosophy," *Methodist Quarterly Review* 4 (1852): 9–37, 169–99; "Instauratio Nova—Auguste Comte," ibid., pp. 329–60; "The Positive Religion; or, Religion of Humanity," ibid. 6 (1854): 329–59; "Auguste Comte and Positivism," *North British Review* 21 (1854): 128–53. See also Holmes's reading lists on Catholicism, in "Excerpts from Various Books," 1850, 1853–88, and in his Diary, 1841–52, Holmes Papers, WPL.

22. Holmes, Diary, 1854; Diary, 22 Jan., 15 Aug. 1856, Holmes Papers, WPL.

23. Holmes, Diary, 16 Nov., 18 Feb. 1862, 10 Jan. 1865, Holmes Papers, WPL.

24. Hammond, Diary, 9 Dec. 1857, Hammond Papers, SCL.

25. Hammond, "Speech Delivered at Barnwell C.H., October 29, 1858," *Selections from the Letters and Speeches of the Hon. James H. Hammond of South Carolina* (New York: J. F. Trow, 1866), p. 356; Hammond to Simms, 22 April 1859, Hammond Papers, LC.

26. Hammond to Simms, 3 April 1860, 22 April 1859, Hammond Papers, LC; see also, Jon Wakelyn, "The Changing Loyalties of James Henry Hammond: A Reconsideration," *South Carolina Historical Magazine* 75 (1974): 1–13, for a summary of Hammond's shifting political positions.

27. Hammond to Simms, 9 March 1861, Hammond to M. C. M. Hammond, 12 Nov. 1860, both in Hammond Papers, LC; Hammond to Simms, 13 Nov. 1860, Hammond Papers, SCL.

28. Simms to W. P. Miles, 2 May 1861, *Letters of Simms,* 4:355; Simms to Hammon, 18 Nov. 1861, ibid., 4:355. Hammond also believed the South deserved the scourge. See Hammond to Lawrence Keitt, 7 Nov. 1862, Hammond Papers, LC.

29. Simms to Hammond, 2 Dec. 1861, *Letters of Simms,* 4:389; Hammond to Simms, 12 June, 30 Aug. 1864, Hammond Papers, LC.

30. Edward Spann Hammond attributed his father's decline to depression over Confederate military defeats. See his untitled memoir on his father's death, Nov. 1864, Ms., Hammond Papers, Simms, "O Tempora, O Mores," Ms., in Hammond Scrapbook, both in Hammond Papers, LC.

EPILOGUE

1. Barbara Welter has described the way nineteenth-century American women served in an analogous manner as "hostages" to the past, embodying traditional morality by representing the immanence of the sacred in a new, profane world dominated by the aggressive man of affairs. But within the role of "true woman" as in the role of intellectual, the cultural tension between pragmatism and idealism was replicated in microcosm. Many "true women" found their moral excellence especially fitted them for the work of mundane reform, just as our intellectuals believed they were destined to be not simply prophets, but stewards. See Barbara Welter, "The Cult of True Womanhood: 1820–1860," *American Quarterly* 18 (1966): 151–74, and Drew Gilpin Faust, "Men and Women in Nineteenth-Century America: Groups, Values, and Social Change," oral presentation at the Berkshire Conference on the History of Women, Radcliffe College, Oct. 1974.

2. On the intellectuals' hostility to revivalism, see James Henry Hammond to Dear Friend, 29 Aug. 1828, Hammond Papers, SCL; Nathaniel Beverley Tucker to his father, 11 Dec. 1824, Tucker-Coleman Collection, EGSL; George Frederick Holmes to D. J. McCord, 24 Oct. 1846, WPL.

3. Victor Turner, *The Forest of Symbols: Aspects of Ndembu Ritual* (Ithaca: Cornell University Press, 1967).

4. See Stow Persons, *The Decline of American Gentility* (New York: Columbia University Press, 1973).

5. See Edward Shils, *The Intellectuals and the Powers and Other Essays* (Chicago: University of Chicago Press, 1972). William Gilmore Simms to Hammond, 10 May 1845, *The Letters of William Gilmore Simms,* coll. and ed. Mary C. Simms Oliphant, Alfred Taylor Odell, and T. C. Duncan Eaves, 5 vols. (Columbia: University of South Carolina Press, 1952–56), 2:61.

Index

THE JOHNS HOPKINS UNIVERSITY PRESS

This book was composed in Linotype Caledonia text and display type by Keith Press, from a design by Susan Bishop. It was printed on 50-lb. Publishers Eggshell Wove paper and bound in Joanna Arrestox cloth by Universal Lithographers, Inc.